POSTAL REFORM AND
THE PENNY BLACK

Postal Reform
and
The Penny Black

A New Appreciation

Douglas N Muir

CURATOR
PHILATELY

NATIONAL POSTAL MUSEUM
LONDON

First published 1990
The National Postal Museum
King Edward Building
King Edward Street
London
EC1A 1LP

Designed by Angela Reeves FCSD FSTD

Printed in the United Kingdom by
Jolly & Barber Limited, Rugby, Warwickshire

ISBN 0 9515948 0 X

Contents

CONTENTS

Foreword

The words 'Penny Black' are words to conjure with in the philatelic world and 6 May 1840 is the red letter day of the philatelic calendar.

The historical and philatelic aspects involved in the issue of the Penny Black contribute much to the most important story in philately. The build-up in dissatisfaction with the postal service and the agitation for postal reform set the scene for the production of the world's first adhesive postage stamp; this, together with the lasting and beneficial world-wide results that accrued, form a fascinating story. Much of a social and postal history nature is involved and the appeal of this book will in no way be confined to those whose main interest is in philately.

Douglas Muir covers the whole field in masterly fashion and the gathering together of the story in one volume is a great advantage to the reader.

Much has been written in the past on this subject following such authoritative works as those of Sir Edward Bacon and some may wonder what more there is to say. However Douglas Muir has not relied, as so many do, on the writings of others, but has gone back to bedrock. The result is the publishing of a good deal of new information, much from the files of the Public Record Office, and especially as regards the authorship of many of the submissions for the Treasury Competition.

The illustrations, too, are outstanding in that a good deal of material is reproduced for the first time, much of it in colour. These illustrations cover many pieces from the Royal Philatelic Collection and also the Phillips Collection at the National Postal Museum.

In all, this important new publication will be much enjoyed by all who read it, whether they be philatelists or those interested in a fascinating story of much social and historical significance.

John Marriott LVO RDP FRPSL

Keeper of the Royal Philatelic Collection

Acknowledgements

Researching and writing a book is never easy. Nor is it the work of one person. Many others provide ideas and give freely of their valuable time to assist. I should like to thank them all – in particular the Manager and staff of the National Postal Museum who have had to put up with the consequences over the past year. Of them, Tony Gammons and John Holman have been of especial help in reading parts of the text and offering advice.

Jean Farrugia and the staff of Post Office Archives were always ready to give valuable assistance, as was John Marriott in giving me access to the Royal Collection on several occasions and for writing the foreword. Thanks must also go to Lady de Bellaigue and the staff of the Royal Archives, Windsor; Robin Francis and the staff of the National Art Library at the Victoria & Albert Museum; the staff of the Public Record Office at Kew; Mrs Lesley Couperwhite of the Watt Library, Greenock (for access to the Wallace papers); and the St Brides Printing Library for help with the technicalities of stereotyping the Mulready.

James Grimwood-Taylor gave particular assistance with the listing of the Uniform 4d. markings as did Mrs D Crawforth with information about letter scales. Dr Jean Alexander kindly provided the index and many helpful suggestions. Thanks are also due to Dr Jack Goodwin and Graham Watson for reading the typescript and being bold enough to make their trenchant observations. I hope the book is more readable as a result. Any omissions or commissions are nevertheless the responsibility of the author alone. The illustrations from the Royal Collection and the quotations from the Royal Archives are reproduced by gracious permission of Her Majesty The Queen. Most of the photography was done by Rod Tidnam of Tony Othen Associates.

A special thanks goes to Angela Reeves for designing the book in her spare time and insisting throughout on the highest quality. She claims she would have done a better job had she not been so rushed due to my late delivery of copy. Lastly, my thanks go to Laura and Mauro without whose sustenance this book would not have been written.

Douglas N Muir, April 1990

CHAPTER ONE

The Posts up to 1830

King Charles needed money. After three parliaments he now ruled alone and the necessary supply was raised and managed by his financial minister Sir Richard Weston, first Earl of Portland. This took the form of fines and the sale of monopolies. But in 1635 Weston died and there was now no curb on Charles's expenditure. As he said he 'would do anything to avoid having another parliament'[1] he had to find further means of raising revenue and so on the last day of July 1635 at his court at Bagshot he issued a proclamation 'for the setling of the lre [letter] Office of England and Scotland.'[2]

It was couched in terms of providing a public service:

Whereas to this tyme there hath bene noe ctayne [certain] or constant entercourse betweene the kingdomes of England and Scotland his Majesty hath bene graciously pleased to comaund his servant Thomas Witherings Esquire his Majesties Postmaster of England for forraigne parts to settle a runing Post or twoe to run night and day between Edenburgh in Scotland and the citty of London to goe thither and come backe agayne in six daies and to take with them all such lres [letters] as shalbe directed to any post towne or any place neare any post towne in the saide roade which lres to be left at the posthowse or some other howse as the saide Thomas Witherings shall thinke convenient.[3]

In essence, however, it was less a service than a new source of revenue, the charges being relatively high: 'twoe pence the single lre if under fourescore myles and betweene fourescore and one hundred and forty myles foure pence if above a hundred and forty myles then six pence and uppon the borders of Scotland and in Scotland eight pence.'[4] And with variations to the rates, mostly increases to pay for Pitt's wars, the Post Office remained a source of revenue to the Government for the next two hundred years. The King's letters and government mail went free, paid for by the public service.

The royal posts did not begin in 1635, rather they were then opened to the public. Postal services had been in operation since at least the end of the fifteenth century for royal despatches both within the kingdom and abroad, and merchants and the universities had their own private couriers. Posts ran intermittently from London to Berwick and thence Edinburgh, with two routes to Ireland, and one to Plymouth. A regular post was established to Dover and the Continent.

After 1635 a central sorting and accounting centre was established in London and nearly all letters passed through that office. Postage was calculated on actual distance travelled, so tended to be higher, sometimes much higher, than had the letter travelled by a direct route. In London the letters were examined by clerks of the roads who assessed the postage on the basis of distance covered and a combination of the number of sheets and weight. They were then sorted into roads and a letter bill was prepared for each post town showing details of each letter and the charges to be collected. A record of the charges against each postmaster was maintained in the London office.

Fowler describes how the mails were then distributed:

Letters for each post-town together with the letter bill were enclosed in a small canvas bag, which would be enclosed in a leather pouch for the post road. The leather pouch would bear a label on which was recorded the time of arrival and departure of the pouch at each post stage. On arrival, the postmaster would extract the canvas bag for his post town and send forward the pouch by post boy on horse to the next post stage. This procedure would be repeated at each stage as the mail was carried throughout the day and night to be delivered at all the post towns on the route.[5]

There was no standardised house delivery service in the post towns. The normal arrangement was the exhibition of a list of letters awaiting collection, but enterprising postmasters quickly established a delivery service for those addressees willing to pay an additional 1d. per letter. Local post boys were used for this service and they also received small gratuities from addressees.

By Grant and Farm

But the public service had barely been established when the Civil War intervened and caused great disruption. The subsequent Commonwealth period (or Interregnum) is characterised overall by central control and rigorous reform and thus in 1653 a Committee for the Management of the Posts reported that the Foreign Post Office should be joined with the Inland Post, and certain inland rates were fixed. The running of the Post Office was to be offered for tender, the undertakers 'to be of known integrity and good affection.'[6]

On 29 June of that year the Committee considered various tenders and on the following day it was resolved 'John Manley to carry all packets, public and private, inland and foreign, according to the terms agreed on between him and a Committee of Council for that purpose, and to enter on the execution of the said office tonight, and receive the profits thereof, and a warrant to be drawn for that purpose; power given to him to stop all mails, i.e. bags of letters carried by any person not authorised by him; and his office for postage of letters to be freed from all taxes.'[7] Manley had to pay £10,000 annually for two years, and had to provide horses and pay his postmasters, but the receipts were all his. Thus the Post Office was first privatised, or 'farmed' (although Manley's predecessor Edmund Prideaux had had to pay a rent of £5,000 a year in his latter years in charge).

In 1657, a bill was laid before Parliament providing for the establishment of one General Post Office and one Postmaster General to be appointed by the Lord Protector. This was the first Post Office Act but it had to be renewed after the Restoration in 1660 to make it legitimate in the eyes of the new state.

The Post Office was farmed out as before, under similar conditions, but the charge had increased considerably. Henry Bishop (Byshop or Bysshopp) of Henfield, Sussex gained the running of the posts at a cost of £21,500 annually. Retrospectively, he was appointed 'Master of Running Messengers' and later Postmaster General (see page 15).

This was a time of great confusion, with many families who had lost their positions during the Commonwealth era petitioning for them to be returned. Many were reinstated; some were not. The atmosphere was one of recrimination and so it is not surprising that many complaints were directed at the new Postmaster General. It was alleged that Bishop was not solely in charge. Rather he owed his position to Major John Wildman, former Agitator, intelligence officer, later imprisoned for treason and finally Postmaster General himself. Wildman was described as having 'the greatest share in the present post farm, solely rules, directs and governs all in it, and the Postmaster (an honest gentleman) [is] little better than the other's pupil.'[8] Certainly it was later proved that Wildman had made use of the Post Office as a 'republican plotting centre in the heart of London, under the nose of the new King.'[9]

The other main complaint against Bishop was about delays of the mail. To obviate this Bishop introduced the postmark, or rather datestamp, as he noted in his reply to particularly strong charges on 2 August 1661: 'and a stamp is invented that is putt upon every letter shewing the day of the moneth that every letter comes to this office, so that no letter Carryer may dare to detayne a letter from post to post; which before was usual'.[10] The earliest examples, from stamps made of wood, date from 19 April 1661 though only the month and the day were shown. Thus began one of the essential elements of the postal system, one which continues, in more elaborate form, to the present day.

In 1663 the revenues from the Post Office were allocated to the
Duke of York, with the exception of several thousand pounds reserved
for King Charles ii and his mistresses. Direct farming of the Post
Office ceased in 1677 when the Duke took it into his own management,
and control was passed to the Treasury. By this time the profit was
considerably greater than when farming had begun some twenty-five
years before. Now, and henceforward, profit to the Revenue was the
prime consideration.

Penny Posts

The Great Fire of London in 1666 devastated large areas of the city,
but it was soon rebuilt, more solid and more extensive than before.
London's population was expanding and about half a million people
lived in the area. However, although someone living in London could
send a letter with comparative ease to Bath or Edinburgh, no provision
was made for sending letters to other parts of London. This severe
lack was met by two private individuals, Robert Murray and William
Dockwra, who set up a postal service which delivered letters and
packets up to one pound in weight all over London for only one penny
per item. The idea probably came from Murray but the scheme was
put into operation by Dockwra and later run by him alone. It has since
come to be associated only with Dockwra.

It began at the end of March 1680 being reported in Smith's
Current Intelligence for 27 March:

On Saturday Last [i.e. 20 March] the Projectors for Conveying Letters to any part of
the City, or Suburbs, for a penny a Letter, opened their offices, whereof the three
chiefest are in Lime Street, about Charing-Cross and Temple-bar; besides several
inferior Offices; at which they have hung out tables to advertise people of the thing.[11]

Initially, the number of receiving houses was limited but the system
was developed until four or five hundred existed for the collection of
letters. Deliveries all over London took place frequently throughout
the day, from six in the morning until nine at night (in the summer).
Letters were also delivered into the General Post for onward transmission through the legitimate Post Office. Two markings were applied
upon receipt in Dockwra's offices. One indicated that the penny postage
had been paid (prepayment being necessary) and this, if somewhat
ingenuously, has been referred to as Britain's first postage stamp.[12]
The other marking, heart-shaped, showed the time of despatch from
the delivery office, an even greater check upon delay than simply the
date, as in Bishop's system.

The business was well organised and understandably popular,
filling, as it did, a great need cheaply and efficiently. But it was not

Henry Bishop, 1611–1691, by Fra. Crake

Ralph Allen, 1693–1764, by T Hudson

John Palmer, 1742–1818, artist unknown

Sir Francis Freeling, 1764–1836, by G Jones

Drawn & Engᵈ by T.L. Busby.

POSTMAN.

Letter carrier of the Inland Office, 1820

1820, for T.L. Busby by Messʳˢ Baldwin & Cᵒ Paternoster Row, & at the Artists Depository, 21 Charlotte Stᵗ Fitzroy

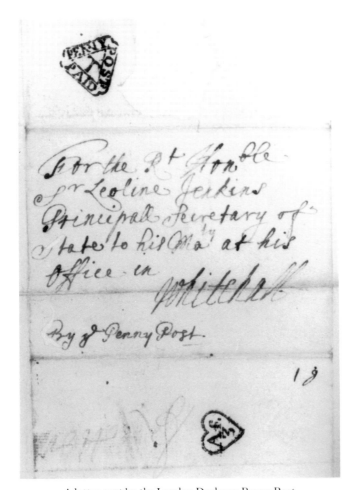

A letter sent by the London Dockwra Penny Post

legal. The Postmaster General and postmasters appointed by him had the sole right to carry the public mails and an alarmed Duke of York saw in Dockwra's Penny Post a loss of earnings.

Thomas Gardiner, Controller of the Inland Office, wrote a survey of the Post Office in 1682 for Colonel George Legge (Baron Dartmouth and a close friend of the Duke) and gave particular attention to the intrusive penny post. The argument that the penny post, though illegal, was still acceptable because it was beneficial, Gardiner delightfully and accurately dismissed as humbug by a clever analogy – 'soe will the erecting a new Custome House and take but half customes.'[13]

However, Gardiner was critical of the lack of service offered to London residents and recommended that the Penny Post be continued under the Duke's auspices. At his second attempt the courts upheld the Duke of York's rights and Dockwra's penny post was closed down on 23 November 1682 to be reopened as part of the Post Office on 11 December. The prepaid penny rate remained and the handstamps were very similar.

This was the first penny post, and the largest. With alterations to boundaries it remained in being until the rates were changed in 1801. Then as the (London) Twopenny Post, it continued as a separate section until uniform postage was introduced. Even then the name and organisation did not disappear. Prepayment had, however, been made optional in 1794.

The Penny Post was revolutionary, efficient and successful and contained most of the elements to be reinstated in 1839. It had a uniform low rate of postage, calculated by weight and not by the number of pages, and this had to be prepaid. The Post Office was only to return to this after many years and more than one long hard campaign. Later, numerous penny posts were established, having been legalised in 1765. The first was in Dublin in 1773, with a private scheme by Peter Williamson in Edinburgh following shortly afterwards.

Expansion and Development in the Eighteenth Century

During the eighteenth century the Post Office expanded and developed largely as a result of the efforts of two energetic and resourceful men – Ralph Allen and John Palmer.

One of the results of the union in 1707 of the Scottish and English parliaments under Queen Anne was the Post Office Act of 1711 creating one unified postal system for Great Britain. The Act was of considerable importance, parts of it still being valid well into the nineteenth century. Increasing the revenue was an aim openly admitted and the Postmaster General had to pay some £700 weekly into the Exchequer. But there were also letters which contributed little or nothing to the overall revenue. As the Act said 'divers Deputy [i.e. country] Postmasters do collect great Quantities of Post Letters called By or Way Letters, and by clandestine and private Agreements amongst themselves, do convey the same Post in their respective Mails or By Bags, according to their several Directions, without accounting for the same, or endorsing the same on their Bills to the great detriment of Her Majesty's Revenues.'[14] Bye or way letters were those from one country town to another which did not pass through London, and for which, therefore, there was no central accounting.

The Act attempted to regulate these. But there was doubtless some relief officially when in 1719 Ralph Allen (see page 15), [deputy] postmaster at Bath, offered to farm all the bye posts for a sum of £6,000 per annum. This was well in excess of the income from such sources at that time which was estimated at £4,000 (later corrected to

£3,700). The contract to farm all the bye and cross road letters was awarded in 1720 for seven years and regularly renewed until Allen's death in 1764. Cross posts served towns near the main post roads. One of the earliest and most important was between Exeter and Bristol laid in 1696 and extended to Chester later. This system Allen extended considerably, and he detailed the new branches in his *Narrative* of 1761. Allen also organised proper controls to check fraud, which meant that as the postal network grew, so did the volume of postal traffic, including 'country' letters going through London for country destinations.

Allen's last contract was in 1761 when the yearly rent still cost him £6,000, but, if receipts from 'country' letters were less than £20,000 annually, Allen was to reimburse the Post Office for the shortage. Robinson considers that 'He was much more than a mere farmer of the by and cross post letters. Allen was the medium through which the Post Office increased the services as the needs arose during the first half of the eighteenth century.'[15] He died a rich man, largely as a result of the Post Office contracts. The system which he had built up on the Post Office's behalf was then taken under direct control and farming ceased.

The other major improvement in the postal system of the eighteenth century came about as a result of the efforts of John Palmer, theatre manager at Bath (see page 15). He proposed to speed up the service on the main routes, now in better repair, by the use of light, fast, armed mail coaches. At the same time, this would be a better protection of the mails against both highwaymen and idle post boys. Stage-coaches and diligences were a normal means of passenger transport, and thus privately (and thus often illegally) carried letters, but they did not carry the public mails.

Through William Pitt, Palmer's plan was promoted against the objections of the Post Office, and the Postmasters-General (now commonly two) were prevailed upon to issue an order on 24 July 1784. It stated that they 'being inclined to make an experiment for the more expeditious conveyance of mails of letters by stage-coaches, machines, etc., have been pleased to order that a trial shall be made upon the road between London and Bristol to commence at each place on Monday, the 2nd August next.'[16] At the same time a new Act increased postage rates. Now single letters cost 2d. for the first stage, 3d. for the second and 4d. up to eighty miles. Double letters with two sheets cost twice this and so on. In 1711, £700 a week had to go to the Exchequer 'in order to raise a present supply of money to carry on the war.'[17] This had continued in times of peace, but was now increased to £2,300 a week. Reform had its price.

The original Bath mail coach, 1784

Five innkeepers on the Bath road contracted to horse the new coach service and on 2 August the first coach set off from Bristol at 4 p.m. loaded with mail and carrying four inside passengers. Outside were the coachman and a guard, both armed. It left Bath at 5.20 p.m. and then continued through the night towards London not deviating from the turnpike road to serve adjacent villages. The General Post Office at Lombard Street was reached at eight o'clock the next morning, a journey time of sixteen hours, much faster than before.

With the success of the new mail coach which 'outruns every conveyance'[18] according to Palmer, further services were introduced. The first was on 28 March 1785 from London to Norwich, and by the end of that year coaches were running to Leeds, Manchester, Liverpool, Portsmouth, Poole, Gloucester, Swansea, Hereford, Carmarthen, Milford Haven, Worcester, Ludlow, Birmingham, Shrewsbury, Chester and Holyhead. They soon spread all over Britain, with conspicuous success until their rapid demise with the coming of the railways.

Palmer was appointed Comptroller General of the Mails under the Postmasters General in 1786. He made various organisational improvements, including the establishment of a Newspaper Office. This was to cope with the vast increase in newspapers, which were carried free, and to ensure that no letters were contained in them to avoid postage.

Francis Freeling, Secretary

One of Palmer's appointments in 1785 was that of Francis Freeling (see page 15) as a surveyor to establish the first cross-post mail coach service between Bristol and Portsmouth via Salisbury. In 1797 Freeling became Secretary to the Post Office, a post he held until his death in 1836 at the age of 71.

Freeling, as a surveyor, made an official visit to Edinburgh in 1790 and there saw in operation Peter Williamson's private penny post, to which the official Post Office turned a blind eye because of its utility. He was convinced by this that an official penny post might be set up in Edinburgh 'with some convenience to the metropolis of Edinburgh and also with some advantage to the revenue.'[19] Williamson's post was subsequently taken over by the government in 1793. At the same time Freeling suggested that it 'would be desirable to try the experiment of opening [penny] posts in some of the great towns of the kingdom' to begin in Manchester.[20] Other penny posts were then set up in Liverpool, Birmingham and Bristol, the area covered by the last being particularly large. These were followed by many more.

Offices were set up in the penny post areas for the receipt of letters and parcels not exceeding four ounces in weight. They were delivered within that area or transferred to the General Post for transmission to any part of the kingdom. In the latter case the penny was in addition to the normal rate of postage.

In general, villages were not well served at this time. To alleviate this, provision was made in the Act passed in 1801 authorising the Postmaster General to make special arrangements in places which were not post towns. These villages or towns could employ messengers to carry letters to and from the nearest post town, agreeing to pay a halfpenny or a penny for the privilege. Permission was granted by the fifth clause of the Act and so these posts were called Fifth Clause Posts or Convention Posts. Gradually, they were superseded by extensions of the penny posts.

However, Britain was now embroiled in war with the French, and money was required to pay for it. Freeling believed in high rates of postage and on his recommendation rates were raised in 1801 again. The London Penny Post became the Twopenny Post and was reduced to a three-mile radius. Further increases in rates took place in 1805 and yet again in 1812. By then, a single letter from London to Edinburgh cost 1s. 1d. while in 1765 it had only cost 6d. As Robinson says 'War had made the Post Office an instrument of taxation.'[21]

Extra taxation nearly affected the mail coaches as well. They had the privilege of not paying tolls on the turnpike roads but the Turnpike

Trustees objected strongly to this loss of revenue to them. Thus, in 1813 an Act of Repeal was passed to change this situation in Scotland. It was entitled 'An Act to Repeal the Exemption from Toll granted for and in respect of Carriages with more than two wheels carrying the Mail in Scotland; and for granting a Rate of Postage as an indemnity to the Revenue of the Post Office from the Payment of such Tolls.' This Act meant that all letters for Scotland, with the exception of certain border towns, were to be charged with a ½d. in addition to the rates already applicable to enable the Post Office to recoup some of its losses. The Act was passed on 3 June. From 9 June this charge applied and resulted in a large number of different markings on letters to indicate the payment required. Rather than stop the mail coaches at each toll the Post Office agreed to pay a lump sum at regular intervals. Despite the additional charge, it was estimated that the Post Office lost more than £5,000 annually because of this agreement.

Postage rates apart, Freeling was a great organiser and born administrator. Everything was committed to paper and instructions of all types flowed from his pen. Instructions to postmasters, instructions to letter carriers, notifications of rate changes or the dissolution of parliaments – all these and many more were the subjects of notices printed at Freeling's behest and sent to those concerned. Many referred to accounting procedures; several to postal practice. A flavour may be gained by three short examples, addressed to all postmasters:[22]

GENERAL POST–OFFICE
30th October, 1820

Notwithstanding the frequent injunctions of the Surveyors, that all Letters shall be plainly and distinctly Stamped with the name of the Post Town, daily experience proves how little those injunctions are regarded. I am, therefore, commanded by My Lords the Postmaster-General, to call your special attention to this essential part of your Duty, in failure of which, you will be held responsible.

And I am to direct you, in every case, to mark the Rates of Postage plainly and legibly on all Letters; and that such as are Post-paid may be invariably marked with Red Ink.

I am,
Your assured Friend
F. FREELING, *Secretary.*

GENERAL POST OFFICE
3rd August, 1821

As certain of the Postmasters are in the habit of Stamping Letters in the Front, it is necessary to issue a General Instruction to all Postmasters, to stamp them on the Back, in order to avoid the possibility of defacing or obliterating any part of the Direction.

And I am to repeat the Postmaster-General's Injunctions, that all Letters shall be stampt legibly, and the Rates of Postage be marked upon them *in the plainest manner, and with as little flourishing as possible.*

By Command of the Postmaster-General

FRANCIS FREELING

Secretary

The late Order issued to all Postmasters to stamp their Letters on the back, is not intended to include the Stamp used by Penny Post Receivers, they are invariably to affix their Stamp in the front of the Letter; – And if such should not be the practice in your Neighbourhood, and if any of the Penny Post Receivers within your delivery should not so stamp them, you will instruct them accordingly, and report any future neglect on their part.

FRANCIS FREELING

Secretary

General Post Office,
September, 1821.

The Post Office in 1830

The Post Office in 1830 was based in London, Dublin and Edinburgh. It consisted of many sections, which had grown up in the ways hitherto described. Its operations were complex and bureaucratic. Its charges were high, not having been reduced after the end of the Napoleonic wars, and open to abuse. The Establishment Book for 1830[23] gives a detailed overall view of the organisation, which was headed by the Postmaster General, Charles, Duke of Richmond, appointed that year at a salary of £2,500 per annum.

A description of his job is couched in defensive terms:

The office of Postmaster General is one of extensive Control and responsibility.

He has the Superintendance of a Revenue of 2 Millions which is not collected as a Tax, but is the produce of a Trade or Business, the success of which depends upon the mode in which it is managed. The Post Office does not receive a single shilling without performing a Service to justify the Demand.

Under the Postmaster General were various offices or divisions, listed here in Establishment Book order:

Secretary's Office – regulating and controlling the whole Department (there was also a Secretary's Office in Edinburgh and the Irish Post Office was independent at this time).

Surveyor and Superintendant of Mail Coaches (later to include railways).

Solicitor.

Riding Surveyors – required to visit and inspect offices in their area frequently and suggest improvements.

Receiver General's Office – to receive the money resulting from postage charged.

Accountant General's Office – to examine all accounts.

Bye Letter Office – to examine the Bye and Cross Road letter accounts.

Letter Bill Office – to keep accounts of letters from and passing through London; the same for the West Indies and America.

Foreign Office – to receive and despatch the foreign mails 'to all parts of the Continent of Europe, the Mediterranean and the Brazil.'

Ship Letter Office – 'For the Receipt and forwarding of Letters to and from parts beyond the Seas, by Ships other than Packets.'

Dead Letter Office – to examine letters that cannot be delivered or have been missent 'to see that the reasons assigned for the non delivery of Dead Letters are sufficient, and that no improper claims have been admitted upon letters alleged to have been overcharged.'

Returned Letter Office – 'Previous to the Year 1811, no Dead Letters were returned to the Writers, but such as were supposed by the Clerks to be of importance the experiment was tried of returning all such Letters and charging the original Postage upon them the result proving that the Plan was advantageous to the Revenue, and beneficial to the Public, this Office was made permanent in 1813.'

Inland Office – (also called General Post Office) the largest and most complex office of all, for the receipt, charging and despatch of mails.

Twopenny Post Office – management of sorting offices and receiving houses in the London area and responsible for their accounts.

Accountant – similar to the Accountant General.

Collector – received the whole of the revenue which he paid to the Receiver General.

Sorting Department – 'There are two Principal Offices, one in St Martins le Grand and the other in Gerrard Street' – to check and sort all letters.

Free deliveries took place in London, and in the penny posts; and in other places there was a very restricted delivery area near the post office. Otherwise, the addressees had to go to the nearest post office to pick up their mail. In London it was very complicated. There were three overlapping systems, with their own receiving houses and letter carriers for delivery. All, however, were based at the new chief office at St Martin's le Grand.

The Foreign branch was the most limited in area of delivery, from Westminster to the Tower, and this was abolished in 1831. Surrounding it, about three miles in diameter, was the area of the urban Twopenny

Post. The suburban post, costing 3d., was on average twelve miles radius from the GPO. In addition to this, there was the Inland service for letters to and from other parts of the kingdom.

Letters were handed in at numerous receiving houses in the twopenny and threepenny districts: 148 in the former, 202 in the latter. These were usually located in shops and were open until 8 p.m. for both paid and unpaid letters. After 8 p.m. they could be put through a slot which had been cut in the shutter.

The receivers had to stamp the letters and the numbers entered on a letter bill. Both letters and bill were collected frequently during the day and taken to the chief office where they were faced, 'candled' (i.e. held up to a candle to see if it was only a single sheet), taxed (if unpaid), sorted and accounted for. Letters for the Inland Office or Foreign Office were transferred to them with appropriate checks and accounts. Deliveries were effected by the letter carriers who collected the unpaid charges and accounted for the money afterwards. Letter carriers were regarded as being in debt to the Post Office and had to make good any deficit in their accounts. They had to 'pass from house to house, at the rate of 4, or not less than $3\frac{1}{2}$ Miles an hour, and where necessary request, but in a civil manner, the persons to dismiss them from their doors without delay.'[24]

The Foreign Office had its own letter carriers as did the Inland Office which also had its own seventy-one receiving houses, sometimes side by side with the Twopenny houses. Letter carriers of the Inland Office carried a bell which they rang in the evenings to collect mail in time for sorting before despatch (see page 16). They were 'not to commence ringing the Bell for the Evening Collection of Letters until Five o'Clock and the Fee is One Penny per Letter; or you may make an Agreement for a Quarterly Sum . . . You are to leave off ringing your Bell, so as to be punctual in delivering your Letter Bag to the Mail Cart at the Time and Place appointed.'[25]

Mail coaches left from coaching inns with wonderful names, such as the Swan with the Two Necks and the George and Blue Boar. They took the mail bags from St Martin's le Grand directly, or had them delivered to their inn, and thence along the main routes to the principal post towns. From these, horse posts and foot posts continued the journeys to the outlying areas which were served. Foot posts could cover vast distances and take several days, particularly in far-flung regions such as the north of Scotland. Naturally, mail returned in the same manner.

Most letters travelled unpaid, money being handed over by the recipient. A large number of items went completely free under the franking system. Some people, by virtue of their position, had the right to frank a number of letters each day as long as these did not exceed one ounce in weight. This included all members of Parliament, Commons and Lords. Some officials had unlimited franking. The system had begun as far back as 1653. Later in 1661 it was reaffirmed, it being noted that 'M.P.s being unwilling to pay portage on their letters during the sitting of Parliament, his Majesty is pleased to direct that single letters, but not packets, to or from members of either House are to go free.'[26] This ceased *immediately* upon the dissolution of Parliament, but in the meantime caused considerable trouble with abuse of the system. Correspondents frequently asked their MP to frank their letters, and in the sorting office they all had to be weighed and counted.

Letters from seamen and soldiers on active service were carried for a penny, if prepaid. This had been allowed since 1795. Newspapers were carried free, but they were taxed separately. However, franked letters could not be put into the penny or twopenny posts without incurring the normal charge.

The system was thus extremely complicated. Bits had been added on over the years but no really rational overhaul had taken place to make it unified. Anomalies abounded, especially in terms of rates.

The Post Office was ripe for reform.

CHAPTER TWO

The Cry for Postal Reform

After the end of the wars with France in 1815 an investigation was set up into all aspects of government revenue. This was a very thorough, if somewhat extended review by a body with the unwieldy title 'Commissioners of Inquiry into the Collection and Management of the Revenue Arising in Ireland and Great Britain.' The eighteenth to twenty-second Reports inclusive concerned the workings of the Post Office. They were published during 1829 and 1830 and described in detail the confused state of the posts at that time.

The Commissioners' eighteenth Report concerned the Post Office in England and Wales, the nineteenth the Irish Post Office, the twentieth Scotland, the twenty-first the Twopenny Post Office in London, and the twenty-second the packet and ship arrangements. Many of the detailed recommendations for the organisation improving were implemented over the next few years; many were not.

The most thorough reforms were carried out in the Irish Post Office which, as a result of this investigation, was consolidated with the main Office in 1831. Corruption and nepotism had been rife and the opportunity was taken to change the entire system. Fixed salaries and proper accounting procedures were now introduced, and general practices were strictly regulated.

However, this thorough revision was not applied elsewhere. One of the recommendations was that the letter carriers of the General and Penny Posts be 'united in one corps and their services made available for the delivery of both descriptions of letters.'[1] This recommendation was implemented in Ireland but a similar proposal for England and Wales was ignored as 'It would be productive of the greatest confusion and delay, and would not be attended with any reduction in the number of persons or expense.'[2]

Other comments by officials were more apt. In the report on Scotland it was proposed 'That the services of all the letter-carriers should be made available to the duties of sorting and stamping.'[3] Innocuous enough it might be thought, but the Postmaster-General observed that 'this would open the door to the renewal of the frauds which led to the dismission [sic] of nearly the whole of the persons employed in some of the departments of the Scotch-office in 1822; and which . . . were committed by a misuse of the stamps, and collusion between the clerks, stampers and letter-carriers.'[4]

Equally, in the report on packet ships the Commissioners complained that the principle of competition was not sufficiently applied in the contracts for building steam-vessels. The Postmaster-General replied with the argument used in dealing with accountants even today: 'Persons at all conversant with shipping are aware that vessels can be built *at any price*, but if a good ship is required, a good price must be given. If the lowest tender is to be accepted, which appears to be the object of public competition, the result would be a very inferior class of ships, which would be the worst economy in a service in which they are required to go to sea when nothing else can.'[5] This showed an admirable understanding of safety first.

Largely, the numerous recommendations were of relatively minor detail. The Post Office changed many practices as a result but argued against some. No major reform was proposed. There was to be no lowering of postage rates, nor any attempt at standardisation. The recommendations and the Postmaster-General's responses were listed in a publication of Parliament of 14 July 1835 which had been made necessary by the complaints of Members of Parliament, Robert Wallace in particular.

Whiting's 'Go-Frees'

The Reports of the Commissioners resulted in greater public awareness of the situation of the Post Office. Later, the reports were to be used by Wallace and other advocates of reform as weapons in their campaigns. Initially, however, the most interesting, practical response came from Charles Fenton Whiting. Little is known of Whiting's antecedents except that he was the son of James Whiting, a printer and publisher. He had worked for Sir William Congreve and on the latter's death had usefully married his widow, thus gaining control of his patents.

Congreve had invented a new kind of printing press of interlocking compound plates, which he had patented in 1820 (patent No. 4520). The first was built for him in the same year by Bryan Donkin. It was formed by cutting a pattern of holes through a plate made of hard metal and pouring softer, molten metal on top to form the second plate. The required design was then engraved on the combined surface. To print from this the plates were separated, inked in different colours, and then combined again to produce perfect bicoloured designs. In 1824, Congreve also patented a method of embossing in colourless relief which could be combined with this bicoloured compound printing. This method of printing was used at Somerset House by the Stamp and Taxes Office to print dies for stamping banknotes. It was an example of one of these banknote dies that Whiting used to illustrate his ideas, the first suggestion of prepaid envelopes.

On 1 February 1830 he addressed a letter to Freeling outlining a plan 'to increase the Post Office's Revenue':[6]

I have respectfully to suggest whether the issuing of Post Office go-frees, or printed franks for forwarding Journals, Gazettes, Pamphlets, Catalogues, Authors proof sheets, Prospectuses of new works etc etc or any description of Printed matter under a stipulated weight might not open a wide field for communication and profit, which is now closed, or diverted into channels on account of the expense inconvenient for the purposes of dispatch and general distribution.

I would therefore propose that the smallest Post frank envelope should be sold for four pence subject to a discount of 20 per cent and entitled to carry a weight not exceeding three ounces of printed matter only.

The next stamp would be five pence (also subject to a discount of twenty per cent) to carry up to five ounces and so on progressively 'according to the convenience or limitation you might deem advisable with respect to the greatest weight to be enclosed in the stamped envelope.'

Whiting then explained why this would be desirable:

Newspapers as a matter of course must be stamped, and pass without expense to all parts of the country; but Literary periodicals not entered as Newspapers do not require to be stamped for Publication, but when required to be sent into the Country the Stamp Office permits the required number to be stamped and when so done the charge for Postage is avoided.

He added, 'Much trouble and many expenses exclusive of the stamp duties are incurred by every Proprietor of a Newspaper annoying to the same and unprofitable to the Revenue, but at present unavoidable.'

To prevent fraud the frank would bear the date and town of issue so that it could not be used twice. Whiting's example was a George IV five-pence die from banknotes produced on the Congreve compound printing press (see page 33). He had cut out the central portion (bearing the royal arms) for the address and had changed in manuscript the 'ONE' at the foot into '5 OUNCES.' At the sides he had drawn indications of date and town stamps. (A mint, intact die print of this same design exists in the Cole papers, so Whiting must have given it to Henry Cole some eight or nine years later as an example of fine, compound printing.)

Being a printer, Whiting was, of course, an interested party. Hence, the otherwise incongruous inclusion of authors' proofs in his proposal. His plan was turned down because of fears that mail coaches could not cope with the extra load, as well as increased possibilities of fraud. This was a very early plan for increasing business and prepayment of postage, if only on printed matter, a basis on which Whiting developed his later ideas for stamps.

The cry for postal reform, in most cases now and later, came from interested parties. Merchants and printers had high postage bills, or would have if they did not evade them (and this aspect was to become much more obvious later); MPS wanted to control the activities of an apparently independent Post Office Secretary; and the intelligentsia wanted to extend written communication to the lower classes. A large proportion of the population, however, especially in England and Ireland, could not write.

Charles Knight and the Society for the Diffusion of Useful Knowledge

The 1820s and 1830s were a period of reform. Advanced social and educational ideas were promoted and societies arose for the general improvement of all people and their surroundings. One of these was the Society for the Diffusion of Useful Knowledge, founded in 1826. One of its earliest members was Matthew Devonport Hill, elder brother of Rowland Hill. Rowland, himself, was elected 'when [the Society] was fully in action.'[7]

As can be inferred from the Society's title, their main aim was that of publication and to this end in 1827 they accepted the services of Charles Knight, that remarkable writer, editor and, above all, publisher. Knight described the members of the Society as 'earnest in the pursuit of a common object, not intent upon personal display or the assertion of petty self-importance; men of cultivated minds, each treating the opinions of the others with respect; the most capable amongst them the most modest; in a word, gentlemen and scholars.'[8]

He soon began a stream of publications: first *The British Almanac*, late in 1827, to counteract the valueless, annual publications of similar titles, and then in 1832 *The Penny Magazine*, dismissed by 'the excellent Dr Arnold' as 'all ramble-scramble'.[9] Knight describes in his auto-biography how the idea came to Matthew Hill, his close friend.

Mr Hill and I were neighbours on Hampstead Heath, and as we walked to town on a morning of the second week in March, our talk was of these cheap and offensive publi-cations. 'Let us,' he exclaimed 'see what something cheap and good can accomplish! Let us have a Penny Magazine!'[10]

It became very successful and influential, especially in postal reform, and lasted until 1846.

Such publications inspired and later supported Rowland Hill's ideas of postal reform. One particular idea of Knight's was of especial importance. Newspaper stamp duties were regarded as a tax on knowledge and there were various parliamentary motions for their repeal. Knight wrote to Lord Althorp, Chancellor of the Exchequer, on the difficulty that would have arisen over the transmission of unstamped newspapers by post. 'I suggested that a penny stamped frank should be issued by the government.'[11]

This proposal was introduced in Parliament by Matthew Hill, now MP for Hull, in a debate on 22 May 1834 when he reported that Mr Knight, the publisher 'recommends that a stamped wrapper should be prepared for such newspapers as it is desired to send by post, and that such wrapper should be sold at the rate of 1d. by the distributors of stamps.'[12]

Details were also given in the *Companion to the Newspaper* published on 1 June 1834 where it was stated:

It will be necessary to make the postage payable by the person sending the paper; for otherwise, a great many papers, especially the very low-priced ones, would be refused by persons to whom they are addressed. It is obvious that a direct payment to the Post-office, by the transmitter of the paper, would be highly inconvenient, if not impossible. Mr Knight's plan of a stamped frank obviates the difficulty; and it would facilitate the transmission of all printed sheets under a certain weight.[13]

This sounds remarkably similar to Whiting's scheme, yet Rowland Hill later credited Knight with giving him the basis for his ideas for prepayment of postage.

Robert Wallace, postal reformer

Robert Wallace (see page 36) was one of the first public figures to campaign for postal reform. Born in 1773, he was the son of a rich West India merchant in Glasgow. He was also a committed Whig and 'vigorous orator,'[14] and as such was foremost in the agitation for political reform which culminated in the Reform Bills of 1831 and 1832. With the eventual passing of the Reform Act he was elected, in December 1832 (first on a show of hands, later by poll), the first member of Parliament for the newly enfranchised town of Greenock.

In his valedictory address to his constituents in 1845 he described how he had become interested in postal affairs:

In the very first year in which I sat in the House of Commons, I was induced to enter upon what eventually became the most laborious of my Parliamentary undertakings – that of Post-Office Reform. The seals of letters addressed to highly respectable parties in Greenock had been violated; I was called upon to investigate and seek redress for this abuse of official authority. The inquiry thus begun, led me to discover that the Post-Office, which was considered the most pure and immaculate of all the various departments of the State, was precisely the reverse, and then disregarding alike the apprehensions of friends and the sneers of opponents, I continued to follow up the investigation closely, and struggling on for years single-handed and alone, brought to light one gross abuse after another.[15]

Wallace's struggles had begun in August 1833 and in support of his arguments he used the large tomes of evidence and recommendations of the Revenue Commissioners. His attacks were so constant that one MP apparently complained that 'he never took up his papers in the morning that he did not find the name of the honourable member for Greenock there with some notice of motion for inquiry with respect to the Post Office.'[16] This was clearly an exaggeration for his speeches in Parliament were sporadic rather than constant.

However, he was widely recognised as being interested in the Post Office. A correspondent from Glasgow in 1835, W Mackenzie, pointed out that foreign letters were often enclosed in envelopes and thus charged double. He had suggested to postal officials that they send a circular to foreign post offices asking them to publicise this. The suggestion was received coldly so he was writing to Wallace 'knowing that if it meets your approbation the General Post Office people will soon be made aware of it.'[17]

In Parliament Wallace's expressed views were that he felt that letters should not be opened on suspicion of being more than one sheet, that Freeling's power should not be uncontrolled, and that the Postmaster-General should be under a Board of Commissioners (a proposal frequently made by Revenue Commissioners).

Apart from complaints about the lack of steam packets from Glasgow to Greenock and the very poor state of the nine mail coaches in Scotland (out of a total of 250 in the United Kingdom) his attacks were general. In these he was supported by Lord Lowther (later a Postmaster-General) and Joseph Hume, Member for Middlesex (later Kilkenny in Ireland, and Montrose in Scotland).

Commission of Inquiry into the Post Office

As a result of Wallace's demands a Commission was appointed in May 1835 to inquire into the management of the Post Office. Over the next three years some ten reports were issued, similar in form to those of 1829 and 1830.

There were three Commissioners, Lords Duncannon and Seymour and Henry Labouchère, and their reports dated from 12 June 1835 up to January 1838. The first three reports concerned the contract for the supply of mail coaches. It was recommended that the contract be thrown open to suppliers other than Mr Finch Vidler, who had the monopoly to build and service mailcoaches, and this was done by the

A printed example of a George IV five pence die for
banknotes, compound-printed

A suggested design by C F Whiting for a 'go-free'
based on the George IV banknote, with centre portion
in place and reversed

Henry Cole, 1808–82

Rowland Hill, 1795–1879,
by Mary M Pearson

John Dickinson envelope and two lettersheets from the Ninth Report of Parliamentary Commissioners, 1837

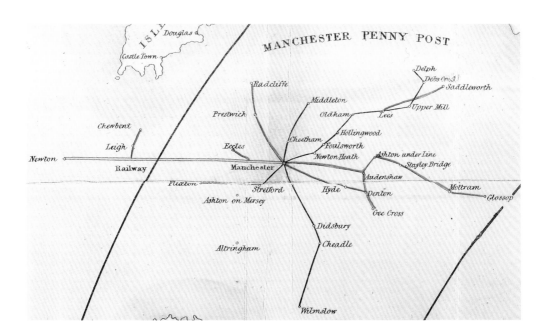

MANCHESTER PENNY POST

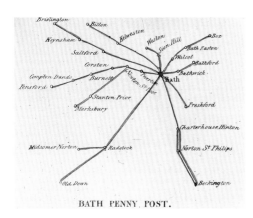

BATH PENNY POST.

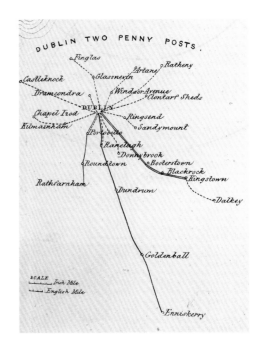

DUBLIN TWO PENNY POSTS.

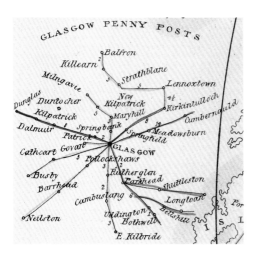

GLASGOW PENNY POSTS

Maps of local penny and twopenny posts, 1838

☐ Rail roads (England) or walks (Scotland)
▨ Mail coaches
■ Horse posts (England) or foot posts (Ireland)
▨ Foot posts
▨ Rides or gigs

Robert Wallace, 1773–1855

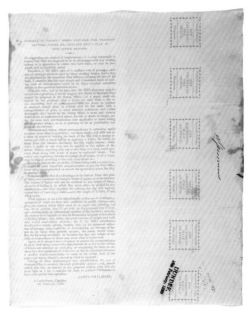

Printed letter from James Chalmers, 1782–1853,
to the Post Office, 10 February 1838

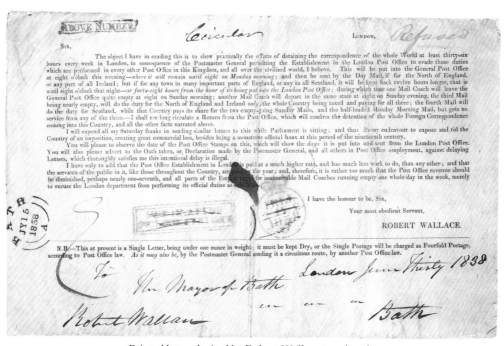

Printed letter devised by Robert Wallace to epitomise
the inefficiencies of the Post Office

end of the year. They then again suggested that a Board of Commissioners should be substituted for the Postmaster-General, and although a Bill to do this was introduced in Parliament it was defeated by the Lords.

The sixth Report concerned the packet and ship letter service. Heavy financial losses were being incurred and the Commissioners were very critical of the running of the office under George Freeling, son of Sir Francis Freeling. It was proposed that the service should be run by those who were actually used to dealing with ships and so the entire department was transferred to the Admiralty, effective from the spring of 1837. By the time the ninth report was in preparation evidence was being taken from Rowland Hill, and this is considered elsewhere. Overall, the emphasis of the Commissioners was on the elimination of losses and inefficiency, and the reduction in the cost of postage. Once again, a detailed abstract of the recommendations of all the reports, and whether implemented or not, was prepared at the behest of Robert Wallace and printed in 1838.[18]

One of the first results of the Commission's reports was the proper regulation of the running of the Post Office. In July 1837 many previous Acts were consolidated and some 125 repealed, thus clearing away much of the confusion surrounding operations. An Act for the Management of the Post Office was passed but this did not constitute any major reform. Postage rates and methods of charging remained the same.

Postal Charges

With the exception of the extensive penny post systems, it was expensive to send a letter any distance. Even a single letter, i.e. one sheet of paper not enclosed in an envelope, cost 4d. for up to fifteen miles and then an extra penny for each of several stages up to 1s. for 300 miles and 1d. for every additional 100 miles. This meant that a single letter to Dublin from London cost 1s. 3d.; to other parts of Ireland, especially via Portpatrick, it could cost up to 1s. 7d. Over and above this there were special toll charges such as the 1d. on all letters crossing the Menai or Conway bridges and the ½d. (on single letters) if they went by way of Milford and Waterford. This last was introduced in June 1836. There was also, of course, the additional ½d. on letters in Scotland. If the letters had to be delivered by the penny or twopenny posts these charges were also additional.

Matters were further complicated by the fact that although postage rates were generally a function of distance, it was not the shortest distance between the two points that was used for calculation. Rather it was the distance the letter had to travel, which was often by a very circuitous route. Invidious anomalies resulted.

Postage of a Single Letter to Horsham

POST TOWNS.

ENGLAND AND WALES.

Towns.	Counties.	d.
A.		
Abbots Bromley	Staffordshire	11
Abbotsbury	Dorsetshire	10
Aberaeron	Glamorganshire	11
Aberford	Yorkshire	12
Abergavenny	Monmouthshire	11
Abergeley	Denbighshire	12
Aberystwith	Cardiganshire	12
Abingdon	Berkshire	9
Acle	Norfolk	10
Alcester	Warwickshire	10
Aldborough	Suffolk	10
Aldborough	Yorkshire	12
Alford	Lincolnshire	11
Alfreton	Derbyshire	11
Alnwick	Northumberland	13
Alresford	Hampshire	9
Alstone	Cumberland	13
Alton	Hampshire	9
Altrincham	Cheshire	11
Ambleside	Westmoreland	13
Amersham	Buckinghamshire	9

38   SCOTCH TOWNS.

Towns.	Counties.	d.
Auchtermuchty	Fifeshire	14
Ayr	Ayrshire	14
Ayton	Berwickshire	13
B.		
Balfron	Stirlingshire	
Ballantrae	Ayrshire	14
Ballachulish	Argyleshire	
Ballendalloch	Elginshire	
Banchory	Kincardineshire	15
Banff	Banffshire	16
Bannockburn	Stirlingshire	
Barrhead	Renfrewshire	
Bathgate	Linlithgowshire	13
Beauly	Invernessshire	17
Beith *Barld*	Ayrshire	1/14, 14
Bellshill	Edinburghshire	
Bervie	Kincardineshire	15
Biggar	Lanarkshire	14
Blackshields	Edinburghshire	14
Blair Adam	Invernessshire	
Blair Athol	Perthshire	14
Blairgowrie	Perthshire	14
Boat of Forbes	Aberdeenshire	
Bonar Bridge	Sutherlandshire	
Bonaw	Invernessshire	15
Borrowmuirhead	Edinburghshire	
Borrowstoness	Linlithgowshire	14
Bothwell	Lanarkshire	
Bowholm	Banffshire	
Bowmore	Argyleshire	

Pages from the Horsham postmaster's rate book, 1836

Printed books were supplied to the postmasters around the country (more correctly termed deputy postmasters) and they had to insert the rates in manuscript. Illustrated are pages from the 1836 book for the post office at Horsham which gives a good impression of the cost of sending a letter from a country town. This excludes all additional charges, however.

The book was printed in May 1836 and thus bore the name of Francis Freeling as Secretary. The following month Freeling died, no longer the admired organiser and administrator. He had believed in high rates of postage and had purposely kept the charges high. Just before he died he set down his views quite clearly:

Cheap postage! What is this men are talking about? Can it be that all my life I have been in error? If I, then others – others whose behests I have been bound to obey . . . Is it not within the last six months that the present Chancellor of the Exchequer has charged me not to let the revenue go down? What! You, Freeling, brought up and educated as you have been, are you going to lend yourself to these extravagant schemes? You with your four-horse mail coaches, too![19]

Freeling was replaced by Lieutenant-Colonel William Leader Maberly as Secretary in September 1836 and the Postmaster-General was now the Earl of Lichfield, appointed in June 1835. These two men were to lead the Post Office through the next few years of turmoil. Both men have been stigmatised for their opposition, in whole or in part, to Rowland Hill's scheme of uniform penny postage. Yet Maberly, although inexperienced, was concerned to have an efficient service. In the severe winter of 1836/7 one of his early instructions to postmasters concerned snow-ploughs, repeating Freeling's instructions of December 1814. On 29 December, 1836 he wrote:

I send you some Copies of a description of a Snow Plough, which has been used with great advantage in former seasons, for the purpose of forcing a passage through the Snow; and I have to request you will communicate with the Magistrates, Commissioners, Trustees and Surveyors of Roads, or other influential Persons, urging their co-operation in endeavouring to remove the impediments to the progress of the Mails.

The Postmaster General relies on all possible efforts being made by yourself and others to secure this important object; and I would suggest whether, amongst other methods, the passage of the Mail Coaches through the Snow might not be facilitated by placing them upon Sledges.[20]

Many suggestions were submitted by members of the public at about this time, some beautifully illustrated.[21]

Unknown to Maberly or Lichfield, at the same time as snow-ploughs were being advocated and their use encouraged in the frozen countryside, Rowland Hill was writing at his desk on a much more fundamental aspect of Post Office work, which was to bring sweeping changes.

CHAPTER THREE

Rowland Hill and his Pamphlet

Rowland Hill (see page 34) was born in Kidderminster, near Birmingham, on 3 December 1795. He was the third of six sons who were to become an exceptionally brilliant and united family. A sickly child, Hill was brought up in Wolverhampton and Birmingham. His father had set up a school on new principles and from the age of twelve Rowland was involved in teaching there. Later, he and his eldest brother Matthew were devoted to educational reform. A new 'model' school, Hazelwood, was opened in 1819. Made famous by the publication of a book by Rowland and another brother Arthur, the Hazelwood system was based on self-discipline and self-government by the boys – a remarkable contrast to the other schools of the day. A branch of this school was opened in Tottenham, north London at Bruce Castle, in 1827.

Discontented to be merely a schoolmaster, Hill turned his mind to invention. His first contact with postal affairs was in 1826 when he devised a plan for sorting and stamping letters in mail coaches while on the road to London. In his autobiography he quotes a memorandum of August of that year:

The mails reach London at six in the morning, and the distribution of letters does not commence till after nine. Might not the mails arrive three hours later, and consequently leave the respective towns three hours later, if the letters could be assorted and marked on the road? And might not this be done by the guard, if he had the inside fitted up with shelves, &c, for the purpose? The charge for postage might be marked with a stamp; as each bag was received, all the London letters it contained would require the same stamp-mark, except in cases of double and treble letters, when the mark might be repeated.[1]

This idea came to fruition in another form as the Travelling Post Office carriage on the London & Birmingham Railway in 1838, as a result of a later suggestion by Fredrick Karstadt.

Then Hill began to work at a more effective rotary printing machine for printing newspapers. This could not be successful unless the method of printing the tax stamp was changed. Now it was impressed on each sheet before printing; to operate with Hill's machine the tax stamp would have to be printed at the same time. Hill's suggestion of how this might be done was turned down by the Lords of the Treasury.

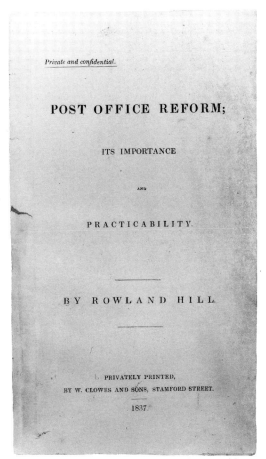

Title-page of the first edition of Hill's pamphlet

In 1835 Hill became Secretary to the Commission for the colonisation of South Australia, a position he held until 1839. At about the same time he began to take a serious interest in postal reform, partly as a result of having been involved in the attempted repeal of the newspaper tax. After writing an initial memorandum, very short in length, his interest was aroused and he began to read the voluminous official reports which had already appeared. At about this time, in 1836, he was introduced to Robert Wallace who furnished him with a cabful of books from which he drew his statistical information. With government revenue in considerable surplus, it was thought time for a reduction in taxation. A lowering of postage rates was an obvious possibility.

'Post Office Reform'

The result of Hill's labours was the pamphlet: *Post Office Reform: Its Importance and Practicability*. It was produced in early January 1837 marked 'Private and confidential' and printed by William Clowes and Sons of Stamford Street, London. Initially, this first edition was circulated to a few of his friends and officials and submitted to the Chancellor of the Exchequer, acknowledged on 4 January. This he did so that the Government might take up the proposals as their own. It was not published for the general public (by Charles Knight) until February of the same year when a second edition was printed with a supplementary paper added.

All in all, there were four editions of the pamphlet, each differing, even if only slightly, in some respect from the others. It has been said that there were five editions as two appeared in February or March of 1837, one dated the other marked 'Second Edition'. The last edition was printed as the fourth edition in 1838.

Post Office revenue had not increased since 1815, yet the population had. Comparatively, Hill claimed in his pamphlet, a loss was occurring of some £2 million per annum. However, as with some of his other calculations, no adequate proof was provided. As a critical survey later pointed out, an increase of population will not produce a proportionate increase of correspondence for some time.

Hill then attempted to establish the 'natural' cost of the transmission of a letter within Great Britain, and took as his basis the cost of sending a letter from London to Edinburgh. This he calculated at 'one thirty-sixth part of a penny'. He argued that as the distance involved was much greater than an average distance, a charge of one thirty-sixth part of a penny would amply repay the expense of transit. (Hill always quotes the distance as 400 miles, though the Post Office calculated it as 399 miles, which kept the charge within a lower band.)

Hill continued (his italics):

If, therefore, the charge for postage be made proportionate to the whole expense incurred in the receipt, transit and delivery of the letter, and in the collection of its postage, it must be made uniformly the same from every post town to every other post town in the United Kingdom, unless it can be shown how we are to collect so small a sum as the thirty-sixth part of a penny.[2]

Further remarks noted that the expenses of receipt and delivery were not much affected by the weight of each letter, within moderate limits; and

as it would take a nine-fold weight to make the expense of transit amount to one farthing, it follows *that, taxation apart, the charge ought to be precisely the same for every packet of moderate weight, without reference to the number of its enclosures.*[3]

There followed a description of the complex operations required to stamp and tax the letters in the London sorting office, and the hurried manner in which they had to be carried out. According to Hill there was no doubt that the chief sources of trouble lay in the complexity arising out of the varying charges for postage and the mixture of paid and unpaid letters. 'The remedy must therefore be looked for in the means of simplification.'[4] This was to be effected by prepayment.

To assist the delivery of letters every house might be provided with a box into which the letters carrier would drop the letters.

The essential elements of his plan were given as 'first a very low rate of postage, to neutralize the objections on the part of the public to its being demanded in advance; and secondly, a uniform rate of postage, to simplify the mode of accounting for its receipt.'[5]

In support of his proposal for a great reduction in rates he gave the example of the *Penny Magazine*:

The distribution of the Penny Magazine is exactly parallel with the proposed primary distribution of letters. The magazine is sent to every part of the kingdom, and in considerable towns is delivered at the houses of the subscribers; but the penny charged for the magazine includes not only the cost of distribution, but the cost of eight large pages of letter-press and wood-cuts; and yet it is well known that the undertaking is a profitable one.[6]

He therefore proposed: 'That the charge for primary distribution, that is to say, the postage on all letters received in a post-town, and delivered in the same, or any other post-town in the British Isles, *shall be at the uniform rate of one penny per ounce*, – all letters and other papers, whether single or multiple, forming one packet and not weighing more than an ounce, being charged one penny; and heavier packets, to any convenient limit, (say one pound,) being charged an additional half-penny for each additional half ounce.'[7] To enable postage to be prepaid he advocated that the number of receiving houses be considerably increased and that they be open shops where all letters were brought to the counter. The reduction in price would mean a huge increase in the volume of traffic and so the revenue would not suffer.

Turning to the postal system as it then existed, he enumerated several defects and anomalies in the methods of distribution. An example of anomalies in postal charges was also provided:

There is a cross-post from Wolverhampton through Dudley, Stourbridge, and other places. Between Dudley and Stourbridge this post passes through the village of Brierly Hill. The postage of a letter from Wolverhampton to Dudley is 4d; but from Wolver-hampton to Brierly Hill, some miles further on, it is only one penny.[8]

A distinction was drawn between what Hill described as the primary and secondary distribution of letters. The primary distribution was between the main post towns, the secondary that which proceeded from those towns to other smaller towns and country villages. Regarding the secondary distribution he declared that no branch of the service should incur a loss and so the country villages would have to defray the extra costs of their letter deliveries. This could be done by charging the expense upon the parish rates, 'or upon each letter.'[9] The extra postage to be collected would only delay the delivery a little, though no mention was made of the breach in uniformity which this charge would entail.

Significantly, no mention was made, either, of the method of prepayment for which Hill is most famous, i.e. the stamped envelopes and letter sheets, and the adhesive postage stamp itself. It was suggested as a possibility that newspapers might be subject to the same rates, but there was no indication that the privilege of free franking should be withdrawn.

Stamped Covers and Labels

Hill's proposals were startling in their simplicity and although he had no direct experience of working in the Post Office they clearly merited proper examination. He had submitted his scheme to the Chancellor of the Exchequer early in January 1837. The Chancellor, Mr Thomas Spring Rice, suggested various modifications and clarifications especially as to the mode of prepayment. Hill supplied a supplement to his paper on 28 January, mentioning for the first time the use of stamped covers which had been originally recommended for newspapers by Charles Knight in 1834.

At this time the Commission Inquiring into the Management of the Post Office was preparing its ninth report, on its investigations into the London Twopenny Post. The Commissioners summoned Hill to give evidence on 13 February. He outlined his plan and expanded on his idea of stamped covers:

Let stamped covers and sheets of paper be supplied to the public from the Stamp-office or Post-office, as may be most convenient, and sold at such a price as to include the postage. Letters and newspapers so stamped might be put into the letter-box, as at present, instead of being delivered to the Receiver.

Covers, at various prices, would be required for packets of various weights, and each should have the weight it is entitled to carry legibly printed with the stamp.[10]

He added that to prevent it being used a second time 'the stamp of the receiving-house should be struck upon the frank-stamp.'[11] Only one objection occurred to him:

Persons unaccustomed to write letters would perhaps be at a loss how to proceed. They might send or take their letters to the Post-office without having had recourse to the stamp. It is true that, on presentation of the letter, the receiver, instead of accepting the money as postage, might take it as the price of a cover or band, in which the bringer might immediately enclose the letter, and then re-direct it; but the bringer would sometimes be unable to write. Perhaps this difficulty might be obviated by using a bit of paper just large enough to bear the stamp, and covered at the back with a glutinous wash, which the bringer, might, by applying a little moisture, attach to the back of the letter, so as to avoid the necessity for re-directing it.[12]

Here is the first mention of an adhesive postage stamp and it was printed thus in the ninth report of the Commission and also in a supplement to *Post Office Reform* which was incorporated in the latter's second edition. This was published and sold to the general public at the end of the same month – February 1837.

The Commissioners considered Hill's proposals ingenious and detailed them at length, even though they were strictly only examining the workings of the London Twopenny Post. They recommended that the idea of stamped covers be carried into effect. Charles Pressley, the Secretary of the Board of Stamps and Taxes, had been interviewed and he was in favour of this, provided a security paper were used to prevent forgery. The paper he suggested was the silk-thread paper manufactured by John Dickinson of the Old Bailey. Pressley and Dickinson himself examined later were of the opinion that this paper should be reserved for government use and that it was almost impossible to forge. It had been invented in 1828 and patented a year later. Originally, the threads were laid at an equal distance from each other and had to be mended when they broke. Manufacture was at Dickinson's Nash Mills in Hertfordshire under Excise supervision as it was used for Exchequer Bonds and government documents which required authentication.

It was recommended that the rates in the Twopenny Post Office be reduced for the whole area to 1d. up to 1 ounce and 2d. up to six ounces if conveyed in stamped covers. Prepayment would not be compulsory, however.

We have appended to the Report specimens of the paper and envelopes which we propose should be introduced for the conveyance of letters by what may be termed 'The London District Post', which at the present, comprises all places within 12 miles of the General Post-office; although we are inclined to believe that it may be found advantageous to extend the deliveries beyond this boundary to several of the towns within 15 miles of London.

In order to afford the public every facility for obtaining the covers, they should be kept at all the receiving-houses, and it will be necessary for the Stamp-office to make such an allowance to the distributors as will induce stationers and others in and around London to vend them. We recommend that the envelopes shall be sold to the public without any additional charge beyond the respective duties of 1d. and 2d.; whilst labels may also be prepared of such a form that they can be attached to other envelopes or covers of any size and description.[13]

The covers that were appended (see page 34) were produced by John Dickinson on his silk thread paper, possibly to designs by Charles Whiting. Each bore a printed insignia indicating that it was for the London District Post. There were two 1d. varieties printed in yellow-buff – one a letter sheet and the other made into an envelope. Accompanying them was a 2d. letter sheet in green.

Also appended to the report were two maps. One was a map of London showing the boundaries of the old Foreign and General Post deliveries and the receiving houses. The other was of the country 15 miles around London showing the limits of the Twopenny and Three-penny Post deliveries. This had been compiled from the Ordnance Survey by James Wyld.

The Commissioners (Ninth) Report was dated 7 July 1837, but produced little immediate response. Hill's proposals, however, had acted as a great stimulant to the argument for postal reform and lower rates and provoked wide public comment. Wallace campaigned in parliament for a select committee to examine Hill's plan but during the debate on the Post Office Bills in June 1837 the Postmaster General, Lord Lichfield, delivered his opinion: 'With respect to the plan set forth by Mr Hill, of all the wild and visionary schemes which he had ever heard or read of, it was the most extraordinary.'[14]

In November 1837 the Select Committee was finally granted.

CHAPTER FOUR

A Very Select Committee

On 23 November 1837 Parliament ordered 'that a Select Committee be appointed to inquire into the present Rates and mode of charging Postage, with a view to such a Reduction thereof as may be made without injury to the Revenue; and for this purpose to examine especially into the mode recommended for charging and collecting Postage in a Pamphlet published by Mr Rowland Hill.'[1]

As Croker later put it in the *Quarterly Review* 'Mr Rowland Hill's plan was certainly worthy of parliamentary consideration, and we only complain that the tribunal was so very *select*.'[2] For the members of the Commission included many prominent postal reformers. The Chairman was Robert Wallace and other members included such knowledgeable reformers as Lord Lowther and Henry Warburton.

Evidence began to be taken in February 1838 and the first thick volume of reports appeared in April. On 1 August, 1838 two further hefty volumes of evidence and appendices appeared from the deliberations of the Commission but their third and final report, although bearing the date 13 August, 1838, was not published until early March 1839. This contained four maps of postroads and deliveries together with the Commission's summing-up and recommendations.

The maps were of Post Office operations in the British Isles. Each was overlaid by circles showing the distances which regulated postage rates under the existing law. In that for England and Wales Leicester 'being near the centre of England'[3] was selected as the point from which the circles radiated. It also did not interfere with the London Twopenny and Threepenny Post limits. Those for Scotland and Ireland were based on Edinburgh and Dublin. Some of the more important penny posts were delineated separately (see page 35). All indicated how the mail was carried – by railway, mailcoach, horse post or footpost, and in the case of Scotland, steam boats and stage coaches. These maps were corrected to January or February, 1838. There was also a postal map of France, dating from 1834.

The Commission's *raison d'être* is summed up in this final report. It begins by expounding some of the 'Moral and Commercial Evils of present high Rates of Postage'[4] especially as to the effects on the poor 'causing them to sacrifice their little earnings to the pleasure or advantage of corresponding with their distant friends, or compel them to forego such intercourse altogether.'[5]

To dispel these 'Evils' the Committee recommended a uniform rate of postage, that payment should be made in advance by means of 'stamps' or stamped paper although this should not be compulsory, and that charges should be regulated entirely by weight.

As to rates, the aim should be a uniform penny rate. But it was recognised that this would be injurious to the Revenue and so an interim 2d. rate should be introduced. The crucial votes on this had taken place on 17 and 18 July, 1838. Members of the Committee were fairly evenly split on the merits of low rates. Initially, Warburton had proposed a 1d. rate but this was defeated (6 to 3). He then proposed a $1\frac{1}{2}$d. rate but was again defeated (6 to 4). At the third attempt on the following day there was a tie (5 to 5) on the motion for a uniform 2d. rate and it was only the casting vote of Wallace, the Chairman, which brought the motion to success.

However, a 1d. rate was recommended for immediate introduction for letters sent up to fifteen miles from the post town.

It was recognised that the privilege of franking and its abuse caused a serious loss to Post Office revenue. The recommendation, therefore, was that 'it would be politic, in a financial point of view, and agreeable to the public sense of justice, if on effecting the proposed reduction of the postage rates, the privilege of Parliamentary franking were to be abolished, and the privilege of official franking placed under strict limitation.'[6] Petitions to Parliament and parliamentary documents would still go free.

These recommendations had resulted from the taking of voluminous evidence. The Committee had examined the main officers of the Post Office from the Postmaster General downwards, directing many important statistical returns to be produced. They had also questioned officers of the Board of Stamps and Taxes, Rowland Hill and 83 other witnesses 'of various classes in society, and of various occupations, professions, and trades, from different parts of the kingdom.'[7] In the selection of these they had been 'much assisted by an association of bankers and merchants in London, formed expressly to aid the Committee in the prosecution of their inquiry.'[8] This was the Mercantile Committee on Postage whose activities are described in the following chapter.

Post Office officials were the first to give evidence as to current operational practice and their views on Hill's plan. Quite some time was spent establishing how many letters were sent illegally, and how. One particularly common practice, it transpired, was for coffee houses in London to hang up bags for the collection of letters bound overseas.

These were conveyed privately to Liverpool and other ports and there put into the postal system or directly on board ship. Considerable savings resulted, though only, of course, to the sender. The Post Office knew about such practices and although they were on a large scale they did little effectively to stop them.

Inland, postage was evaded by use of private carriers, booksellers' parcels etc. Numbers could not be estimated but they were thought to be very high.

The examination of T Lawrence, Assistant Secretary of the Post Office, elicited remarkable information about postage rates. He explained that as a result of a recent change single letters paid 2d. for distances up to eight miles between post towns, 4d up to fifteen miles, 5d up to twenty miles and so on. 'Packets of one ounce weight are charged as four single letters. If a single sheet exceed one ounce it is charged according to its weight.'[9]

He was asked by Wallace 'if a mail goes a circuitous route, the person receiving a letter pays an additional sum for the additional inconvenience?'[10] He agreed, adding that in some cases there were two different routes from and to the same places, with different rates, frequently a penny more. When asked if he had not had many complaints about that mode of charging he tersely replied 'A great many.'[11]

Hill was first examined on 12 February and taken through his plan in detail. He was particularly questioned about his distinction between primary and secondary distributions and he seemed unclear as to where to draw the line between them. On reflection he withdrew this, removing the supplementary charge for secondary delivery and throwing all his calculations out of kilter.

Because of lack of official statistics Hill had had to estimate the number of chargeable letters which he noted in his pamphlet. This he did at about 88 million per annum. The Post Office preferred their estimate of under 60 million. After the Commissioners ordered accounts to be kept for two separate weeks they decided that a truer figure was $77\frac{1}{2}$ million, as well as some 7 million franks and $44\frac{1}{2}$ million news-papers going free. Hill revised his figures to similar amounts'. This was important inasmuch as it determined how many letters would be required to be sent to sustain the revenue at its present level. Hill thought five and a quarter fold; Lichfield, the antagonistic Postmaster General, twelve-fold.

The attitude of Maberly, the Post Office Secretary, was summarised as follows:

He considers the whole scheme of Mr Hill as utterly fallacious; he thought so from the first moment he read the pamphlet of Mr Hill; and his opinion of the plan was formed

Earl of Lichfield, Postmaster General 1835–41

long before the evidence was given before the Committee. The plan appears to him a most preposterous one, utterly unsupported by facts, and resting entirely on assumption. Every experiment in the way of reduction which has been made by the Post-office, has shown its fallacy; for every reduction whatever leads to a loss of revenue, in the first instance; if the reduction be small, the revenue recovers itself; but if the rates were to be reduced to 1d., the revenue would not recover itself for 40 or 50 years.[12]

Strongly put, and somewhat exaggerated, but in essence this was nearer the truth than Hill's less qualified remarks. The trouble was that although it was clear that there would be some increase of correspondence on the reduction of rates, what size that increase would take was mere supposition.

When it came to the method of payment, the Committee only accepted Hill's proposals in part. They agreed that it should be paid in advance though this would not be made compulsory. If prepaid it should be by means of stamped envelopes or sheets, stamped paper, or labels. They also recommended Dickinson's paper for fear of forgery.

Post Office Reaction

Publication of the Committee's third report gave great impetus to the movement for postal reform and caused quite a flurry of activity. Early in April 1839 the Lords of the Treasury asked Lord Lichfield, as Postmaster General, to comment on the effect to the revenue if the Committee's recommendations were carried into effect. By this time there was no longer a surplus in government revenue, there having been a deficit for the previous two years. Ironically, Lichfield reported on 6 May, 1839, a year to the day before the fruition of his opponents' plans with the issue of prepaid stationery and labels.

Lichfield seized upon the inconsistencies in the Report occasioned by the need for compromise. There should be a 1d. charge for the first fifteen miles, and a uniform 2d. everywhere thereafter. How were these overlapping and interlocking radial distances to be determined? The aim of simplicity would be lost. Penny posts, moreover, were to remain as they were, for want of a uniform system, even though the Committee did not like them. But no replacement was suggested. Rather defensively he detailed some of the changes already made, including the lowering of some charges, but he challenged the view that a vast reduction in rates would lead to an immediate, large increase in the number of letters, large enough to offset the loss. Experience taught him otherwise, and he felt that only solid experience provided any reliable guide.

He concluded:

I can only repeat that it is my firm conviction that on the gross Revenue the deficiency would be very great if the plan recommended by the Committee were adopted, while in the net the sacrifice would be still larger from the expenditure rendered necessary by increased business. That there would be an augmentation of correspondence I have no doubt, but the amount of it must be wholly conjectural, though I think myself warranted in asserting that neither the present number of Letters would be increased nearly fourfold nor the present net Revenue be realized from the altered rates of postage for some years to come. Admitting therefore that there must be a large increase of Letters I must differ in opinion with the Committee, and instead of arriving at the conclusion with them that you will risk nothing by the reduction proposed I am compelled to state my firm conviction that the greater proportion of the net Revenue of the Department will be hazarded by the adoption of their recommendation.[13]

But realism, if small-minded, had been overtaken by political necessity. The Lords of the Treasury annotated this long report simply 'No directions necessary'.

CHAPTER FIVE

Henry Cole and the Mercantile Campaign

Pressure for reform came largely from merchants and businessmen, who naturally had a great deal to gain from lower postage rates. They formed a high proportion of the witnesses called before Wallace's Parliamentary Committee. This was because in London they had been organised into a Committee for the express purpose of gaining as much publicity as possible for postal reform, and thus influencing the parliamentary committee. The Mercantile Committee on Postage was to have a decisive influence.

It was proposed and set up by George Moffatt, a large tea merchant in the City and later an MP for a number of constituencies. In February 1838 he informed Rowland Hill that he had prevailed upon Joshua Bates of Baring Brothers to be Chairman of his proposed committee. Hill then approached Henry Cole to be Secretary and William Ashurst became Solicitor. Both Cole and Ashurst were to work with great zeal on behalf of the Committee.

Henry Cole was an exceptionally energetic and gifted man (see page 34). Born at Bath in 1808, he worked in the Record Office as a senior assistant keeper under Lord Langdale. He was interested in almost everything – drawing, wood engraving, writing, medieval art. Later, he was a leading member of the Society of Arts, member of the executive committee of the 1851 Exhibition and, as a result, the founder of the Victoria and Albert Museum in South Kensington. As the *Dictionary of National Biography* puts it 'Cole's duties at the record office did not absorb his whole energy.'[1] His output was prodigious and remarkably effective. (He was also married, with a large family, eight children surviving him.)

Throughout his life he remained altruistic and high-minded and failed to take many opportunities of making money. He had a warm personality but this was masked by a hectoring manner. Later he was the subject of a number of cartoons emphasising his flowing white hair, dishevelled appearance and small yapping dog which was his constant companion.

Charles Dickens regarded Cole as gloriously absurd. He introduced him as a school inspector in *Hard Times*, written in 1854:

The interior of the General Post Office, 1840

Examples of different printing methods for lettersheets
suggested by C F Whiting in 'The Post Circular'

Treasury Competition entry by George Dickinson

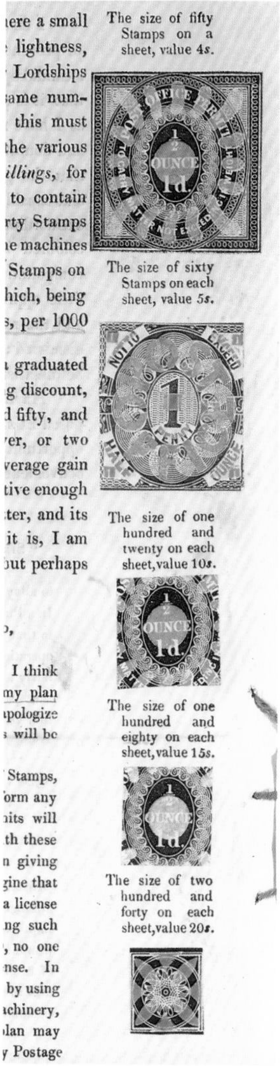

ıere a small
: lightness,
Lordships
ame num-
this must
the various
illings, for
to contain
rty Stamps
ıe machines
Stamps on
hich, being
s, per 1000
ı graduated
g discount,
l fifty, and
er, or two
verage gain
tive enough
ter, and its
it is, I am
out perhaps

I think
my plan
ıpologize
; will be
Stamps,
orm any
ıits will
th these
n giving
gine that
a license
ng such
, no one
nse. In
by using
ıchinery,
ılan may
y Postage

The size of fifty Stamps on a sheet, value 4*s*.

The size of sixty Stamps on each sheet, value 5*s*.

The size of one hundred and twenty on each sheet, value 10*s*.

The size of one hundred and eighty on each sheet, value 15*s*.

The size of two hundred and forty on each sheet, value 20*s*.

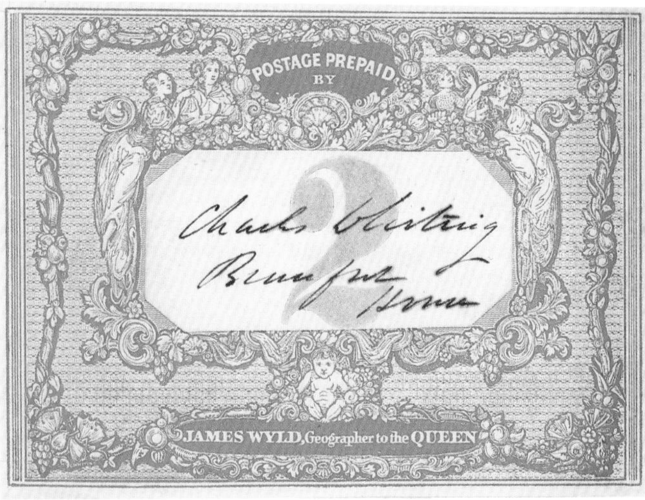

C F Whiting's suggestion for a letter sheet

Left, above and below:
Printed examples from C F Whiting's entry to the Treasury Competition

The Post Circular.

OR, WEEKLY ADVOCATE FOR A CHEAP, SWIFT, AND SURE POSTAGE.

No. 1.   WEDNESDAY, MARCH 14, 1838.   Price 2½d.

LORD ASHBURTON on presenting a petition from merchants, bankers, men of science, and others, of the metropolis, to the House of Lords, May 29, 1837, thus addressed their Lordships: "The petition was on the subject of the Post-office; one most important, yet one which had been unfortunately neglected. Its object was to state to their Lordships the inconveniences which arose from the presen tcharges for the conveyance of letters—inconveniences which disturbed social life, and strewed impediments in the way of science. He concurred in the view of the case taken by the petitioners; for he considered a tax on the transmission of letters, when carried to such an extent as it was in this country, to be most ill judged and pernicious. The system required thorough reconsideration and an entire reform. He recommended to their Lordships the perusal of a pamphlet written by Mr. Rowland Hill; that pamphlet confirmed the impression which he had, that the grievances complained of might be remedied without a sacrifice of the revenue. The remedies suggested by that gentleman were—1st, a great reduction of charges; 2nd, the payment of the charges in advance; 3rd, equalisation of the rate of charging. The expense of a Post-office establishment was the same whether the letters were conveyed twenty or two hundred miles—the only difference caused by distance being the expense of conveyance; and Mr. Hill had shown that the expense of carrying a letter to Edinburgh did not amount to more than the one-thirty-sixth part of a penny, or the one-ninth part of a farthing. He thought, therefore, that it was an injustice to persons in distant towns to impose on them the present charges. Mr. Hill proposed that no payment should be made at the Post-office, but that covers or stamped envelopes should be purchased which should carry the letter free. Mr. Hill had calculated that a penny for a letter not weighing more than half an ounce would prove sufficient. He requested the noble Lords connected with the Government to give the matter their consideration, if it were only from the fact that the revenue was injuriously affected by the present system. In the year 1835, that revenue was 130,000l. less than it was in 1825, notwithstanding the increase of population and wealth, and the spread of education. It was clear, therefore, that the charge was too heavy, and also that it was fraudulently evaded. It certainly therefore was necessary, as well for the comforts of the people as for the sake of the revenue, that the matter should be seriously considered; and had it not been that the session was so far advanced he should have deemed it his duty to move that Mr. Hill's plan for remedying the evils complained of should be referred to a select committee."

ADDRESS.

To the subject of Postage and its numerous important bearings on all departments of national policy and civilization, this publication is to be chiefly devoted; it is therefore hardly necessary to observe that all political discussion will be studiously avoided in its columns.

The POST CIRCULAR will attempt to carry out its object by impartially inquiring into the merits of Mr. Rowland Hill's plan of an uniform Penny Postage, payable in advance, and the probable effects of this plan on the present system of Post-office administration and Post-office revenue—by carefully collecting all facts strengthening or controverting Mr. Hill's plan—by recording the proceedings of the legislature, the presentation of

The average of the present postage (taking in all chargeable letters) is sixpence halfpenny per letter.

The average cost of the actual carriage to any post-town in Great Britain is about one-tenth of a penny; and even allowing the whole present cost of the Post-office establishment, the tax is above 200 per cent.: a rate of tax which experience has demonstrated always produces an evasion of the law.

No law is so extensively evaded as this; and so general has the practice become, that even the best-regulated minds do not think they are committing offence by violating it.

It is proposed to call witnesses to prove—

The great extent to which the practice of violating the law by the irregular conveyance of letters and evading postage is carried, and to give evidence of those modes, taking care to protect parties who may furnish this testimony.

That this correspondence, if the reduction be made, would immediately be transferred to the Post-office.

In addition to the very great increase in the number of of the retail dealer; whereas now such orders are not sent, or the wholesale houses are obliged to charge the postage upon them. And that, to the very numerous classes engaged in those trades into which silk, cotton, and woollen enter, this would be a most important convenience, and the cause of very great additional correspondence.

That it would lead, in all trades requiring extended publicity, to an immense increase in the postage as a mode of advertising, because a thousand circulars, with a letter on the fly-leaf, could be despatched for 4l. 3s. 4d. to parties thought by the senders most likely to become the purchasers. This would be particularly the case with publications addressed to men of science, and to particular classes or sections of society, and yet would not supersede the more extended appeal to the public through the medium of advertisements.

That to all religious and charitable institutions, particularly to those having branch societies, it would afford most essential aid in bringing their works of benevolence directly

Masthead of the first issue of *The Post Circular*

A mighty man at cutting and drying, he was; a government officer; in his way (and in most other people's too), a professed pugilist; always in training, always with a system to force down the general throat like a bolus ... he had it in charge from high authority to bring about the great public-office Millennium, when Commissioners should reign upon earth.[2]

As an intelligent man interested in current affairs he had read Hill's pamphlet in March 1837 soon after it was published. Later that year he met Hill and was taken to see one of his new printing machines in construction at Oakley Street. In February 1838 Hill proposed that Cole should assist him in 'Post Office Agitation' and a few days later offered him the secretaryship of the Mercantile Committee on Postage. This Cole accepted, with the agreement of Lord Langdale. It was a post for which he was paid fifty guineas a session.

He immediately, and characteristically, threw himself into organising the Committee. Invitations were sent out to merchants and bankers to subscribe. Many did, mostly offering £10. With the money thus provided he gained offices in Freemans Court, Cornhill, City of London, and arranged for a newspaper to be published.

This was called *The Post Circular. Or, Weekly Advocate for a Cheap, Swift, and Sure Postage.* (*Weekly* was dropped after three numbers.) Written and edited by Cole himself it cost 2½d. and was sent through the post to other newspapers, subscribers and MPs. Printed petitions and circulars would have been costly to send by post so the idea of a newspaper containing the same but going free was particularly apt. As

Cole later remarked 'The Post Office . . . would thus become the chief instrument for reforming itself.'[3] The publisher was Henry Hooper and the printer Charles Whiting. The latter offered to take the risk of the paper provided that the Committee took 500 copies of each number, and paid six guineas for each edition.

The first issue of *The Post Circular* was dated 14 March 1838. It contained in four pages an explanation of the aims of the Committee and a digest of Hill's plan. The whole back page consisted of a list of books published by John W Parker, West Strand and inside a few snippets of 'news'. This last constituted the legal basis by which *The Post Circular* could be termed a newspaper and thus pass free through the post. With the first issue, however, there were some problems for, although the paper had been properly stamped at the Stamp Office, the Post Office had not been informed. Thus, a number, including one to Robert Wallace's wife, were charged postage. After immediate complaints the Postmaster General allowed that it was indeed a newspaper and so it passed free, but it enabled Wallace to write that it was the Postmaster General who decided what was, and what was not, a newspaper.

James Chalmers' Slips

In the fourth issue of the 'newspaper' a letter from James Chalmers, bookseller and printer of Dundee, was reprinted on the front page. In December 1837 he had written to Wallace (and later in February 1838 to Maberly) with a suggestion for what he termed 'slips' to indicate the prepayment of postage. These he also designed and printed alongside his printed proposals (see page 36). This was to be the source of a parochial controversy that raged in the latter part of the nineteenth century and remarkably still continues to this day.

Chalmers suggested:

> that sheets of Stamped Slips should be prepared at the Stamp Office, (on a paper made expressly for the purpose), with a device on each from a die or cut resembling that on newspapers; that the sheets so printed or stamped should then be rubbed over on the back with a strong solution of gum, or other adhesive substance, and (when thoroughly dry) issued by the Stamp Office to town and country distributors, to stationers and others, for sale in sheets or singly.[4]

To prevent the 'slips' being used twice postmasters should put the town stamp across the slip, as he illustrated on one of his examples. A version of his design was also printed in *The Post Circular*.

Subsequently, Chalmers submitted different designs in the Treasury competition in 1839 and his descendants, and some other Scots, have claimed that he was the inventor of the adhesive postage stamp.

Propaganda for Reform

Some eight editions of *The Post Circular* appeared regularly until the end of May, 1838. They were filled with parliamentary reports, commentaries thereon, and letters from readers and fellow reformers refuting various Post Office statements. Numerous petitions were organised and sent to willing MPs, who then laid them before Parliament. In June there was a break and the last of the first series, No. 9, appeared on 5 July. This was smaller in format, now pamphlet size, and cost 6d. No more were published that year.

At the same time Robert Wallace, despite being Chairman of the Parliamentary Committee, was still actively campaigning. He sent out a circular designed to show as many as possible of the iniquities of the present system. In the form of a sealed letter sheet, the front was printed with a long text explaining how it had been posted (see page 36):

This will be put into the General Post Office [in London] at eight o'clock this evening – *where it will remain until eight on Monday morning*, and then be sent by the Day Mail, if for the North of England, or any part of all Ireland; but if for any town in many important parts of England, or any in all Scotland, it will be kept back twelve hours longer, that is until eight o'clock that night – *or forty-eight hours from the hour of its being put into the London Post Office*, during which time one Mail Coach will leave the General Post Office quite empty at eight on Sunday morning.

The example illustrated shows that this is what happened. On the reverse is a datestamp for 30 June with a handstamp on the front indicating that it had been put in after seven o'clock at night. The FREE handstamp was applied on 2 July but Wallace had clearly posted too many because this was crossed out in manuscript and a handstamp 'Above Number' applied. MPs were allowed to send ten letters a day free under the system and receive fifteen, none to exceed one ounce in weight. Wallace's circular, which he had addressed to the Mayor of Bath was charged ninepence, because he had sent more than his allocation. The Mayor naturally refused to accept this and so the circular was returned, bearing the Bath datestamp of 5 July. Happily, the circular had been kept dry. It was just under one ounce in weight and Wallace noted that if it were not kept dry it would be over the limit and be charged fourfold. All this encapsulated the reformers' complaints against the postal system.

Cole spent the latter part of 1838 working on articles and arranging petitions. One of his ideas was a scene which he wrote for the Christmas pantomine performance of *Fair Rosamond*. It does not seem to have been performed, however. Mr Young, the 'pantomimist', was supposed to have performed it at Covent Garden Theatre but although Cole notes in his diary that he went to the theatre on several days in December, the scene was either not ready, or had been omitted.

Later in 1839 he was more successful with another scene. It was an imaginary reception by Queen Victoria of Rowland Hill, Lord Lichfield and Lord Melbourne at Windsor Castle. The Queen questions Hill on his plan and asks Lichfield to explain the high rates and why nothing has been done about it. She then shows remarkable knowledge of the Reports of the Parlimentary Committee and details to Lord Lichfield how the number of letters carried could be increased twelvefold without increasing Post Office expenses twelvefold as Lichfield thought.

In a version of the scene published by Henry Hooper, the Postmaster General then submitted himself entirely to 'your Majesty's compassionate correction. Your Majesty is much more enlightened about the Post-Office than your Majesty's most humble servant the Postmaster-General. With your Majesty's leave I will retire.'[5] At which point Lichfield exits and the Queen remarks to Lord Melbourne, the Prime Minister, 'It is clear to me that his Lordship had better retire from the Post-Office.'[6] She also thought that the loss of Colonel Maberly to the Post Office would be another great gain to the public.

Cheaply printed as a pamphlet or sheetlet, the scene was amusing and widely read.

Another of Cole's ideas was designed to show the absurdity of some of the rates. Two printed letters were prepared headed 'Specimen of Postage Charges in 1839. *To be Preserved among the Curiosities of any Museum, &c.*'

One was a large sheet of paper, thirty-five inches by twenty-three inches, weighing under one ounce. If kept dry it was charged as a single letter, but, as with the Wallace letter, if it became damp it would weigh more than one ounce and therefore be charged fourfold.

The second letter consisted of two pieces of thin paper, four inches by two and a half inches, weighing only seven grains but attracting double postage. Cole describes with glee the scene at Charing Cross post office when fifty of each were taken to be posted.[7]

The Climax of the Campaign

In March, 1839 Wallace's Parliamentary Committee published its delayed final report and immediately the Mercantile Committee met at the Exchequer coffee house to plan their next campaign. It was agreed to publish another issue of *The Post Circular* with extracts of the Report. It also called for the signing of petitions and deputations to Members of Parliament.

A remarkable number of petitions were organised and presented to Parliament. In 1837, there had been only five on the subject of

Cole's caricature of the Edinburgh mail

postal reform, but the following year saw some 320. However, by July 1839 over 2,000 petitions had already been presented with over 250,000 signatures. Members of the Mercantile Committee kept in their papers examples of the various posters produced.

The campaign continued with an issue of *The Post Circular* dated 30 April, 1839. Cole cleverly illustrated how a small number of letters paid for the carriage of a much greater bulk of newspapers and parcels. He produced a drawing of the Edinburgh mail of 2 March, 1838 entitled 'Great Weight and No Price! Little Weight and All Price!!' It was designed for the particular instruction of the Postmaster-general 'who, notwithstanding he stands at the head of the Post-office class, has shown that he is at the bottom of it, in respect of knowledge of the rudiments of his business.'[8] Cole showed that the number of letters could be drastically increased without overloading the mail.

Printed in the same issue of the newspaper were examples of Charles Whiting's ideas for the prepayment of postage (see page 53). First, in blue, there was a design inscribed 'Post Office Permit Price 1d $\frac{1}{2}$ Ounce'. This was from a letterpress block and was to be reproduced in several forms and colours throughout the year. (A letter sheet in yellow had been produced the previous year by John W Parker, a bookseller in West Strand, London, and included in William Ashurst's booklet 'Facts and Reasons in Support of Mr Rowland Hill's Plan for a Universal Penny Postage'.) The other design was printed by the bicolour Congreve method.

Public clamour now demanded some action on the part of the Government. On 2 May a large deputation of MPs and members of

UNIFORM PENNY POSTAGE

A PUBLIC MEETING

Of the Bankers, Merchants, and Traders, of the City of London.

Will be held at the

EGYPTIAN HALL OF THE **MANSION HOUSE,**

ON

Friday, May 31,

AT TWO O'CLOCK PRECISELY.

TO PETITION PARLIAMENT FOR THE ADOPTION OF MR. ROWLAND HILL'S PLAN OF A UNIFORM PENNY POSTAGE,

As recommended by the Select

Committee of the House of Commons.

THE RT. HON. THE LORD MAYOR

WILL TAKE THE CHAIR

The Metropolitan Members are expected to attend.

Above
Poster of the Mercantile Committee
announcing a meeting

Right
Poster of the Mercantile Committee
for a petition

UNIFORM Penny Postage

THE FOLLOWING

PETITION

TO THE

HOUSE OF COMMONS,

To Pass this Important Measure without delay,

Lies here for Signatures.

READER,

Sign the Petition without a moment's delay,

BECAUSE

IT MUST BE PRESENTED BEFORE FRIDAY NEXT, JULY THE 12TH

*To the Honourable the Commons in Parliament
assembled.*

The humble Petition of the undersigned Inhabitants of Westminster.

Sheweth,

THAT, an Englishman having invented the
Uniform Penny Postage Plan, your Petitioners feel that
the United Kingdom should not be behind France, and
Belgium, and Prussia, and the United States, in getting
it; they, therefore, humbly pray your Honourable House
to give effect to the Uniform Penny Postage, payable in
advance, *during the present Session of Parliament.*

And your Petitioners will ever pray.

the Mercantile Committee called on Lord Melbourne to persuade him to bring a bill before Parliament. Henry Warburton, MP for Bridport led the delegation, mainly supporters of the Government. When he said 'It would be a concession so wise, that it would be well calculated to make any Government justly popular, and he would strongly urge it as a measure which a Liberal party had a just right to expect from a Liberal administration' he was loudly cheered.[9] Melbourne said he would think seriously about the business but only six days later the Government resigned. Peel was asked to form an administration but refused and so Melbourne was back within a month.

To keep up the pressure a meeting was summoned at the Mansion House in the City. The following day a petition from the City was prepared and received more than 12,500 signatures within a few hours. But in the meantime Lord John Russell, Home Secretary, had announced the Government's intention to propose a resolution in favour of uniform penny postage. This was regarded as a procedural device to get over the session without a bill and incensed Moffatt and Cole. In the budget debate at the beginning of July a Bill was at last promised. It was a relatively easy sop to radical opinion within the Liberal party. The Select Committee's recommendation of a uniform 2d. rate had been overtaken by overwhelming public pressure.

CHAPTER SIX

Success of the Reformers

Given all the drama and agitation that went before it, the Postage Duties Bill had a remarkably painless and swift progress through Parliament. It was introduced by the Chancellor of the Exchequer in the House of Commons on 18 July and received the Royal Assent on 17 August.

The Report of the Select Committee had been received and agreed on 12 July, by majorities of 102 and 59 respectively. Spring Rice, the Chancellor, stated that the real question at issue was not the reduction in postage charges but rather which tax should be imposed to safeguard the revenue from the loss which this would entail. He asked for a guarantee from the House to make good any shortfall.

On 22 July, the Chancellor moved the second reading of the Postage Duties Bill. In it he asked that powers be conferred on the Treasury to make such reductions and warrants as necessary to introduce uniform penny postage when they felt it suitable. Details were to be worked out later. This vagueness occasioned some opposition, but Spring Rice pointed out that none of the powers conferred on the Treasury by this bill would survive the next Session of Parliament. It was an experiment which would be renewed or otherwise in the light of experience.

Sir Robert Inglis, Member of Parliament for the University of Oxford, and Sir Robert Peel led what opposition there was. The former asked the Chancellor to state 'whether he did not bring forward this measure in opposition to the Postmaster-general, and all those officers, whether past or present, who had been, or were connected with the fiscal arrangements of the Post-office?'[1]

This was a plan, not to aid the poorer classes, but rather for the benefit of the great traders. It was a plan which had been brought forward to obtain public favour.

With regard to MPs' privilege of franking he did not see why 'because a tax was to [be] taken off others, a tax was to be imposed on Members.'[2] There he found little sympathy, even from his own party. Peel was against the continuation of the privilege of franking for MPs and even more against the sending of bulky parliamentary papers free.

He thought, however, that there should have been an experiment of a partial reduction first. But he did not wish to push matters to a vote and so the bill was read a second time without division. Two days later it went through its Committee stage in less than three quarters of an hour (according to Cole)[3] and on 29 July it was read for the third time, and passed.

When it came before the Lords on 5 August, Lord Melbourne himself introduced it. In his speech he was assisted by notes prepared by Cole and Hill. He was cautious as to the effects on the revenue and did not wish to go into details as to how the plan might be put into effect but he nevertheless recommended it.

The Duke of Wellington then rose and pointed out the dangers to the revenue when trouble in Canada required the presence there of 40,000 troops. After a long rambling speech he concluded 'notwithstanding I feel so little confidence in this measure, and notwithstanding that I must continue to lament that it should ever have been adopted, when all the circumstances are considered, I, nevertheless, earnestly recommend you to pass it. It is a measure which has been most anxiously looked for by the country.'[4] The circumstances he was referring to related to its being a money bill, which, by agreement, was the prerogative of the House of Commons. The Lords could not oppose this unless they wished to have a full-scale constitutional battle with the Commons. Even then they would still lose.

One of the last speakers was Lord Lichfield, the Postmaster General. He sought to remove the impression that he was opposed to the measure 'with perfect consistency with all that he had said or done.'[5] He now approved of uniform penny postage 'on the simple ground, that the demand for the measure was universal . . . So obnoxious was the tax on letters, that the people had declared their readiness to submit to any impost that might be substituted in its stead, and on these principles [sic] he agreed to the plan, assuring the House he would use his best exertions effectually to carry it out.'[6] Postal reformers might have been forgiven for making a few derisory remarks.

The Bill was read without a vote being taken and on 9 August at its third reading it was passed. As mentioned above, it received the Royal Assent on 17 August 1839. Basically, the Act gave temporary powers to the Lords of the Treasury up to 5 October 1840 to arrange the reduction of rates to a uniform penny, regardless of distance, but measured by weight, no amount being specified. It allowed for the abolition of franking and the use of stamped paper, stamped envelopes and stamps affixed thereto. These now had to be designed and produced. A competition was arranged by the Treasury to effect this, the results being described in the following chapters.

Francis Baring, Chancellor of the Exchequer

Rowland Hill at the Treasury

To put the Act into operation the Government turned to Rowland Hill. The new Chancellor of the Exchequer, Francis Baring, invited Hill to join the Treasury in an ill-defined post for two years at the rate of £1,500 per annum. He was to be 'attached' to the Treasury 'with reference to the proposed alterations in the Post Office'[7] but had no direct control. This was agreed on 14 September. Shortly thereafter Hill asked Cole to be his assistant, at the same time resigning from the Secretaryship of the South Australia Commission. Though they were to work together closely over the next few years, they never really liked each other. Cole thought that Hill could not get on with people and when he subsequently read Hill's autobiography he described it as 'correct, impassive, foggy like himself'.[8]

One of Hill's immediate actions upon his appointment was to visit the General Post Office in the company of Francis Baring to see postal operations for the first time (see page 53). It was quite clear that the office was too small and needed to be enlarged. Hill suggested raising the roof and adding another floor but this did not come about for some fifteen years. Conditions were cramped and hot and not conducive to efficient work.

The following day, on 17 September, Hill arrived at the GPO at 6.20 am, unannounced. In his diary he describes the situation:

Less bustle and confusion than on the previous night, the morning being, they said, unusually slack; still the office was felt to be inconveniently small. The checking of the taxation was done with great rapidity. The stamping at the rate of 5 or 6 letters per second probably (they had previously been arranged), and the sorting appeared to be again by far the longest operation. A letter-carrier was called upon to check the charge raised against him on certain letters; he cast the amount in two minutes – was wrong. Another man was then called upon to cast the amount, the letter-carrier standing still the while. This took 3 minutes more. The letter-carrier afterwards took 9 minutes to arrange the same letters for delivery. (They had been assorted to his walk by another person before he cast the amount.) The heat and closeness of the rooms not so bad as the previous evening but still very unpleasant.[9]

Hill spent the first half of October in Paris looking at the operations of the French Post Office, and later reported on them.

Cole joined Hill officially on 13 October after he had finished his submission to the Treasury competition, although he had been spending some of his free afternoons at the Treasury from September. Both he and Hill now set about drawing up a plan for the introduction of uniform postage and to this end visited the Post Office to discuss matters with Messrs Bokenham and Smith, the Superintendants of the Inland Office and Twopenny Post respectively.

The attitude of Post Office officials to this situation was ambivalent. Now that the question of penny postage was settled they had to deal with the consequences. Thus they said they would do their best to make the plan succeed. However, when Cole visited St Martins le Grand on 30 October he noted in his diary:

Mr Bokenham showed me over the Newspaper and Inland Office. He was very courteous in showing every thing. At the same time it was clear that he still disliked the P[enny] P[ost]. He spoke of 'Mr Hill as our Ruler'. He thought PP wd be a total failure.[10]

On 2 November, Rowland Hill submitted a memorandum to the Lords of the Treasury on an interim measure, preparatory to the introduction of the uniform penny post. This was accepted almost *in toto* by the Treasury, thus fulfilling Baring's promise that he would 'find from myself and the Board that confidence and cordiality which will be necessary for the well working of the proposed alterations.'[11]

Hill had been mindful of certain prerequisites. The measure should be bold enough to satisfy public expectations. All the alterations should be in the direction of the final goal, and none should require to be subsequently unravelled. It should be independent of the need for stamps and it must not involve any immediate extension of the office

Draft memorandum in Rowland Hill's handwriting

in St Martins le Grand. Other requirements were that it should test the practicability of prepayment and introduce the practice of charging by weight.

Interim Treasury Minute

The Treasury minute containing Hill's proposals is dated 12 November. It begins by referring to the Act of August 1839 and saying 'Since the prorogation of Parliament My Lords have turned their unremitting attention to the measures necessary for carrying into effect the intention of the Legislature.'[12] It had been the intention of Parliament that the necessary alterations be carried into effect with the least disturbance to normal Post Office operations. But they had:

always been aware that the cotemporaneous adoption of the charging letters by weight and the reduction of Postage to an uniform rate of One Penny, would be attended with much practical difficulty. The time occupied now at the large Offices and at the Forward Offices in charging and sorting the letters has been reduced, for the public convenience to as narrow limits as possible. To alter the mode of charge from that to which the Officers of the Post Office have been long accustomed, must of itself for a time be accompanied with some inconvenience. My Lords apprehend it would be imprudent to increase that difficulty by adding at the same moment so large a number of letters as must naturally arise from the immediate reduction to the Penny rate . . .

However satisfactory, therefore, and however desirable in many points of view it might be to carry into execution cotemporaneously, the complete plan, their Lordships upon a full consideration have come to the conclusion that by adopting some inter-mediate measure and bringing into operation the mode of charging the letters by weight previous to the entire reduction of the rate of postage, their Lordships will not only avoid the risk to which the other course is liable, but materially facilitate the introduction of the remaining parts of the plan.[13]

Therefore, with as little delay as possible, charging by weight was to be introduced. This would be accompanied by a reduction of postage which would not interfere with the discharge of duties of postal officers. However:

In giving their sanction to the proposed arrangement My Lords consider it as a temporary measure only, and as a step to the introduction of the uniform Penny charge and their Lordships will continue their anxious efforts to give effect to the whole of the intentions of the Legislature with as little delay as is consistent with the due consideration of the public convenience.[14]

As a result, all letters posted on or after 5 December next would be subject to the following regulations:

General Post Letters shall be charged by weight as follows:-
1.   Letters not exceeding $\frac{1}{2}$ oz One Postage
    „   „   „   1 „   2   Do.
    „   „   „   2 „   4   Do.
    „   „   „   3 „   6   Do.
and so on adding 2 Postages for every ounce up to 16 oz. beyond which no packet subject to postage shall be received.
2.   All single Postage rates between places within the United Kingdom which now exceed 4d shall be reduced to that sum – inferior rates to remain undisturbed, but the letters to be charged by weight. Additional charges to which General Post letters are now liable if posted or delivered beyond the limits of the General Post free delivery as also the additional halfpenny on Scotch letters and the additional penny for passing the Menai and Conway Bridges to cease.
3.   All Letters and Packets exceeding the weight of 1 oz. to be prepaid and delivered in at the window – if not so prepaid and delivered to be charged double postage.
    Foreign letters and Packet letters will be charged according to the preceding scale of weight.
    Letters to and from the British West Indies to be charged 1/- per single rate, the same charge to attach to Letters from and to Gibralter [sic], Malta, and the Ionian Isles conveyed by Packet and not transmitted through France.[15]

The whole question of rates on foreign letters was reserved for future consideration. It was hoped that foreign postal authorities might be induced to make corresponding reductions in their charges on letters to and from the United Kingdom.

All Ship Letters between parts of the United Kingdom including the Channel Islands and the Isle of Man were to be charged by weight and according to the rates chargeable on Inland letters.

Other Ship letters were to be charged by weight, the single sea postage rate remaining as before, and the Inland rate being regulated as for inland letters.

In the London District the rate was to be reduced to 1d. in both the Twopenny and Threepenny Post areas, provided that it was prepaid and that the letter did not exceed half an ounce.

The minute concluded with a reference to privileged mail continuing to go free: 'My Lords have no intention by the present arrangements, to make any alteration with respect to Newspapers, Franked letters, or Parliamentary Papers, which will still continue to enjoy the same privileges and be subject to the same charges as at present.'[16]

Post Office Instructions

Printed notices to the public and instructions to postmasters explaining the new rates and conditions were sent out at the end of November and the beginning of December. That from William Bokenham, Superintending President of the Inland Office, amplified the Treasury instructions. He explained what the postmasters should do with letters already accepted but not yet delivered on the introduction date of the uniform system:

The Letters arriving on the Morning of the 5th, will of course be charged by the Deputies, and delivered for the present Rates of Postage, this will partially continue for Four or Five Mornings, according to the Distances of the Towns from London, as no Letters posted anterior to the 5th will be liable to the new Principle; this will also apply to Charging Packet and Ship Letters Inwards, depending as it must upon the Out-Port at which they may be Landed.[17]

All officers were asked to pay careful attention to the changes detailed. Unless ill, they were not to take leave of absence on the first day and possibly several days thereafter so that they could supervise the changeover and the considerable increase in letters which might reasonably be expected:

Every possible arrangement will be made to facilitate the duty, and to meet any great influx of Letters, by the employment of extra conveyances to bring up an early supply from the Branch Offices and Receiving Houses, and also by the aid of additional Stamps, &c, although it will, doubtless, be difficult at first to be fully prepared for every contingency that may result from so material a change of the System, and probable great increase of the Business of the Department.[18]

Further amplification was given in the Post Office London Directory for 1840 (published in December 1839). Apart from the texts of the

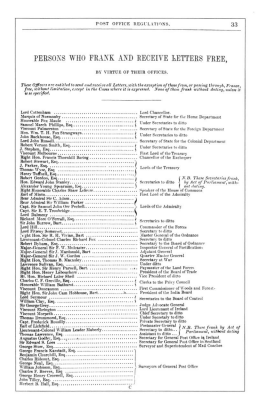

Act and notices it listed all the rates for overseas destinations and the numerous still complicated exceptions. For instance, no penny postage would then be charged upon letters passing through the General Post except on those which were franked. Franks, however, would still be liable to the local rates of 1d. or 2d. when passing through Penny Posts in the country or the local Posts of London and Dublin. Complete lists of post towns were also given together with rates, not only of Great Britain and Ireland, but also of France, 'Central Germany' and Switzerland. Times of delivery in the London District Post, routes and departure times of mail coaches and trains both from London and in cross mails, were all detailed. There was also a complete list of all those (other than Members of Parliament and the Royal Household) still entitled to frank and receive letters free, some with particular limitations. They, of course, were the last to enjoy such privileges.

Reduction of Postage Rates

The reduction in postage rates came into effect on 5 December. On the following day Hill noted in his diary:

There was an increase of about 50 per cent in the number of letters dispatched from London on Thursday as compared with the previous Thursday, & a loss of about

£500 out of £1600 in the total charges. The number of paid letters in the District Post has increased from less than 9,000 to about 23,000. The number of unpaid letters remaining about the same as before, viz : 32,000. No doubt the increase is greater at present than it will be in a day or two, as comparatively few letters were written the day before the reduction; still, the result is as yet satisfactory.[19]

The next day he noted that the increase was down to about twenty-five per cent.

In fact, in the four weeks from 8 December, 1839 to 4 January, 1840 the number of chargeable letters which passed through the London General Post, inwards and outwards, was (with the corresponding figures for the previous year in brackets):

Unpaid	Paid	Total
1,566,434	505,847	2,102,281
(1,299,789)	(201,127)	(1,500,916)

Letters were charged at the 4d rate irrespective of whether prepaid or not.

For the London District Post where the charge had been reduced to 1d. *if prepaid* the figures were:

Unpaid	Paid	Total
477,273	825,282	1,302,555

Hill quotes a comparable figure for the year before (four weeks ending on 1 January 1839) as totalling 970,953. Overall, there was thus an increase of about a third.

It was said that Maberly was 'boasting at the Traveller's Club of the fulfilment of his prophecies.'[20]

Uniform 4d Post Charge Markings

Uniform fourpenny postage was an interim measure and did not last for more than five weeks. Letters from this period are not numerous and most of them bear charge markings in manuscript. Certainly, in England and Wales there was no central ordering of handstamps to be used in local offices. A few towns had handstamps made locally but even these were used infrequently. The London Twopenny Post conspicuously used manuscript throughout. There, of course, the fourpenny rate only applied to letters going outside the London area. Within that area letters cost 1d. if under half an ounce and prepaid, 2d. if unpaid. All penny posts also remained at their lower charges, as did letters travelling only a short distance.

A very few places had more than one type of handstamp. All are rare. Normally the 4 was struck in black to indicate the letter was unpaid. One is known in red to indicate paid – from Huddersfield, and two towns used blue ink. Double- or treble-weight letters were charged in manuscript.

Uniform 4d marking of 5 December 1839
from Birmingham in manuscript

Uniform 4d period: double-weight letter
from Leith charged in manuscript

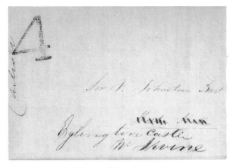

Uniform 4d handstruck 4
from Carlisle

Uniform 4d standard
handstruck 4 from Edinburgh

Examples of handstruck markings are known from:

Arundel	Ipswich (2 types)
Ashburton	Kington, Radnor
Ashby (?)	Leamington (?)
Baldock	Leominster
Blackburn	Norwich
Carlisle	Nottingham
Catterick (blue)	Oxford
Chester	Rushyford
Cullompton	Scarborough
Dorchester (2 types)	Sherborne
Grimsby	Stockton
Guildford	Wakefield
Halifax (blue)	Welshpool
Hawes	Whitchurch
Hertford (3 types)	Woodbridge
Hoddesdon	Worcester
Horsham	

The situation in Scotland and Ireland was somewhat different. In Scotland the contract for the production of such handstamps was held

*Illustration of the superior distinctness of the
Journal Post Office Stamps, when used upon Red,
to that of other Colours*

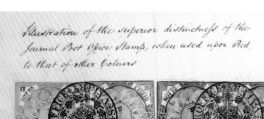

*Illustration of the Use of the Adhesive
Stamp, instead of a Wafer.*

Cole's submission to the Treasury Competition with labels
printed in compound printing by C F Whiting

*Rough Illustrations, shewing a Mode of preparing,
Smaller Adhesive Stamps, upon Compound Plates.*

*Four
Adhesive Stamps*

*Four
Adhesive Stamps.*

*Three
Adhesive Stamps.*

Cole's suggestion for small stamps in compound printing

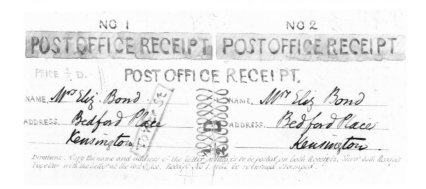

Cole's suggestion for a Post Office Receipt

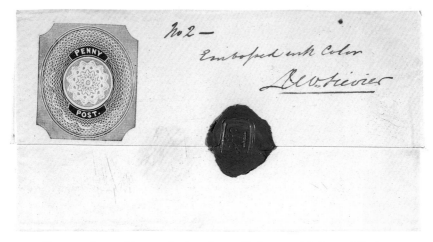

Treasury Competition entries from James Chalmers and Robert W Sievier

by Alexander Kirkwood & Sons in Edinburgh.[21] Their proof books have survived and include large and small 4s marked 'not accepted'. The accepted type was cursive, though as each was individually cut there are minor variations between them.

There are impressions of some twenty stamps in the proof book, though only one is marked for a particular destination (Stonehaven). Several stamps were used in both Edinburgh and Glasgow and other towns known to have used the standard type were Aberdeen, Ayr, Dundee, Haddington (in blue and black), Inverness, Leith (in blue), Perth and Stonehaven. Locally- or privately-made handstamps are known from Coldstream, Galashiels, Golspie, Hawick, Kirkwall, Port Glasgow, Stromness and Wigton.

All examples (with the exception of those from Leith) are in black. None are known in red. Some Scottish handstruck 4s are much more common than those from England, though there are only one or two examples known from such places as Ayr, Coldstream, Galashiels, Golspie, Hawick, Kirkwall, Port Glasgow, Stromness and Wigton.

In Ireland, as in Scotland, there was a standard type used in Armagh (in blue), Belfast, Derry, Drogheda, Dundalk, Enniskillen, Newry and Roscrea. Other types were used in Ballymena, Cork, Dublin (two types according to Mackay,[22] and one in blue), Galway (three types) and Stranorlar. In addition, Dungannon is also listed by Whitney[23] and Rosscarberry by Lillywhite.[24] All Irish 4s (except from Dublin) are as rare as the rarest English.

Letter Weights and Scales

The principle of charging by weight was not new. Foreign letters were already charged by that method as were certain inland letters. Because of this the Post Office already used weights and scales in its every day operations. Indeed, on 1 January 1835, Francis Freeling sent out a directive to all postmasters which had resulted from an Act recently come into force. This had said that 'all Weights and Measures whatsoever used for buying and selling, or for the collecting of any Tolls or Duties, or for the making of any charges on the conveyance of any Goods or Merchandize, shall be examined and compared with one of the copies of the Imperial Standard Weights and Measures'[25] to be provided by magistrates for the use of inspectors appointed under the Act. Freeling was 'commanded to direct, that you will without delay, cause the Weights used in your Office for weighing Letters and Packets, to be inspected by the Proper Officer.'[26]

In the Incidental Bills register of the London office there are half yearly payments to William Mary de Grave and Son for 'Scales weights and balances supplied and repaired.'[27]

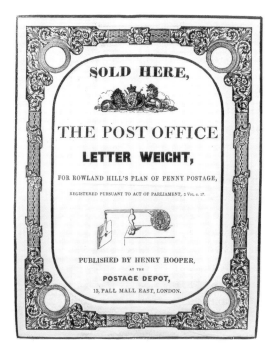

Henry Hooper's letter scale

However, with the new principle of charging all letters by weight, scales would be needed universally. Hill notes in his diary for 22 October that the Chancellor of the Exchequer had authorised him to 'incur any moderate expense in the construction of machinery in weighing letters.'[28] Remarkably shortly thereafter, Edwin Hill, another brother of Rowland with an inventive frame of mind, had produced just such a 'machine' and this was shown to the Chancellor at the Treasury on 26 October. Later, it was shown to officials at the Post Office and to de Graves who voiced some objections. Nevertheless, Rowland Hill managed to get the Chancellor's authority to have thirty or forty of his brother's weighing machines made by someone else if necessary.

On 18 November de Grave agreed to make the scales, but the only other apparent reference to them is the payment of a bill to William Mary de Grave & Son for 11 sets of scales and weights supplied on 5 January 1840 (at a cost of £35 15s).

It was also now desirable for merchants and even private individuals to be able to weigh their own letters and thus know what the Post Office charges would be. Several enterprising scale makers and others therefore proceeded to produce a number of different scales for home and office use.

One of the first was Henry Hooper, the publisher and postal reformer. Even before the Postage Duties Bill became law he was constructing a scale, or at least having one constructed for him. Cole may have had a hand in it, as he mentions discussing an agreement with Hooper on 9 August 1839, and they went together to register it on 12 August.

Based on the bismar principle it was for weighing letters up to 4 oz with markings for $\frac{1}{2}$ oz, 1 oz, 2 oz, 3 oz and 4 oz. Made of brass, there was a fixed coin-like counterweight inscribed 'The Post Office Letter Weight' and on the reverse 'For Rowland Hill's Plan of Penny Postage. Registered No1 Pursuant to 2 Vic. Ch.17 For H. Hooper 12 Aug. 1839.' and then in smaller letters 'Silvester & Co 27 Strand', who were seal and copperplate engravers to the Queen.

It came in four versions: with steel clasp (3s. 6d.); with spring holder (4s. 6d.); with spring holder on a clamp (8s.); and on a table stand (10s. 6d.). All were packed in appropriate cases. In a prospectus of November 1839 Cole explains the method of operation:

The letter or parcel is fixed into, or suspended from, the clasp, at the end of the lever. The lever is adjusted on the foot or fulcrum, according to the gradations marked on the lever. The amount of weight is at once shown by the rising of the lever out of the horizontal line. Of course it is necessary to place the machine at the edge of the desk or table, so that the parcel or letter may be fairly suspended. This machine supersedes the necessity and inconvenience of moveable weights. The whole weight of the machine itself, in a light case, is under two ounces, and therefore quite portable for the pocket; and it will pass free by post to *any part of the United Kingdom.* [his italics].[29]

There was also another plainer version of this registered (No. 68) in October 1839. It was for letters from $\frac{1}{2}$ ounce to 2 ounces and cost 1s. 9d. (with steel clasp) or 2s. 6d. (with spring holder).

A note in Cole's diary shows that these letter weights were very popular. On 28 November they were already out of stock at Hoopers.

Other types followed, some quite elaborate. A gilded pendulum, marked 0, 1, 2, 3 and 4 has 'No 113, Nov 28 1839 G Riddle London' on the weight arm. Another stamped 'H B Wright, No 130, London. Dec. 20 1839' and marked $\frac{1}{4}$, $\frac{1}{2}$, 1 oz, 2 oz, 3 oz and 4 oz is a telescopic

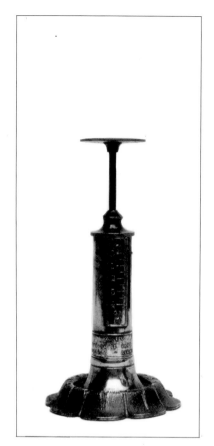

Candlestick letter scale
by Robert W Winfield

Letter scale on a call bell
by Joseph and Edmund Ratcliff

steelyard supported by a boy holding a scroll of foliage. These were obviously expensive.

Somewhat cheaper were a number of later candlestick letter weights made by Robert W Winfield of Birmingham. These consisted of a central cylinder housing a spring. Attached to this was a short brass rod, with a circular, flat plate on top. A vertical slot had a graduated scale from 0 to 4 ounces and the brass band at the base bore the inscription 'No 170 January 13 1840. R W Winfield Birmingham'. Other candlestick letter weights were made by Joseph and Edmund Ratcliff, also of Birmingham. With markings from 0 to 2 ounces, one example is mounted on a call bell.

Among those scales patented was one by C E Dampier, an attorney (No 8342, dated 14 January 1840). Called the 'Geometric Balance' this was a circular plate acting as a bent lever or pendulum beam and applied to a pendulum letter balance or other weighing instruments.

Weight-collecting letter scale
by Ratcliff

Stamped $\frac{1}{2}$, 1, 2, 3, 4, 5, 6, 7 and 8 ounces and up to 1s 4d Prepaid, it was sold by an agent R T Hughes of 158 Strand.

Another scale manufactured by Ratcliff was patented (No. 8384 on 12 February 1840) by Robert Willis, a professor at Cambridge University. It was a weight-collecting scale made of brass with a mahogany or marble base. The weights were of rolling-pin shape, each graduated to allow for its distance from the central pivot point. Depending on the number of weights, the first is picked up when the letter is over half an ounce and the beam moves above 1 on the pence markings on the left. If the letter is over one ounce then the second weight is picked up and so on. Should the letter weigh more than five ounces the spare cylindrical weight is added and the scale is turned round with the higher rates being read off from the other side. No weight values were shown.

Three designs are known using three, five or seven weights. According to Crawforth[30] the prototype appears to have been made by Holtzapffel & Co.

The production of all these scales, and other subsequent ones, indicates the widespread popularity of the new postage measures. At the same time as these scales were being introduced for private and business use, official steps were being taken to provide adequate means of prepayment of letters.

CHAPTER SEVEN

The Treasury Competition

As far back as 1829 it had been recognised that prepayment of letters was desirable. When in 1837 Rowland Hill recommended that postage rates be reduced to one penny he also suggested that the charge be prepaid by means of various forms of stamps and stamped paper. In the two years prior to the passing of the Act some designs had even been submitted. Now it was necessary to put these ideas into practice.

On 23 August, 1839, very shortly after it had been empowered to put Hill's plan into operation, the Treasury announced a competition to suggest the best plan for covers under the Uniform Postage Act. By this Act the Lords of the Treasury were 'invested with a power of carrying into effect the reduced and uniform rate of Postage contemplated by Parliament either according to the present mode of collecting the Postage or by prepayment collected by means of Stamps Compulsory or optional.'[1]

Much would depend upon the stamp to be employed:

> For the convenience of the Public it is of the greatest importance that the mode which should be selected should afford every facility for obtaining and using the stamp. It is also clear that the charge which will fall upon the purchasors in the shape of increased expense and of extra payment on account of the Stamp itself in addition to the penny rate must also vary according to the nature of the stamp adopted. In the course of the inquiries and discussions on the subject several plans were suggested viz stamped covers, stamped Paper and stamps to be used separately to be applied to any letters of whatever description and written on any paper.
>
> Before My Lords can decide upon the adoption of any course either by Stamp or otherwise it will be useful that Artists, men of Science and the public in general may have an opportunity of offering any suggestions or proposals as to the best manner in which the Stamp may be practically adopted. With this view My Lords will be prepared to receive any proposal for consideration which is to be sent in to them on or before the 15th day of October 1839.
>
> All persons desirous of communicating with My Lords on the subject are requested to direct to the Lords of the Treasury, Whitehall, marked Post Office Stamp.[2]

It was proposed that a 'premium' of £200 be awarded to the best suggestion and £100 to the next best. The points considered to be of the greatest importance were:

1 The convenience as regards the public use.
2 The security from forgery.
3 The facility of being checked and distinguished in examination at the Post Office which must necessarily be rapid.
4 The expense of the production and circulation of the stamps.

It was noted that foreign as well as native artists could enter. This minute was published in full in *The Times* on 6 September, 1839.

Entries were supposed to be sent direct to the Treasury. Some, however, were sent to the Postmaster General, and these were later forwarded. All communications received were recorded in the Treasury registers[3] and allocated a number. The registers give the sender's name, the date of his letter and the date of its receipt. Normally, the subject of the letter was also recorded and what was subsequently done with it, but those entering the competition were so numerous that they were simply designated 'Penny Post Plan' or some similar description. Quite a number were submitted anonymously or only with initials or some strange name such as 'Fortuna.' Some came from overseas, especially France.

The entries were interspersed with communications on other Treasury business and so the numbers allocated to them sometimes have large gaps. However, they run from 18609/39 (27 August 1839) through to 29865/39 (31 December 1839) although strictly any suggestion received after 15 October would not have been an entry to the competition.

Entries were not properly considered until November and Hill's resulting report was not submitted until the beginning of the following month. Often, enclosures such as designs or stamped envelopes were also given the same number as the accompanying letter (so that they might be kept together) though it is impossible now to prove that this was invariably the case. Suggestions continued to be received the following year (in the /40 sequence.)

What happened to most of the entries is a mystery. A few remained with the official files and are now in the Public Record Office. Some were retained by Hill and Cole. Most 'went missing' at some point in the nineteenth century and a large number of the designs found their way into private collections, often rudely torn from the original descriptive sheets. A vast number have not survived. Today, of those originals still extant, most are in the Royal Collection with some others in the National Postal Museum, the Victoria and Albert Museum, and a few in private hands. Many of the items in private collections normally thought of as Treasury Competition entries are in fact reprints, or even items never actually submitted to the Treasury.

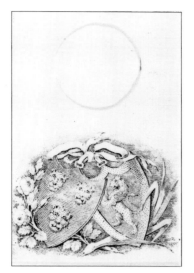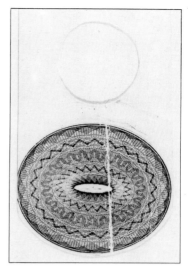

Two engraved designs for appliqués by Francis Coffin

Coffin and Bogardus, and similar suggestions

One of the first entries to be received came from Francis Coffin of Bucklersbury, in the City of London. It was sent on 29 (or 30) August with a further letter on 4 September.[4] Exceptionally, both are noted in the Treasury register as including labels, the second 'with Specimen of a Steel engraved label for the Penny Postage.' Coffin also wrote to the Post Office at the same time and, as with several of the competitors, appears at least four times in the registers. In his letter to Rowland Hill he said that 'the Engraving might be the Queen's head as on the coins, or the arms of the United Kingdom or any other that might be chosen.'[5]

Three of the labels have survived, all being on the same principle though with two different designs. A label was 'to be attached by the upper part to the cover, and to be sealed through the circular hole on to the flap.'[6]

The idea was apparently that of James Bogardus, also of the City, who had taken out a patent on 26 August. In this he described the label's use:

if it be required to affix one to any letter by means of a wafer, let the wafer cover a portion of the label and the rest of the wafer will seal the letter . . . but a better method is to cut or pierce a hole in the label, which hole, being placed where the wafer or wax is placed to seal the letter, the act of sealing the letter affixes the label.[7]

One of the designs consists of an engine-turned device in the form of a transverse oval. The other shows two armorial shields surrounded

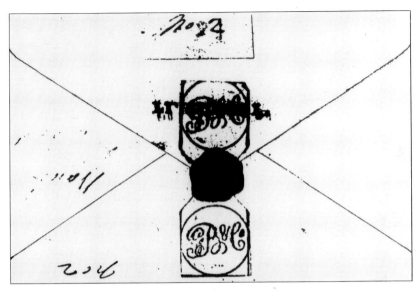

Gummed label suggested by Egerton Smith

by flowers and ribbons. Both were printed in black on a lead white glazed card with a circular hole at the top.

Subsequently, a steel die with the name Bogardus on the reverse was found in Rowland Hill's papers. It showed an outline engraving of Queen Victoria and lithographic impressions were taken from it. No contemporary prints are known, though Bogardus submitted an entry to the competition on 14 October.

Suggestions came pouring in to the Treasury. It was later estimated by Hill and Cole that between 2,600 and 2,700 entries were received. It has been possible to list some 2,400 of these but only a small proportion have survived.

Many suggested the use of labels or covers to indicate prepayment, sometimes (as with Coffin) utilising the seals which were commonly used at this time to close the letters. One such was a gentleman from Liverpool with the remarkable name of Egerton Smith.[8] His suggestion was the use of gummed labels in combination with wafers or seals. The labels would seal the letter and at the same time prepay postage. They would also be cancelled by the town stamp. Simple directions as to use would be printed on the reverse. Smith also suggested that the labels be provided in sheets of sixty and he had little to say of possible forgery. The design he used was simply that of a cypher seal.

George Dickinson made quite a number of submissions to the Treasury and also wrote to the Post Office.[9] His idea was to have a number of different labels for different rates. Each would bear the value and possibly the destination. The labels which he submitted

Charles Whiting's design for an envelope, cancelled by his Go Free marking

were individually drawn in ink along the lines of the existing newspaper stamps (see page 54). All had a crown in the centre with the royal cypher but superimposed were the words One Penny, Two Pence and so on up to Four Pence, or specific inscriptions such as American Letter (1s.), Foreign Letter (1d.) and even French Letter (6d.). Others indicate surcharges, money letters or 'Past Seven O'clock.' These also had a tag pierced by a circular hole for attachment by seal or wafer.

Charles Whiting

Another prolific writer was Charles Whiting, the printer, whose work was also used by several other competitors, one being Henry Cole. Whiting produced a large number of designs, some of which were simply examples of printing techniques. He also reprinted items from *The Post Circular*, and later reprinted many of his designs. It has thus become very confusing as to what is one of Whiting's competition entries and what is not.

Whiting's main submission (see page 54) was sent on 9 October, in printed format with a covering letter (Treasury No. 22864).[10] In it he recounted his previous contacts with the Post Office and the Treasury, going back to his 1830 plan for 'Go-frees,' and also covering his evidence to the Parliamentary Committee on Postage. He then detailed his solution to the three possible methods of prepayment as proposed by Hill, viz. stamped covers or envelopes, stamped paper, or what he regarded as more important 'small stamps either to be pasted, gummed, glued, or wafered on the letter.'[11] Both Hill and Cole had been closely connected with Whiting over the past two years through the Mercantile Committee and the printing of its publication *The Post Circular*, so all were familiar with each other's ideas.

For stamped covers 'A plate should be made for relief-printing as difficult as possible of execution, but capable of being multiplied *ad libitum*, technically called stereotyping; then the largest sheet of paper that can be made of a practicable size should have repeated, in the manufacturing of the same, the words "V.R./Post/Office./1840" or "Post/Office/1d./½ Ounce" as many compartments as the sheet would cut up into fitting sizes for each envelope. If the sheet would cut into twelve envelopes, then there would be repeated twelve water-marks.'[12] These watermarks would be the best protection against forgery. They would then be printed with a suitable design 'and by changing the colours of the various denominations of envelopes in the printing, the Post Office examinations will be most easily effected and checked; thus, a blue envelope might denote a 1d. stamp, a red 2d., a green 3d, a brown 4d., and so on.'[13] The envelopes referred to were almost certainly of an elaborate design inscribed 'JAMES WYLD, Geographer to the QUEEN.' Examples exist in several different colours in the Royal Collection and in the Cole papers they are marked as being 'prepared by C. Whiting.' Some are also cancelled with the insignia shown at the end of Whiting's submission inscribed 'Post Office Go Free' in black surrounded by a circle of pricked dots. One cover is printed in blue with a large '2' in the centre.

For stamped paper Whiting suggested the use of the Congreve machines, which Whiting and the Stamp Office both had. 'Should it be deemed advisable to use these machines in any way, I then claim, as a matter of justice only, the right to be employed in all connected with their application.'[14]

In terms of small stamps he referred to his letter of 10 June (which had actually been written by Cole) and to his offer to produce about 2,000,000 stamps a day at no more than sixpence a thousand. This depended entirely on the size of the stamp determined on and Whiting printed five different examples ranging from 50 to a sheet to 240. All were printed by the bicoloured Congreve method. A typical printing sheet size was also appended. This bore a number of variations of small-sized designs.

As regards forgery:

all that I will add is that it is a fallacy to say that any one person can produce what another positively cannot; and as I have no doubt but that your Lordships will be presented with numberless graphic panaceas and doubtful patents . . . I beg to add, as a general remark, that the greatest amount of difficulty that can be produced by combined labour and talent, and capable of being impressed at one operation, is the best.[15]

If watermarked paper were adopted he felt very little apprehension as regards forgery. Very similar sentiments were expressed by Cole.

Whiting ended his communication with remarks about the sale of stamps and covers, and the discounts to be allowed.

Henry Cole

Henry Cole had had a great deal of experience in dealing with ideas for postal reform, and being a very practical man had already worked these out with Hill and Whiting, amongst others. He first set out the reasons for prepayment being compulsory. One was that advertisers would avail themselves of cheap postage to bother the public:

Without prepayment the public would be perpetually teazed by advertisers clamouring for notice and patronage. Release the hungry quack from the obligation of paying the postage of his request, and no delicacy will deter him from inflicting a penny. The public have a right to claim protection, if possible, against being made to pay for the impertinences of the Joseph Adys and the Doctors Morrison of the day. Prepayment gives this protection.[16]

Some of his other reasons were prevention of fraud, economy of time in delivery and gain to the revenue when stamps were destroyed or lost by negligence. He concluded that 'prepayment of postage by stamps seems to be a rare instance where payment before value received, is a good thing to both parties.'[17]

Much of Cole's submission was concerned with the question of forgery, the possibility of which he endeavoured to prove would be slight:

I submit that the small temptation, the regulations of sale, the difficulty of uttering, the certainty of official examination, the clue to detection conferred by the address of the letter, and the check of the number of letters passing through the Post Office, present an aggregate of impediments to forgery which would prove so protective as to render the artistical difficulties of the stamp itself, in this case, a matter of little anxiety. To make assurance doubly sure, the stamp itself should present all the difficulties that could be attached to it.[18]

Cole then explained in detail how the composition of the stamp might be effected so as to avoid forgery. In sentiments very similar to those of Whiting, but in words rather better chosen, he wrote:

The papermakers, engravers, and printers, are the parties chiefly interested in the manufacture of the stamp. In the progress of my inquiries and observations during the last eighteen months on the subject of the stamp, I have found all papermakers say, 'there is no security in any stamp;' and all printers, that 'There is no security in any paper.' Each individual papermaker, engraver, and printer, equally asseverates that the nostrum for security is known only to him. It would be folly and presumption to assert to your lordships, that what one human agency has done cannot be effected by another . . . but in calling in the aid of the papermaker, the engraver and printer, I believe a sufficient preventive to forgery may be obtained in the stamps, specimens of which I offer to your lordships.[19]

The stamps which Cole submitted were produced by Whiting by the Congreve compound printing method in blue and red, green and red and black and red (see page 71). Four examples in different colours were appplied to one letter and cancelled. This was marked by Cole 'Illustration of the superior distinctiveness of the Journal Post Office Stamp, when used upon Red to that of other Colours.'[20] Another single stamp showed how an adhesive stamp might be used instead of a wafer. (This same design was also used by Whiting to illustrate part of his entry.) Cole also submitted labels of existing firms' designs to provide specimens of 'glutinous wash' on various papers.

However, one further interesting set of designs for adhesive stamps accompanied his submission.

Cole had been at work on his Treasury Competition entry since the beginning of September. In his diary on 5 September he noted 'In the Evg [evening] making design for a letter stamp.'[21] The next day he was at Whitings for nearly three hours and then went to 'Perkins & Heath with Specimen.'[22] On 11 September he visited both again and Robert Branston (son of Sir William Congreve's partner) 'who said he could turn the Spicyclidal pattern. He thought the engine turning ought to cover the whole surface & thought Hill's machine available for printing them.'[23] Subsequently, he visited the Perkins Bacon premises in Fleet Street on several occasions.

Although his letter to the Treasury was dated 30 September it was not received until 10 October. Cole's diary explains the delay. He noted on 4 October 'Perkins & Bacon did not send as they promised so I closed the Postage Letter,'[24] though the final transcript was sent on 8 October.

In this Cole stated that the only machines able to print by the Congreve compound method were at the Stamp and Excise Office and at Beaufort House (Whitings):

The colours blue and red, are selected because either one destroys the other by accidentally overlaying it, an effect very likely to follow in any clumsy imitation. The only objection to this stamp [Whiting's Post Office Journal] is its size; and I had hoped to have laid before your lordships specimens of another stamp only *one-fourth* of the size of this specimen, but there has been an unavoidable delay in its preparation, and I am unwilling any longer, on the chance of succeeding with the stamp in pro-jection, to postpone the delivery of this statement. Should the stamp be effected in time, and seen to be one worthy of your lordships' notice, I shall claim the indulgence of transmitting it.[25]

It seems certain that this refers to the specimens not yet arrived from Perkins but they must have come in time, for in the Royal Collection there are three further designs printed in red and black by the Congreve method and bearing the same Treasury number as the other parts of Cole's entry (see page 71). They are described as 'Rough illustrations showing a Mode of preparing Smaller Adhesive Stamps upon Compound Plates'[26] making up four or three stamps. Designs are basic, showing the numeral 1, or Post 1d. or something similar.

The probable course of events is that they were designed by Cole, the compound plates then prepared by Whiting and Branston, the engine-turned engraving done by Perkins and Heath and the final printing again being undertaken by Whiting. Correspondence with Perkins, Bacon & Petch at this time refers to dry printing, i.e. without the paper being dampened.

Cole also submitted a proposal for a Post Office Receipt (see page 72). This had been originally suggested by Rowland Hill in evidence to the Parliamentary Select Committee on Postage to ensure the safe delivery of letters. Cole's design was to incorporate some engine-turning as protection against forgery. They would be sold in books by postmasters and licensed stamp vendors and cost a halfpenny each. This idea of a certificate of posting was not taken up by the Post Office until 1877. According to Cole[27] some officials in 1839 thought that the scheme was impracticable, in particular that it interfered with the registration of letters. However, he was still suggesting the idea in January 1840 when he prepared a new design, probably the one preserved in his papers featuring two halves, one part to be given to the sender, the other to remain on Post Office files.

Stamped covers were discussed in other parts of Cole's submission, where he suggested the use of Dickinson's paper and watermarks for both covers and stamps. Stamped paper he was against because of loss of security and general inconvenience.

James Chalmers

In the list of entrants to the Treasury competition are a number of names of prominent postal reformers. One such was James Chalmers who had first written about his ideas for 'slips' in December 1837. He now wrote twice with details of the plan which he had 'now more fully matured.'[28] The slips were now circular rather than rectangular and were attached to letters on the sealed side.

Chalmers submitted a number of slightly different designs with values of 1d. and 2d. in red and black (see page 72). Most are cancelled DUNDEE and then the date (either 30 September or 7 October 1839) and some also are marked USED, all in black ink. He proposed:

that these stamps should be printed on paper the size of small post, and that each full sheet should contain 120 stamps or slips, each of which slips will be nearly 2 inches long by 1½ broad – the *blank* on the length being for the purpose of inserting under the fold of the letter – the stamp to be wholly exposed.[29]

He believed these stamps to be better than stamped paper or covers (letter sheets and envelopes).

Benjamin Cheverton

Benjamin Cheverton, a frequent contributor to the correspondence columns of the *Mechanics' Magazine*,[30] was also not in favour of stamped paper and covers. He proposed separate stamps which would be 'affixable by means of the back of it being coated with a composition which is smooth and firm when dry, but which becomes extremely glutinous when wetted with the finger. The most refined need not scruple to use the tongue, as in wafers, for the substance is "the jujubes" as prepared for lozenges.'[31] A solution of gum would not serve so well.

Where Cheverton's idea was ingenious was in his proposals for the stamps' manufacture. He suggested a long narrow coil of paper, perhaps a mile long, on which a device would be stamped repeatedly. If necessary Dickinson's paper could be used:

The immense number of impressions which may be made in a day by means of a rolling-press would be incredible, if it were not attested by an experiment which I instituted for the purpose. I passed a slip of paper between the cylinders taking medallic portrait impressions from the raised and hollow dies or matrices on their surfaces, and, without the least detriment to the goodness of the impression, produced a series of them at the very moderate velocity which is usually allowed to mechanical motions, viz. 220 feet per minute. This would give us twenty-five miles of stamps in a working day of ten hours, or rather more than 2,000,000 in number.[32]

As to the design 'It should be executed, in the original by one of our best sculptors, in a fine, bold, and massive style of relief. The subject to be a head of Mercury, and the design, if need be, may be changed every year.'[33] He explained that as the eye was 'educated to the perception of differences in the features of the face, the detection of any deviation in the forgery would be more easy – the difference of effect would strike an observer more readily than in the case of letters or any mere mechanical or ornamental device, although he may be unable, perhaps, to point out where the difference lies, or in what it consists.'[34]

Cheverton's submitted specimens no longer exist. A die was found by a relative, Eliza Cooper, which showed the head of a young woman (possibly Queen Victoria) and this was illustrated by Crawford in 1910, and a few impressions were taken from it. Also attributed to Cheverton is an embossed design of lace patterns in colourless relief. This shows the VR cypher surmounted by the crown in the centre and POST OFFICE below. Neither of these accords with the description given in the submission.

Most of Cheverton's letter was concerned with administration, distribution and the prevention of forgery, though the letter itself only exists in draft form, having been reconstructed by Crawford.

Other Ideas

Of the large number of other designs and proposals submitted no great detail can be given here. Many correspondents based their designs on the Royal Arms or Cypher. Some were quite beautiful, others extremely crude. Few were practical.

Some of the most beautiful were by Robert W Sievier, an engraver and sculptor. Later an example was used by Cole in the *London and Westminster Review* when he was writing about the forthcoming stamps. There were three designs with an embossed pattern in the centre surrounded by an engine-turned design in two colours, with the words PENNY POST (see page 72).

One of those submitted anonymously contained a series of at least eleven envelopes. Each bore a different design and was intended for a different destination. Legends such as 'No. 2, General London Envelope' or 'No.7, General Ireland Envelope' and 'No. 8 District Scotland Envelope' are written in manuscript above rather beautiful designs featuring aspects related to them such as Irish harps or the Arms of the City of London (see page 89).

A more interesting and practical idea was the crude submission of John Little. This consisted of a book of 1,000 stamps costing £4 3s 4d. The design was a scribbled head within a circular band. The booklet comprised twenty pages of blue wove paper, each page numbered.

Another interesting suggestion, which has been preserved in the Cole papers, came from L Schönberg. Unfortunately, it bears no date, but a letter from 'Schonberg and Bishop' was received by the Treasury on 16 October. The design showed a helmeted head facing left, with the inscription 'POST OFFICE ½OZ ONE PENNY.' Although the (originally four) examples were from the same die, each bore a different number. A sketch at the bottom of this letter makes this idea even more explicit. 'In order to render the marginal differences more striking,

Sample of Dickinson paper used in Hill's Report

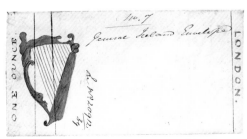

Anonymous entry to the Treasury Competition (20912/39)

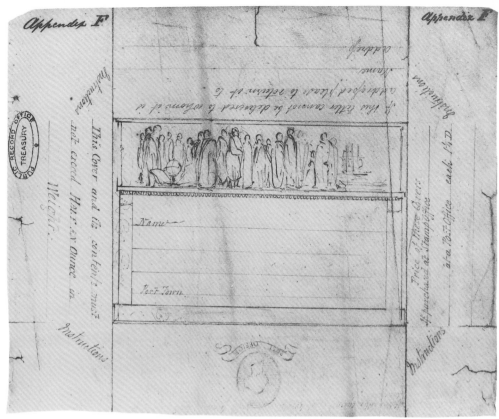

Sketch by Cole for the lettersheet, in Hill's Report

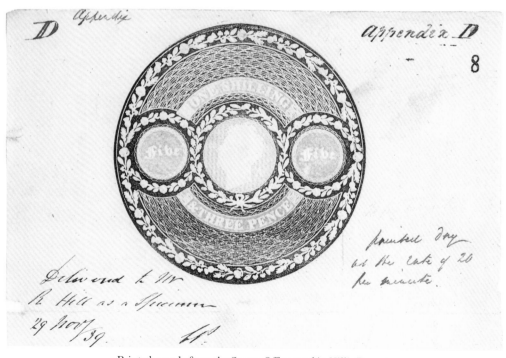

Printed sample from the Stamp Office used in Hill's Report

First day of Uniform Penny Postage: entire from London

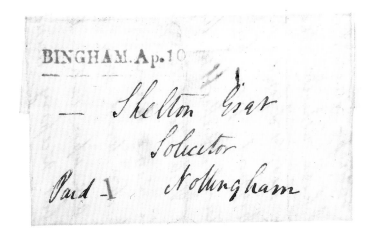

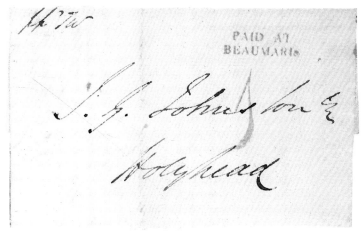

Uniform Penny Postage covers from Bingham and Beaumaris

Brass recess plate from which Mulready stereotype plates were made

William Mulready, 1786–1863, by John Linnell

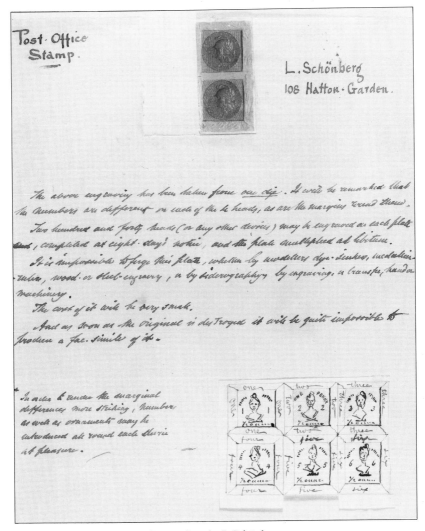

Suggestions by L Schönberg

numbers as well as ornaments may be introduced all round each device at pleasure.'[35]

From all these ideas, and the many others, Hill had to sift out the essentials and eventually fit together the component parts of the postal stationery and postage stamps as finally produced. A listing of Treasury numbers is given in Appendix Two together with a number of illustrations but it is impossible to detail all known entries here (and there are some that cannot be attributed).

Hill's Report on the
Treasury Competition Entries

As soon as they had been recorded in the Treasury minute book all the entries to the Treasury competition, due to be completed by 15 October, were passed to Robert Gordon, newly appointed as one of three Secretaries to the Lords of the Treasury. All other correspondence referring to the Post Office and penny postage was also sent to or from Gordon. He passed the entries on to Hill and Henry Cole, Rowland Hill's assistant at the Treasury as of 13 October. They would need to have been collated and sifted as several correspondents wrote on many occasions, some well after the official closing date.

Despite the fact that he had been a competitor himself Cole began reading the 'Proposals' papers on 4 November,[1] helping Hill to sort and analyse them. Indefatigable as ever, he was at the same time preparing the prospectus for Hooper's letter weight and acting as amanuensis to Hill. In helping Hill to prepare his report he even produced the first design for a cover.

On 27 November Hill informed the Chancellor that 'the communications to the Treasury respecting the construction of the Stamps are now ready for final adjudication of the prizes.'[2] Tuesday, 3 December was set aside for this. Robson Lowe states (without giving any source) that of the 2,600 suggestions only forty-nine concerned the adhesive postage stamp and that of these nineteen were selected as having sufficient merit to deserve future consideration.[3]

In his report Hill summarised the suggestions submitted by the public and judiciously fitted them into his own preconceived plan for three different methods of prepaying postage. This had been published in its fullest form in his letter 'On the Collection of Postage by means of Stamps' printed and circulated in June 1839 by the Mercantile Committee on Postage. (Rather confusingly both Hill and Cole used the term 'stamps' to include adhesive labels, stamped covers and stamped paper, Cole in particular often referring to the cover or envelope as the 'stamp.')

The report[4] on the entries to the Treasury competition is illustrated by examples submitted by John Dickinson, and items specially produced for Hill. It was addressed to the Chancellor of the Exchequer, Francis

Baring, and after due consideration during December it resulted in the issue of postage stamps and postal stationery in May 1840.

Dated 6 December 1839, it began:

Several of the communications which have been addressed to the Lords of the Treasury in consequence of the Minute of the 23rd of August last, display much ingenuity and contain many useful suggestions, still I am not aware that any plan has been proposed which, however excellent, is, as a whole fit for adoption. I hope to be able, however, by combining the suggestions of many, to propose a plan which will secure the objects which their Lordships had in view in framing the Minute.

A large majority of the writers advocate Stamps of some kind or other: of this majority a few recommend that the public should be allowed to send paper to the Stamp Office to be stamped; several advise that the Government should manufacture and issue stamped covers; and the greater number prefer small stamps to be attached by various means to the letter when written; it appears, however, to have been assumed by nearly all, that the public must be confined to the use of one kind of Stamps only.

The Possibility of Forgery

As far as forgery was concerned he referred specifically to the papers submitted by Cole and Cheverton:

Many contrivances have been suggested as affording protection, and a selection of the most promising has been made; but the greater part of these schemes require new and untried machinery, and I should have little hope of bringing them to bear in the short time allowed for preparation. There is one large class of contrivances which I think may be at once discarded – the security which they profess to afford depends on certain chemical or mechanical processes which it is assumed can be carried on in secret. A reliance on such security would, I am of opinion, be exceedingly unsafe.

It was important that the design and execution of the 'stamp' should be such that imitation would require the combined skill of the greatest possible number of the best artists, thus increasing the risk of detection and the difficulty of effecting it:

The difficulties of imitation and the risk of detection will be greatly increased, if it can be made necessary for the forger to employ extensive, costly, or extremely delicate machinery . . . In devising means for preventing forgery, it is very necessary to keep these facts constantly before the mind; the question is not what are the difficulties the forger must overcome in a process similar to that which produced the genuine Stamp, but what are the difficulties in the way of the easiest means of imitation open to him; the genuine stamp itself being before him, ready for any use to which he may think proper to apply it.

Several peculiar kinds of paper had been proposed, some of which were manufactured by secret processes. The paper proposed by Messrs Pewtress & Low and that recommended by Mr Delisser fell into this category:

I have already expressed an opinion that it would be unsafe to rely upon the preservation of a secret, but it is said that these papers also require the aid of peculiar and costly machinery in their production. How far this is correct, not being acquainted with the processes, I am, of course unable to determine.

The most remarkable kind of paper was that proposed by Mr John Dickinson:

In the Appendix I have given a specimen of Mr Dickinson's paper [see page 89] together with an imitation of it which was effected by cementing together two thin sheets of paper, between which the threads are placed. It is true that in his communication Mr Dickinson has proposed a modification of his plan, which consists in bringing the threads alternately nearer, to first one and then the other side of the paper; a peculiarity which undoubtedly very much increases the difficulty of imitation, if it does not render it impossible by any other means than those used for producing the genuine paper. Still this peculiarity is not apparent to the eye (it can be discovered by tearing out the threads) and paper so manufactured is essentially dearer than that in ordinary use.

On the other hand, it is stated by the officers of the Bank of England, that the water-mark of their Notes has never been successfully imitated; that the difficulties of an illicit manufacture of a peculiar paper, and the risk attached to the possession of the sieve required for the water-mark are such that they are practically insurmountable by the forger, who invariably makes use of paper of the ordinary description.

After a careful consideration, therefore, Hill proposed that paper manufactured 'in the ordinary manner, but with a very well defined and peculiar water-mark be employed for all Franking Stamps issued by the Government.'

Manufacture of the Stamps
He then turned to printing:

Several of the gentlemen, who have addressed Papers to the Lords of the Treasury, advocate Sir William Congreve's mode of printing in various colors as now practised at the Stamp Office. The Papers of Mr Cole and Mr Whiting may be referred to as affording the most complete information on this head. Several other parties have proposed improvements in this mode of printing, which consist, for the most part, of more difficult and more various combinations of colors. There is no doubt that this mode of printing greatly increases the difficulty of imitation by transfer from a genuine impression; still, means have been pointed out by which imitation may be effected without much difficulty, and in a hasty inspection, the complex and confused appearance of the design tends to the concealment of defects, which, in one of greater simplicity would be readily apparent. I think it not improbable that some of the new proposals for printing in various colors may not be open to these objections; but they are as yet untried, and much time would probably be necessary to decide the question. In the Paper already referred to I suggested this mode of printing in colors, but I am now of opinion that it would be inexpedient to rely on the security which it affords; not that I have any reason to doubt that the forgery of Stamps printed in this manner is extremely rare, but because I think other arrangements equally easy of adoption may be resorted to which afford greater security.

Hill believed that what provided the most security was a combination of embossing and printing somewhat similar to the specimens he attached, one of which was supplied from the Stamp Office (see page 90), and the other by Whiting:

In these specimens the embossing and printing are both executed at one blow of the press, there is consequently no difficulty in keeping the most exact register between the two, and it is the exactness of the register which would interpose the chief difficulty to the forger, for although he might imitate the embossing by a cast from the genuine stamp and the printing by a transfer from the same, he would, I think, find it impossible to devise any means by which the two processes could be separately effected with a register sufficiently exact to deceive a tolerably careful observer, if the design were made, as it might be, so as to shew more decidedly any deviation therefrom.

Other specimens in which printing in two or more colours is combined with embossing might be seen in the communications of Mr Sievier, Messrs Myers Sparrow & Co, and Mr Dyer.

With regard to the design he quite agreed with Mr Oldham that it should be:

as beautiful a specimen of fine art as can be obtained; also that there is nothing in which minute differences of execution are so readily detected as in a representation of the human face. Some excellent remarks in support of this opinion will be found in Mr Cheverton's letter to the Lords of the Treasury, and in that of Mr Radford the beneficial effects on the national taste of continually bringing under observation beautiful specimens of fine art are ably pointed out. I would therefore advise that either in the embossed or in the engraved part of the Stamp or perhaps in both, a head of the Queen by one of our first artists should be introduced; the best course to adopt would probably be to employ Mr Wyon to execute a die from which the embossed impression would be obtained, and from which, by means of Mr Bate's machine an engraved plate might also be made. By the use of the powerful press at the Mint, exact facsimiles of the die might be obtained in any number, and by a process somewhat similar, the engraved plate might also be multiplied without limit.

Hill then went into some detail as to how the stamps and covers should be distributed. He thought that they should be sent out to all postmasters from the London post office and from the Stamp Office to its distributors and sub-distributors. Forgeries might be discovered upon examination of the letters as they passed through the post.

Covers and Envelopes

As to the actual stamps and covers he gave precise details.

At first I shall confine my attention to Penny Stamps only, leaving those of higher denomination for consideration hereafter.

Covers – To be of the size of half a sheet of Quarto letter paper, namely 9 inches by 7½ inches. The paper to be of rather inferior quality for the sake of cheapness with a watermark ("Post Office") across the middle. To have the most beautiful design that can be obtained engraved in relief, with the addition of certain engine work and printed in such a manner that when the cover is folded, the design shall form a border round its face, with the Queen's head at the back just below the seal. The form already mentioned for the name and address of the writer to be placed above the seal, and instructions for the use of the cover with a short statement of the more important Post Office regulations to be printed on the other folds. A rough sketch of a cover shewing the arrangement here described is given in the Appendix [see page 90].

The design now described, which is intended to serve the purpose of a Stamp, could not be made very difficult of imitation; but the water-mark and the low price compared with the cost of production (I mean to the forger) would, I am of opinion afford ample security.

The printing may be executed by an ordinary printing machine at the rate of about 20,000 covers (12 to a sheet) per hour, or by my own press at the rate of 200,000 per hour. The latter press possesses this additional advantage that it may be combined with the Paper machine so as to print the paper before it is dried. Under either arrange-ment there would be no difficulty in connecting a counter with the printing machine so as to record the number of impressions.

The total cost of these covers would, I am informed, be at the rate of about 15 for a penny, and I would recommend that they should be supplied to the Government in a finished state by contract, and by Government sold to the Vendors, at a slightly higher rate to cover carriage, book-keeping etc. (say 14 a penny or rather, including the Stamps, 14 for 15 pence.)

The Deputy Postmasters, Distributors and Sub-Distributors might be required to sell the Covers retail, at a price not exceeding $1\frac{1}{4}$d each, (which would afford them a profit of nearly 17 Per. Cent. on the cost price) and in larger quantities at a lower rate, say 11 for 1s. This arrangement would, perhaps be better than to leave the price to be determined by competition as suggested in the printed paper already referred to.

In the printed Paper just referred to, I have recommended that another variety of covers should be supplied, viz: pieces of paper of a lozenge form such as are required for envelopes. As they would take but little more than half as much paper as the covers above described, they might be supplied at a considerably lower rate, so as to admit of their being formed into envelopes by the stationers, and yet sold to the public at a price not exceeding that of the covers. The plates for printing them might be cast from the same original as would be used for the Covers, consequently their supply would be attended with little additional trouble. A different arrangement of the water mark in the paper alone would be required.

Stamped Paper

Stamps to be struck on paper etc. sent in by the public. As regards these Stamps it is obvious that no security can be derived from the paper; it is the more important, therefore, that the Stamp itself should be difficult of imitation. I propose that it shall be similar in construction to those exhibited in Appendix E, but with an embossed head of the Queen in the centre struck from a die to be cut by Mr Wyon, and an engraved head obtained from the same die by the use of Mr Bate's machine as before suggested. I have already stated my reasons for considering this form of Stamp very difficult of imitation.

The stamp must be so placed as that when the letter is folded it shall fall just above the seal. This will bring it at the edge of the sheet (the most convenient place for the Stamper) and at the back of the letter.

The cost of striking stamps on letter paper is estimated by Mr John Wood, late

Appliqué sealed on a letter

Chairman of the Board of Stamps, at 1/- per 1,000. One machine will execute about 1,800 per hour. The Stamp Office already possesses five machines of the kind required (now almost useless) and Mr Whiting has a sixth which he is willing to part with. These six machines working 10 hours a day would produce about 100,000 stamps, a number which considering that this description of stamp appears to be much the less popular of the three, would probably suffice. If not the presses might be worked incessantly until others could be provided.

The distribution of this kind of Stamp would of course, in some degree rest with the parties who sent the paper; but as Licenses to vend stamps are given gratuitously to all respectable applicants, there would be no great hardship if it were thought necessary in placing these Stamps under the same restrictions as others with respect to their sale.

It would of course be necessary to require that the paper sent to be stamped should come in large quantities. A ream (480 sheets or £2 worth of penny Stamps) might be made the minimum.

He suggested that 'stamps' of this sort might also be made in Dublin, Edinburgh and Manchester as well as in London.

'Appliqués' and Labels

Small detached Stamps. (Appliqués). To be $1\frac{1}{2}$ inches long by $\frac{3}{4}$ inches wide with the stamp at one end and a hole at the other, by means of which the stamp would be attached to the letter, as shewn in the Appendix, in sealing it either with wax or wafer, 120 of these stamps arranged in the manner shown in the Appendix to be printed on one sheet, the price of which would be 10s.

I propose that in order to save the cost of punching the holes and to increase the difficulties of imitation, the sheets be manufactured in the first instance with holes in them, the practicability of which I have ascertained. This would give to every stamp the security afforded by the rough edge; but in a form more convenient than that of the long narrow strips ingeniously suggested by Mr Cheverton. Each stamp should also have a small watermark, a crown for instance, and the sheet a larger one forming the words 'Post Office'.

The printed part of the stamp to consist of a head of the Queen to be engraved by Bate's machine in the manner already described, together with the price of the Stamp, the weight it is intended to frank and a distinctive mark which will be described hereafter – the whole sheet being printed at once from a steel plate.

A plate thus engraved would afford ample security against forgery.

In the appendix to the report was a letter from a Mr Martin, a lithographer:

distinguished for the fineness of his execution, which removes all apprehension of the stamp being imitated by the lithographic process, while the great combination of skill and of machinery required for the production of the plate renders forgery by similar means practically impossible. It may perhaps be thought that the forger might succeed by engraving, by hand, a small plate or die large enough to print a single stamp, and then covering the sheet with repeated impressions; but this would at once be detected by the absence of the distinctive marks which in the genuine sheet would make each stamp slightly different from every other. The same absence of variety would be discovered if he should cut up the sheet before offering his stamps for sale, even if he were not deterred by apprehension of the suspicion which would certainly be excited by an attempt to vend any considerable number of separate stamps.

But even if he should succeed in selling his Stamps in spite of these difficulties, the more frequent recurrence of a certain distinctive mark would be noticed at the Post Office of the District, and thus the forgery would speedily be detected.

As the steel plates for printing the labels can be multiplied without limit and as they would be worked by an ordinary copper plate press there can be no doubt as to the practicability of obtaining a sufficient supply. Messrs. Perkins and Co. are willing to contract to supply the necessary number at a rate not exceeding 8d per thousand stamps, including the plates but not including the paper, which would probably cost 2d. or 3d per 1,000 more.

These stamps I propose should be sold retail at 1d each, the Vendor being allowed a small poundage (on the average 3 per Cent.) which as well as the expense of distribution must be added to the cost of production. As the stamps are larger and of a more expensive construction than those which I described in my printed Paper of June last, their cost will somewhat exceed that estimate; the total need not however be more than 4 per. Cent. (my estimate was $3\frac{1}{2}$) on their value; still they would, to the Government, be far the most expensive, and therefore the use of other kinds should be encouraged. Some further security against forgery might be afforded by stamping the back of the sheet with a single impression from the die used for the letter paper. If the sheets were printed out of the Stamp Office (which I think would be unavoidable) this would be a means of recognising the validity of the stamps.

The distinctive mark on each stamp might be obtained by using the several combinations of the letters of the Alphabet and the first five numerals – the whole taken in pairs; these combinations would suffice to distinguish 960 stamps or 8 sheets full. The eight different plates should be numbered from 1 to 8. One use of the distinctive marks has already been pointed out, another would be this; it would afford the means of sufficiently identifying letters in any checks on the letter carriers which it might be thought advisable to establish . . .

These labels have been suggested by six different parties and one of these, Mr Bogardus, has taken out a patent for the invention. This patent was sealed on the 26th of August prior to the date of either of the six communications and the title is such that the patentee will, I fear, be enabled to include in his specification, which is not yet enrolled, not only this but any other kind of Appliqués which may be adopted unless published prior to the date of his patent. The necessary steps have, however, been taken to ascertain the extent of the patentee's right. Unfortunately, the price asked by the Patentee for the manufacture of the Labels is so high (2s per 1,000) that there appears little chance of overcoming the difficulties of the case by making him the contractor.

If it should appear that the Government is debarred from the use of the Label, the next best form of Appliqué appears to me to be a small stamp, partly embossed and partly printed, somewhat resembling the French wafer and to be attached to the letter like that wafer by means of a glutinous wash at the back. A cement every way fit for the purpose has been proposed by Mr Philipps. This kind of Appliqué would be cheaper than the Label, but the machinery necessary to produce it would require two or three months to prepare. It could not, I believe, be included in Mr Bogardus's Specification, inasmuch as I proposed it long ago in my evidence before the Postage Committee.

Another kind of Appliqué which also would be secure against any exclusive claim might be made by using plates similar in all respects to those from which it is proposed to print the Labels, except that the stamps would cover the whole sheet instead of leaving one half plain; the sheet would therefore, contain 240 instead of 120. These stamps would be attached to the letters by a glutinous wash at the back. Their cost likewise would be less than that of the Labels.

As this latter kind of Appliqué would require little or no peculiar preparation, as it would be less costly than the label, and in some respects more convenient in the readiness with which it might be attached to the letter (after it had been sealed for instance) I am inclined to recommend its issue even though the Labels should be adopted. It appears to me that in the first instance it will be advisable to issue as great a variety of Stamps as is consistent with a due regard to economy; if it should be found that there is a demand for all such demand will clearly shew that all are required; if there is not a demand for any kind the supply of that kind can be discontinued, I see no other way in which the wants of the public can be ascertained with certainty.

Influenced by this view of the matter, I am inclined to recommend what I have latterly considered unnecessary, that Twopenny Stamps of each kind shall be issued as well as Penny ones. Dies and Plates similar to those employed for the Penny stamps and copied mechanically from the same originals (the figure marking the value being inserted by hand) would suffice; and as a means of readily distinguishing the 1d. and 2d. stamps, they should be printed in different colors. Stamps of a higher denomination would, I think, be quite unnecessary. They would rarely be wanted and Appliqués used in sufficient numbers would serve all purposes. If the smaller Appliqué be issued, 16 Twopenny ones (the number required for a pound parcel) would occupy a space only three inches square and even if the labels be the smallest stamps issued, the space occupied would be only 6 in by 3 in.

I suggest the twopenny stamps partly for the reason assigned above and partly in deference to what appeared to be the opinion of the Board when the question was discussed on Tuesday last. At the same time I think it right to state that although the 2d. stamp may possibly prove convenient to the public, they will probably, to some small extent, be found inconvenient to the Post Office. Thus, it will not I imagine be thought expedient to forbid the use of two of the penny Stamps instead of one Twopenny stamp: (the course which, if open to them, I expect the public will generally prefer) – two modes of paying for letters will therefore be introduced and the counting of letters or rather of Stamps, either by mechanical or other means as they pass through the Post Office, rendered more difficult and complex. With only Penny Stamps, every blow of the Journal Stamp would be counted as a single letter.

In all the stamps which have been proposed, the distinguishing and essential feature is the Queen's head; engraved it is true in different styles, but still of uniform size and from the same original die. At the Post Office, therefore, the object to be looked for will be invariably the same, and I have so arranged as that it shall always be found in as nearly as possible the same part of the letter – viz: at the back, and in the place of or just above or just below the seal. The back of the letter has been chosen for *all* the Stamps, because the Label, if used, *must* be placed there, and if the stamp were sometimes at the back and sometimes at the front, the letters would require to be "faced" twice over. The Label is also unavoidably *below* the seal – for this reason the Queens head on the covers is likewise placed there – and a similar arrangement would have been extended to letter paper, but that this would have required the Franking Stamp to be struck near the middle instead of the edge of the sheet which would have retarded the operation. If for any reason the Labels should not be used, then all the Stamps might either take the place of the seal or stand above it. An Instruction as to the proper position of the stamp should be printed on each.

The Queen's head being the essential part of the stamp and that which presents most difficulty to the forger it appears to be unavoidably the part which must be struck with the Journal stamp of the Post Office.

Against forgery a particular number of wire lines might be employed in the paper:

Again, a new stamp might be issued periodically, say every year and the old ones called in. Thus an exact account of Stamps consumed would be obtained, and a comparison with the number of letters posted in the same period would detect the existence and extent of forgery. If the stamps were uniformly called in on a certain day, there would be no hardship in throwing a small portion of the loss on the holder which would tend to diminish the waste.

And lastly a Notification may be printed on every kind of Stamp, that certain parties only are authorized to vend them. And that any one buying or selling them at less than their nominal price, or a number of Appliqués otherwise than on the sheet would expose himself to suspicion of fraud. I do not consider any of these additional securities necessary or desirable, but merely enumerate them as practicable.

Hill's report was to be accepted, almost in its entirety, and he and Cole were put in charge of arranging for the design and production of the various component parts.

Uniform Penny Postage

During the early part of December 1839 Hill monitored the increased volume of letter traffic which had resulted from the introduction of the first part of his plan. There was a loss of revenue, as expected, but a reasonably satisfactory increase in the number of letters sent. Official government reaction was relaxed as reflected in Lord Melbourne's daily conversations with his young Queen. 'Of *course* a *decrease* of income. "I knew it would work easily enough" said Lord M.'[1]

On 16 December Hill suggested to the Chancellor that the penny rate be introduced without waiting for the stamps to be ready. He proposed 6 January as the date and that franking should be abolished as soon as prepayment became compulsory. Francis Baring, the Chancellor of the Exchequer, approved in general terms but thought that the date was rather too early and named 10 January in preference. He also preferred abolishing the franking privilege immediately.

Baring then wrote to Lord Melbourne on 19 December outlining his plan:

The Stamps it appears will take much time and upon the due consideration I can give the subject I have come to the conclusion that it will be most expedient to bring the penny rate into operation as soon as possible independent of the stamps – and to introduce the stamps as they may be made . . .

This move will I know create some surprise among a large number [?] of our friends who really have persuaded themselves that the 4 penny rate was intended as a permanent arrangement.[2]

Melbourne read this letter to Queen Victoria two days later and agreed with his Chancellor. '"I am entirely of that opinion", said Lord M., and that it should be carried into execution, before the Meeting of Parliament, for else, he said, they would be asked about it, and people would say they had made us do it.'[3]

Queen Victoria's Franking Privilege

In his letter Baring went on to question whether the Queen should retain her own franking privilege. Initially he thought that arrangements might be made for this, subject to reasonable checks:

Subsequent consideration has lead me to doubt how far this will be expedient – I don't mean as to revenue – nor as to legal difficulty for I apprehend that the Queen not being mentioned in the act the Law cannot extend to her as to taking away the privilege of franking. But whether it will have a good effect when all other privilege is sacrificed that the Queen should retain it – I should not think it could be a very large matter in money amount when the charge is reduced to 1d. – a few hundred pounds will go a great way and the question is whether it is of sufficient importance to keep the privilege with the risque of being counted shabby.[4]

Politically this was astute. Queen Victoria's journals suggest that she was not entirely in favour but that Melbourne persuaded her. 'Baring also talks of Sir Henry Wheatley's having asked him if he might not have the privilege of franking for *me*, still, – but Lord M. advised me as everybody gave it up, to do so also.'[5] This decision was later portrayed as Victoria's enthusiastic endorsement of penny postage, and proved a popular action.

The Treasury Minute

In his autobiography Hill amusingly describes how the Treasury Board came to its decisions:

Few fictions, I suppose, are more complete than the minutes purporting to describe the proceedings of the Treasury Board. There was certainly a large and handsome room containing a suitable table headed with a capacious arm-chair, the back bearing a crown, and the seat prepared, as I was informed, for the reception of the Sovereign, whose visits, however, scarcely seemed to be frequent, as the garniture was in rags. On this table, according to the minutes, the Chancellor laid such and such papers, making such and such remarks; sometimes the First Lord of the Treasury [the Prime Minister] appeared as taking a part, though only occasions of some little importance, such, for instance, as my appointment; then deliberation seemed to follow, certain conclusions to be arrived at, and corresponding instructions to be given. This had a goodly appearance on paper, while the simple fact was that two or three Junior Lords being seated for form's sake, papers were read over which were to go forth as the resultant minutes of the said meeting, but which, having all been prepared beforehand, had received the signature of the Chancellor of the Exchequer, or of one of the Secretaries of the Treasury, the attending Lords giving their assent, as a matter of course, without a moment's thought or hesitation.[6]

This is largely what happened with consideration of the Treasury Competition entries and the introduction of Uniform Penny Postage. As has been noted Hill records in his diary that he laid a memorandum on reducing the postage rate to one penny before the Chancellor of the Exchequer on 16 December. Two days later he accompanied Baring to his house at Lee and worked with him until after one o'clock in the morning considering the necessary arrangements. The adjudication of the competition was also settled at this point. On the following day Hill prepared the minute and on 20 December handed this to Baring.

That part of it referring to the new postage regulations was sent to Maberly. He objected 'in a very decided manner to the proposed course on the ground that it will be impossible to manage the receipt of pence for prepaid letters, especially in the country. He says that when Mr Baring talked the matter over with him 3 or 4 days ago he did not understand that prepayment was to be encouraged by demanding a higher sum on delivery.'[7] Maberly then met Baring and Hill and a compromise agreement was arranged over the details. It was finally agreed on 26 December and published on that day in the *Globe* and *Sun* newspapers.

The minute[8] began by describing the results of the Treasury Competition:

The communications (more than 2,600 in number) received in consequence of this Minute [23 August] have, for a long time, occupied the attention of their Lordships. Many of them display much ingenuity, they are highly satisfactory as evincing the interest taken by men of science, and by the public in general in the measures now in progress for the reduction of postage, and they have afforded much useful information with reference to the details of the new arrangements. Upon full deliberation, however, their Lordships do not think it will be advisable to adopt any one of the specific plans proposed without modification and combination with other arrangements.

Despite the terms laid down at the outset the Lords of the Treasury, or rather Hill, decided to award four equal sums of £100. The recipients were Messrs Bogardus and Coffin 'who have acted together', Benjamin Cheverton, Henry Cole and Charles Whiting. Cole had been informed by Hill of his award on 19 December as he recorded, without comment, in his diary.

'As far as practicable' postage was to be prepaid by means of 'stamps' of which four varieties were to be prepared:

First. Stamped Covers – The Stamp being struck on pieces of paper of the size of half a sheet of quarto Letter paper:-

Second. Stamped Envelopes – The Stamp being struck on pieces of paper of a lozenge form of which the Stationers and others may manufacture envelopes:-

Third. Adhesive Stamps – or Stamps on small pieces of paper with a glutinous wash at the back which may be attached to letters either before or after they are written; and,

Fourth. Stamps to be struck on paper of any description which the public may send to the Stamp Office for that purpose.

The paper for the first, second and third kinds of Stamps to be peculiar in its watermark or some other feature, but to be supplied to Government by competition.

It was stated that experiments were already far advanced to obtain such 'stamps' but that it was feared 'that a considerable time will be required for completing the preparation of the Dies, Plates and Machinery (much of which is unavoidable of a novel construction) necessary for the manufacture of the Stamps, and being desirous of affording to the public with the least possible delay the full advantage of the intended reduction in postage their Lordships propose at once to effect such reduction.'

Their Lordships were therefore pleased to direct that new regulations would come into force on 10 January 1840:

The scale of weight already established for General Post letters to be extended to the London District and other Local Post letters.

The charge on all letters passing between one part of the United Kingdom and another whether by the General Post or the London district or other local post, to be one penny per single rate.

Such postage to be prepaid, if not prepaid to be charged double on delivery.

The minute then proceeded to detail foreign rates and to deal with parliamentary and royal franking:

Lord Melbourne states to the Board Her Majesty's desire that such measures may be taken with reference to Her Majesty's privilege of franking as my Lords may consider advisable for the public service and in conformity with the other regulations which they may lay down with regard to franks.

My Lords are pleased to direct that from and after the 10th January next, the privilege of franking both Parliamentary and official shall cease.

Various exceptions having to do with Parliamentary Proceedings and addresses to the Queen and such like, were then detailed. The warrant bringing these regulations into force was published in the *London Gazette* on 28 December.

Notices were printed informing the public of the new regulations but these were not publicised until 7 January. If prepaid, letters would now cost 1d. if not exceeding half an ounce, 2d. up to one ounce and 4d from one ounce to two ounces with an additional 2d. for every additional ounce up to sixteen ounces. Double rates were to be charged if the letters were not prepaid.

It was thought that the volume of mail might cause the Post Office severe difficulties and so it was decided:

to hold out an inducement to the public not to delay the posting of letters to a late period, by restricting the benefit of the full reduction to those letters which shall be posted early. And their Lordships with this view are pleased to authorize the Postmaster General to close the letter boxes throughout London at 5 o'clock, and in the country, an hour or half an hour earlier than at present according to the circumstances of each place.

Fees for late letters were: 1d. extra if posted between the former hour of closing and the new one; and 2d. extra if posted later than that, unless the present fee were already greater in which case that fee should continue.

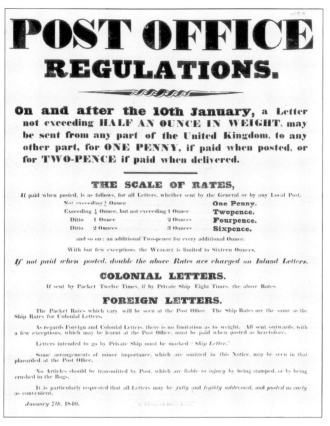

Poster informing the public of the introduction of Uniform Penny Postage

This was a somewhat complicated formula. In reality what happened in London is shown by a notice to the public dated 6 January. The boxes at the receiving houses were to be closed for the receipt of General Post letters at 5 pm. Those at the branch offices at Charing Cross, Old Cavendish Street, and the Borough were to be closed at 5.45 pm. Lombard Street and the main post office in St Martin's-le-Grand shut at 6 pm. At the last, however, letters could be received until 7 pm on payment of an extra penny, and until 7.30 pm on payment of an extra sixpence.

10 January 1840

At this time Cole was engrossed in discussions with William Mulready, the artist, John Thompson, the engraver, Charles Whiting and others about the production of envelopes with watermarks. So engrossed was he that there is no mention of the introduction of uniform penny postage in his diary.

Prepaid letter received after 7 pm with 6d. extra fee

Hill, on the other hand, was exultant. In his diary he wrote:

Jan: 10th. Rose at 8h 20' Penny Postage extended to the whole kingdom this day! Very able articles on the subject in the Chron:, Advertizer, & Globe. The Tory papers for the most part sulky. Standard abusive of the C[hancellor] of the Ex[chequer] & lying as to the cause of delay in the stamps. The C. of Ex. much pleased with Mathew's admirable article on Postage in the Edinburgh Review published yesterday.

I have abstained from going to the P.O. tonight, lest I should embarrass their proceedings. I hear of large numbers of circulars being sent, & the Globe of tonight says the P.O. has been quite besieged by people prepaying their letters. I guess that the numbers dispatched tonight will not be less than 100,000, or more than 9 times what it was this day twelve months. If less, I shall be disappointed.[9]

In his triumph, Hill, here and elsewhere, exhibited that less than admirable trait of thinking intelligent and able only those who agreed with him. However, he was not to be disappointed as to the number of letters. The following day he noted that 112,000 had been posted, of which all but 13,000 or 14,000 were prepaid. 'Great confusion in the Hall of the P.O. owing to the insufficiency of means for receiving the postage.'[10]

The scene at St Martin's-le-Grand was depicted in the February number of the *Westminster Review*:[11]

A night or two after the change to a penny, we ourselves witnessed the scene at St. Martin's-le-Grand. The great hall was nearly filled with spectators, marshalled in a line by the police, to watch the crowds pressing, scuffling and fighting to get first to the window. The superintending President of the Inland Office, with praiseworthy zeal, was in all quarters, directing the energy of his officers where the pressure was greatest. Formerly, one window sufficed to receive letters. On this evening, six

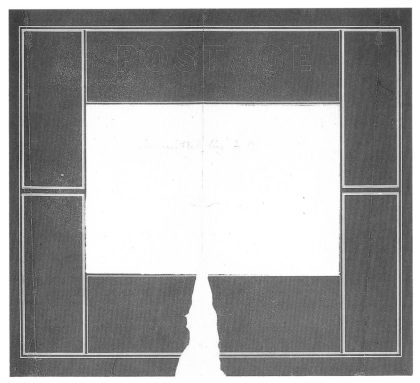

Early suggestion for possible layout for the Mulready

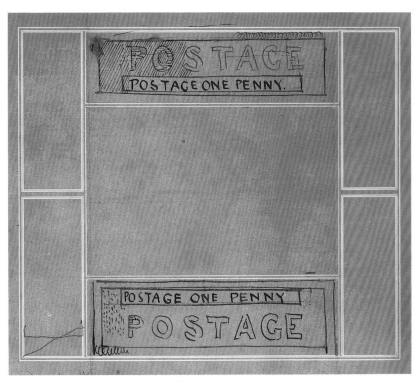

Mulready layout proof in red with hand-drawn annotations

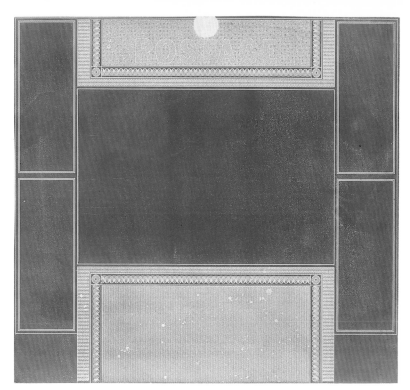

Mulready layout proof in blue

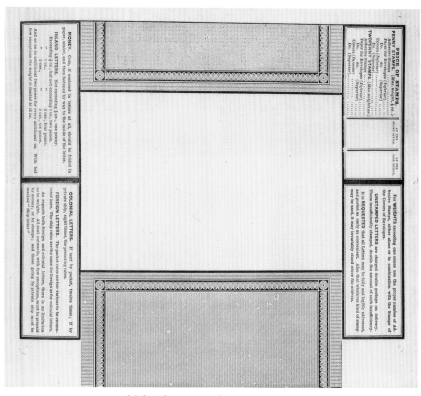

Mulready typographic proof in blue

windows with two receivers at each, were bombarded by applicants. As the last quarter of an hour approached, and the crowd still thickened, a seventh window was opened, and, that none might be turned away, Mr Bokenham made some other opening, and took in money and letters himself. To the credit of the Post Office, not a single person lost the time; and we learnt that on this evening upwards of 3,000 letters had been posted at St. Martin's-le-Grand between five and six. A witness present on the first night of the Penny Post described to us a similar scene. When the window closed, the mob, delighted at the energy displayed by the officers, gave one cheer for the Post Office, and another for Rowland Hill.

In the two four-week periods from 5 January to 29 February the number of chargeable letters which passed through the London General Post, inwards and outwards, was (with the corresponding figures for the previous year in brackets):

Four weeks ending	Unpaid	Paid
1 February	787,139 (1,326,304)	2,217,127 (217,071)
29 February	462,647 (1,345,725)	2,875,427 (212,175)

In the London District Post the numbers were:

Four weeks ending	Unpaid	Paid	Total	(Previous total)
1 February	331,589	1,207,985	1,539,574	(1,067,358)
29 February	312,757	1,312,379	1,625,136	(572,742*)

*two weeks ending 12 February 1839

These figures[12] showed a 100 per cent increase over the comparable figures for 1839 (50 per cent in the case of the London District Post). While some of this could be attributed to the elimination of free franking, most was the clear result of the reduction in postage. The best indication of this was the change from the majority's being sent unpaid, to the vast majority's being now prepaid.

Parliamentary Envelopes

On Monday, 13 January Hill called on the Speaker of the House of Commons in answer to a note sent to the Chancellor of the Exchequer on the previous Saturday, one day after free franking was abolished. Members of Parliament were clearly concerned about the inconvenience of taking letters to the Post Office with cash for prepayment, as Hill had recognised as early as 1 January when he had conferred with Mr Vardon, the Librarian of the House of Commons. Hill arranged with the Speaker and other parliamentary officers 'for a sort of stamped cover for the use of the Members & had specimens prepared at the Stationary [sic] Office.'[13] These he submitted to Baring for his approval. This must have been forthcoming, for on the following day (14 January) the arrangements for the Houses of Parliament were settled with Maberley, Bokenham and Smith.

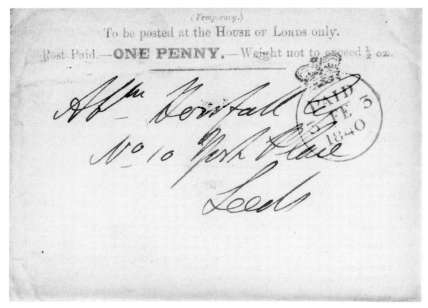

1d. House of Lords envelope

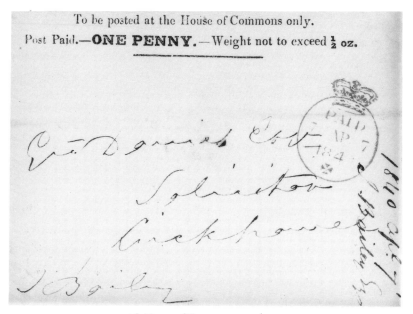

1d. House of Commons envelope

These envelopes came into use on 16 January when Parliament reassembled and were thus the first items of prepaid stationery to be produced under Hill's plan. MPS were informed that letter covers had been prepared for them and might be bought at the office for the sale of parliamentary papers in the Members' Waiting Room. They were sold at the cost of the postage but could only be used if posted at the Houses of Parliament.

On 18 January, in reply to a question in the House of Commons, Baring said 'he proposed, that each Member should sign his name on the cover. That regulation had been omitted by some accidental error.'[14] The librarian, Mr Vardon, was to sell the covers 'to none but Members and to receive none but such as had the Member's name in the corner.'[15]

The envelopes were hand-folded and thus varied in size; the inscriptions were printed letterpress after they had been made up. There were two varieties at 1d. and 2d. simply inscribed 'To be posted at the Houses of Parliament only./Post Paid. – [value in words] – Weight not to exceed [$\frac{1}{2}$oz. or 1 oz.]'. Printing was in black on greyish or bluish watermarked paper. The 1d. black version also exists with a line under the inscription and three minor varieties are recorded.

Later in the month other varieties were produced: 1d. and 2d. in vermilion for the House of Lords and 1d. in black for the House of Commons. No 2d. envelope for the Commons has been recorded. At least seven varieties of the 1d. House of Lords envelope are known and no fewer than eight of the 1d. House of Commons.

Hill noted on the first day that arrangements were working very smoothly and then went on to quote Queen Victoria's speech opening the new session of Parliament. 'I have lost no time in carrying into effect the intentions of Parliament by the reduction of the duties on Postage, & I trust that the beneficial effects of this measure will be felt throughout all classes of the community.'[16]

Plans for the Increased Postal Traffic

At about this time a number of ingenious plans were suggested to the Post Office to enable them to cope with the great increase in postal traffic. Even at this early date people were thinking of machines taking over the work of men and doing it more efficiently.

One such machine was suggested by John Hiscox to aid sorting. His invention was called the 'Alphasorter'. Receiving houses and post offices were to be provided with this 'machine' which was:

an instrument or upright Wooden Case, of a parallelogram form, to be internally lined with tin and to be supplied underneath with Castors; such Machine containing various separate internal divisions above; and figured letter boxes externally, . . . a space of only 4 feet 10 inches by 5 feet 8 inches, would comprise thirty divisions; thus:-'[17]

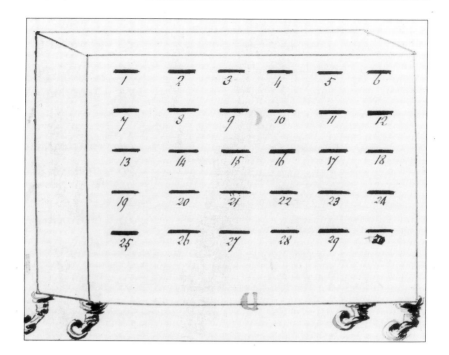

The numbers represented sorting divisions into which all towns of England and Wales would be allocated. Numbers from 25 to 30 were reserved for Ireland, Scotland, East and West Indies, the colonies, foreign and 'Doubtful'. In essence, these were to be filled up during the day when business was slack so that the rush after five o'clock could be coped with. Areas nearer London would have their own system. However, because Hiscox had received no definite information about numbers of letters he was unable to indicate how many sorters might be saved by introducing his invention.

Another suggestion for mechanical aids was to assist in the 'stamping' or postmarking of letters. A letter dated 3 January 1840 from Mr S White[18] of Lambeth contained a plan for a machine to stamp letters at the rate of 100,000 to 800,000 per hour. Two webs were placed round drums which propelled them along. The letters were placed in twos between the webs and marked as they went along by self-inking stamps held in place by collars. There is no indication that this was ever tried out in practice. Instructions were given that a reply be sent to White saying that all such matters were in the hands of the Treasury. Nevertheless, both areas of stamping and sorting were suitable for mechanisation and all major postal authorities in the world have since found it necessary to introduce rapid and complex machinery for both activities.

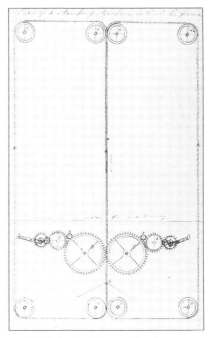

White's plan for stamping letters

Uniform Penny Post Markings

As with the 4d post, handstruck markings were used in the period of Uniform Penny Postage to indicate whether postage had been prepaid or not. In contrast to the former period nearly every town in the United Kingdom now introduced its own handstamps. These spread gradually and many different types continued in use over a period of years. Paid handstamps from previous periods also continued in use.

Normally, the handstruck marking indicated 1d. paid, though occasionally 2d. paid stamps were also produced. All should have been struck in red to indicate prepayment. Markings in black indicated that postage had not been paid. As this fee was now double, handstruck 2 stamps were slowly introduced to show that postage was due.

Not many offices had new stamps in January 1840. Of those that were introduced many consisted of a simple single stroke, of varying length and thickness, to stand for 1d.. Some had the d or D added; others incorporated the word Paid or P; and some included the town name. Most stamps were probably procured locally. Markings illustrated (see page 91 and page 116) show the wide variety that came into use.

These markings generally did not cease with the introduction of prepaid labels and stationery in May 1840. Rather they continued in various forms for many years. A detailed listing is given in the Robson Lowe encyclopaedia.[19] Prepayment in cash remained possible for at

A selection of different Uniform Penny Post paid markings

least ten years, being withdrawn from provincial offices in 1851 and from London at differing dates.

Envelopes and Letter Boxes

There were two developments resulting from uniform penny postage that were largely unforeseen. One was the popularity of envelopes. Prior to this reform an envelope was very seldom used because it counted as another sheet of paper and thus doubled the already high postage. Wafers and seals were used instead to fasten the single sheet. Now a letter could be easily accommodated within an envelope and still be under the half ounce allowed for the lowest rate of postage.

Envelopes were in use by 1835. One of the first references to them occurs in a letter from Fanny Dickinson, daughter of the papermaker

John Dickinson, who wrote to her brother on 13 March 1835 'on blue notepaper enclosed in a *pocket*.'[20] A year later she noted in her diary that she was busy making envelopes all day to send out invitations to a party. In 1837 she inscribed the fly leaf of her diary 'Envelopes at 2/6 per 100, to be had at 209 Regent Street.'[21] The paper was sold flat and ungummed, the four corners folding to meet under the seal. With prepaid penny postage envelopes became the rule rather than the exception.

The other development was the insertion of letter boxes into the front doors of houses. This had not been necessary before as the letter carrier always had to call to collect the fee. Now, with the fee already paid, it was quicker to pass the letters through a slit in the door. Hill had suggested in his pamphlet that every house might be provided with a box into which the carrier would drop the letters. On the introduction of penny postage Harriet Martineau wrote in a letter:

We are all putting up our letter-boxes on our hall doors with great glee, anticipating the hearing from brothers and sisters, – a line or two almost every day. The slips in the doors are to save the postmen's time – the great point being how many letters may be delivered within a given time, the postage being paid in the price of the envelopes, or paper. So all who wish well to the plan are having slips in their doors.[22]

Nevertheless, it was still not universal in 1848 when Hill arranged for the Postmaster-General to publish a circular encouraging the inhabitants of London to provide letter boxes. This circular offended some including the Marquis of Londonderry 'who indignantly demanded whether the Postmaster-General actually expected that he should cut a slit in his mahogany door!'[23]

CHAPTER TEN
Mulready's 'Poetic' Design

On 4 December 1839 the Chancellor of the Exchequer authorised Hill to apply to William Wyon, William Harvey and another artist to be selected by the President of the Royal Academy to design the stamps. Later, on 11 December 1839, Hill was authorised to commence preparations for them, i.e. adhesive labels, stamped paper and prepaid stationery. However, even before this his assistant, Henry Cole, had been making various contacts. As has been seen he had prepared his own design for a cover for Rowland Hill's report of 6 December.

He had known John Thompson, 'the wood engraver', since May 1838. Thompson was in fact perhaps the foremost wood engraver of his day. Born in Manchester in 1785, he was apprenticed at fourteen to Robert Branston Senior, another great engraver. He aimed to rival the effect of metal in engraving black lines, but was also a prolific metal engraver of stipple and mezzotint plates. Amongst a huge output of works of great quality, he cut on steel in 1852 the figure of Britannia on English banknotes.

In a letter to him at the end of November 1839 Cole wrote:

I am happy to say there is a wish to have all the beauty possible to be got into the Stamped Envelope and I want to consult you about setting about it. I hope the result will be that J Thompson's name will go all over England &c in connexion with the Penny Postage. Who can be applied to for a design? R.A. or otherwise – & what is there of antiquity which might be appropriated for the purpose. Pray say when I can have the pleasure of seeing you in the Evg soon.[1]

Cole then notes in his diary that on 28 November 1839 Thompson came to talk about the design for the envelope and the following day discussed the matter again and 'brought some hints for subjects.'[2] Cole now consulted Sir Martin Archer Shee, the President of the Royal Academy, who recommended as designers Sir Richard Westmacott, a sculptor, Charles Cockerell, an architect, and Henry Howard, Charles Eastlake and William Hilton, all artists and all Royal Academicians.

He tried to contact Westmacott first but failed to do so for some days. In the meantime Henry Corbould, the landscape artist and portrait painter, called on 9 December with a design which he sub-

Henry Corbould's design for an envelope

sequently took away to alter. On 11 December Cole noted 'Mr Corbould brought his design for envelope.'[3]

This design is preserved in the Cole papers in the Victoria & Albert Museum. Classical in format and allusion it shows a central figure of Britannia with on her left a naked Mercury, messenger of the gods, and on her right probably Ceres, goddess of tillage and corn, resting on a horn of plenty. The design is balanced by two of Neptune's tridents with the central area being left free for the address. Instructions were to be placed at the four corners clear of the design and the Queen's head would appear beneath (on the back when folded).

No contemporary comment on Corbould's design has survived but it cannot have pleased Cole or Hill for on the day after its delivery Cole went to see William Mulready at the behest of Francis Baring, the Chancellor.

William Mulready (see page 92) was Irish, born in Ennis, County Clare, in 1786. His family had moved to London by 1792, part of the great immigration of cheap Irish labour. Despite poor beginnings he became a successful landscape and genre painter and part of respectable society, being elected RA in 1816. However, he was very sensitive about his Irish origins and tried hard to obscure them. The Irish in Britain at the time suffered from poverty and hostility and Mulready

William Mulready's first 'poetic' design

Mulready's initial faint drawing at an early stage

distanced himself from them as much as possible. He had a wild and passionate side to his nature and a roaring temper, together with a taste for bad company. His wife left him in 1809.

According to Cole Mulready 'readily entered into the idea'[4] of what was required for the envelope and on the Sunday, three days after Cole first approached him, he produced his first design. This was ambiguously described by Cole as 'highly poetic' though Hill 'seemed to like it.'[5] The sketch showed a central Britannia (as in the Corbould drawing) but sending out messengers to all corners of the Empire. Elephants indicated India and a group of Red Indians America. The latter group seems to have come from Benjamin West's drawing of William Penn's treaty with the Indians, a copy of which had been engraved by Perkins & Heath. At the foot of the drawing a small steam tug is chugging across an aqueduct.

Discussions about this design took place between Cole, Mulready and Thompson and it was altered slightly, the main changes being the removal of the aqueduct and translation of the cherubic messengers into angels. It was not noticed at the time that one of these angels only had one leg. Later, when the original drawing was presented to Thomas Baring MP this was corrected. An interim, very faint, sketch exists with the general layout of the figures but without the angels.

Mulready's design was approved by the Chancellor of the Exchequer on 4 January and engraving by Thompson commenced. When a proof was submitted to Queen Victoria Mulready appended a commentary:

This Design is intended to convey the idea that the measure it assists in carrying out, emanated from Great Britain, and that it is a very wide spreading benefit, facilitating our friendly and commercial intercourse with remote lands, and bringing, in a manner, our separated brethern closer to the sick beds and cheerful firesides of home.[6]

It is sometimes reported that Mulready claimed he was not paid for his design, or that he received £200. In fact, Cole's diary makes it quite clear that he was paid £352 10s on 17 June 1840, after the public ridicule had broken out.

Paper and Security Devices

When it came to the production of all the forms of stamps it was agreed that someone should oversee this. Rowland Hill suggested that his brother Edwin could fill this role and he was confirmed on 31 January as Superintendant of stamp production at the Stamp and Taxes office.

Edwin Hill would now work with Cole and Rowland Hill to effect the production of the stamps. Cole was more concerned with the design and printing of the envelopes and covers. For some time he had been discussing the use of a watermark in the paper for these. He had sought advice from George Magnay, the paper maker who had mills near Rickmansworth and Guildford and who had given evidence to the Select Committee. During the latter part of December 1839 Cole's diary records that he was preparing a 'model sheet' for the watermark and this continued into January. Examples of a large watermark 'postage' in lozenge form (for envelopes) exist, each marked in writing exactly the same as Cole's Treasury Competition entry. The legend

Drawing (probably by Cole) for a watermark in the envelope

reads 'A sheet $25\frac{1}{4}$ inches by 36 inches containing 20 lozenge shaped divisions the diagonals of which are 11.3 inches by 7.4 inches with a watermark "Postage" in letters one inch long inserted in each division, such watermark being placed $2\frac{1}{4}$ inches from the bottom and one inch from the side of each division.'[7] A similar drawing with different dimensions exists for lettersheets. This is probably the watermark 'model' drawn by Cole, although the date applied to the examples is February 1840, the time when watermarks were being seriously considered. Other examples of watermarked paper from Magnays are preserved in the Cole papers.

The supply of paper, however, was put into the hands of the Excise department. A Treasury minute of 28 January explains that as the manufacture of paper was already under the control of the Excise department they should take under their control the manufacture of the paper required for the various stamps to be printed.

In the first instance a supply sufficient for at least six months' consumption should be obtained. This was estimated at 9,000 reams for covers (in sheets of twelve); 6,000 reams for envelopes (in sheets of twenty); and 500 reams for adhesive stamps (each sheet making 240). A ream consisted of 480 sheets. Moulds required for making the paper were to be supplied at the cost of the contractor but they would remain the property of the Excise office:

Whilst My Lords have selected a watermark as the most suitable distinguishing feature of the paper, their Lordships will not preclude manufacturers from making tenders of paper in which any other mechanical peculiarity affording a security against forgery is substituted for the watermark.[8]

This was not to include proposals dependent on secrecy.

The size of the sheets of paper intended for the covers and envelopes was found to be inconveniently large for ordinary printing machines and so a further minute on 5 February reduced these but made a corresponding increase in the number of reams. The revised requirements for tender were: 15,000 reams for covers (in sheets of eight); 9,000 reams for envelopes (in sheets of twelve); and the same 500 reams for adhesive stamps.

The tenders had to be supplied by 20 February. Some six firms sent in tenders, including Stacey Wise and John Dickinson. But nothing came from Magnays who had been working with Cole and Hill to produce machine-made paper with a watermark. Hill remarked in his diary that he suspected that Magnay was 'conscious of some difficulty with regard to the water-mark – he says the conditions are too stringent.'[9]

Schedule of Tenders[10]

Tenders by	Reams Envelopes	Reams Covers	Delivery	Price
Stacey Wise	9000	None	From 1st June 1840	£2 2 7
Francis Giles	1500	1500	500 Reams on or before the 1 May 1840	£1 10 0Cv
			and 500 Reams on or before the 1st of each succeeding month	£1 11 0Ev
Harris & Tremlett	9000	—	500 Reams from 30 May to the 30 Novr.	£1 8 6Ev
John Key & Co	9000	15000	500 Reams in 6 Weeks & 500 in every succeeding 14 Days	£1 8 3Cv / £1 9 9Ev
Venables Wilson & Tyler	—	3000	500 Reams in one Month from date of Order & 500 per month	£1 7 0Cv
John Dickinson & Co.	3000	3000	Reams	
			500 March 17 Covers	£1 3 6
			500 March 27	
			500 April 18	
			500 May 2	
			500 May 20	
			500 June 8	
			3000	
			500 March 17 Envelopes	£1 4 6
			500 March 31	
			500 April 15	
			500 April 30	
			500 April 30	
			500 May 20	
			500 June 4	
			3000	

As Hill noted Dickinson offered the lowest price and the earliest supply for paper for covers and envelopes. It had in any case already been decided (on 17 February) that the paper to be used could only be produced by Dickinson's patent machinery, and the other manufacturers had been informed of this.

Accompanying the tenders were letters of explanation from the paper manufacturers. The most interesting were two from John Dickinson where he explained the significant features of his silk thread paper:

The specimen of Protective Paper annexed to our tender is manufactured with colored threads, worked into the body of the sheet, by means of peculiar machinery, simultaneously with the formation of the Paper; and not by any process of *stiching* two sheets or webs of paper together with threads between them; and an imitation of our process by this latter mode, beside being difficult and expensive, admits of easy detection, either by separation of the sheets, if they are merely pressed together in a wet state, or in case of some cement being used, by the adhesion of the thread to the substance of the paper.[11]

He claimed that his paper had several advantages over the ordinary watermark. It was more difficult to produce or imitate, it was novel, it could be reserved for government use as the machinery was patented and could be immediately detected by the public:

Threads of any color might be introduced and any arrangement of these colors; *also any adjustment of the distances of the threads, so as to avoid any distinguished frank of the present stamp.*

It will be seen that the threads made use of in this sample are in fact compounded, viz: blue and white twisted together. We propose so to introduce them into the paper that eight threads may traverse each cover and six threads traverse each envelope. This thread is very expensive, and it takes nearly two yards to a cover, beside waste; and the introduction of it renders damaged paper entirely useless; so that the competition, *in price only,* with ordinary water-marked paper is hardly a fair thing.[12]

Dickinson proposed to supply printed covers and envelopes and undertook to deliver envelopes on 1 May and covers on 16 May. Thereafter, production rates would be 300,000 envelopes a day and 260,000 covers.

There were apparently problems in the negotiations with Dickinson subsequent to his tender. Rowland Hill, exasperated, noted in his diary:

Dickinson is a most impracticable fellow – he seems to think that all the arrangements are to be remodelled expressly to suit his convenience for making the paper, a view of the matter in which he is, in no small degree, encouraged by Mr Wood [of the Excise Office]. We meet again tomorrow morning at my office, but I do not expect to arrive at any satisfactory conclusion. Among other matters, Wood & Dickinson want to carry some of the blue silken threads right across Mulready's design.[13]

Despite Hill's premonitions the meeting went well and satisfactory arrangements were made. 'Dickinson behaved very well at last.'[14] The Treasury minute authorising the acceptance of the tender was dated 9 March. This minute also dealt with the paper for the adhesive stamps:

With regard to the paper to be employed for the Labels or Adhesive Stamps, My Lords would prefer, for the sake of uniformity of plan, that it should be of the same description as that used for Covers and Envelopes; but as it appears that Dickinson's paper if employed for this purpose would be very expensive, from the great number of threads that would be required in order to give at least one to each label, and that it would in some other respects be objectionable, My Lords are pleased to confirm the intention expressed in the Minute of 19th ult. of employing a watermarked paper for the Adhesive Stamps or labels.[15]

As a result that contract was awarded to Stacey Wise.

It was not until 22 May that the contract with John Dickinson was actually signed. The delay was due to difficulties in preparing and agreeing the wording. But already by 13 June demand for the end products had ceased and the initial order for paper had not yet been fulfilled. The Excise department, under whose auspices the paper was being manufactured, wrote to the Treasury for guidance.

They pointed out that Dickinson's tender, as accepted, was for 3000 reams of paper for envelopes and another 3000 reams for covers. As urgent supplies had been required to print the Mulreadys,

deliveries were made before the contract was ready for execution, and as it was supposed from the rapidity with which the paper was called for, that the whole of the first 6000 Reams would speedily be delivered, the contract was simplified by being drawn as a general one subject to be put an end to by notice as above stated.

In the meantime Messrs Dickinson have only as yet sent in 2670 Reams for Covers and 2220 Reams for Envelopes, & there remain to be delivered 1110 Reams to make up the first tender of 6000 Reams.'[16]

By the terms of the contract Dickinsons were entitled to supply the remainder.

On 7 July the Excise department wrote again.[17] Dickinsons had applied for the paper they were holding to be removed. This now comprised 420 reams composed partly of half sheets making 383 reams for covers and 370 reams for envelopes. No other use could legally be made of this paper by the manufacturers and so it was felt that it should not be left in their hands. The original contract had been altered because of a change of plans for printing. Covers were intended to be produced in sheets of eight but it was decided to print them in sheets of twelve. The tender requirements had therefore been reduced from 15,000 to 10,000 reams.

It was eventually agreed to pay Dickinson for this paper but it was not considered desirable to terminate the contract. The Treasury wrote that 'their Lordships are of opinion that the manufacture of the paper should be altogether discontinued for the present, but they do not consider it impossible that a further supply of paper, in a somewhat modified form perhaps, may be required.'[18]

Method of Production

John Thompson, who had been consulted by Cole about the design, made enquiries of various printers as to how the covers and envelopes should be printed. As a result he suggested that they should be printed from stereotype plates moulded from a brass original. Stereotype is a word compounded from two Greek words – *stereos* solid, and *tupos* impress. Thus, stereotype printing takes impressions from a fixed, immovable forme. A mould is made from the relief surface. Molten metal is then poured upon this to obtain a cast of which the surface is in relief, identical to the original. As many of these casts or stereos are taken as are required to create the printing forme. The quality of the final product would depend on the original plate, and on the care taken by skilled workmen in the production of the various stages, and on the purity of the materials. A mobile foundry could be set up to produce the stereos without great difficulty.

One of those Thompson asked about printing was Robert Branston, son of the wood engraver of the same name to whom Thompson had been apprenticed. Robert Edward Branston was a noted engraver who had formed a partnership with Charles Whiting. By 1840 he had left Whiting and had set up with James Henry Vizetelly in Fleet Street.

Branston suggested hard metal rather than stereotype moulds which did not deliver the ink as well. However, the lozenge-shaped envelope might be polytyped in two pieces. He gave a series of detailed answers to questions about stereotyping, particularly in reference to their quality and wear. If type were to be used it would be best to have it stereotyped first and then fixed up with the brass original to be moulded from. He also quoted the price of brass required for the original die (5s.).[19]

Edward Cowper gave a detailed and critical description of the problems of stereotyping:

unfortunately Stereotype Metal is often either made of bad materials or not well mixed, & the consequence is that either the lead becomes rotten from the presence of Sulphur, or the Antimony remains in separate small hard particles that when the plate wears instead of wearing with an even surface, it has a surface like *Chalky Sand* by the sea shore, the Antimony forming innumerable little *rocks*, which you may not [find] very good for Printing – I have spoken to Messrs Clowes frequently on the subject but although their plates are better than they used to be, still I do not venture to print more than 20,000 from them.[20]

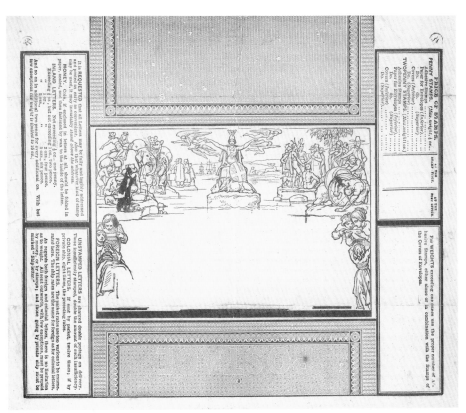

Unfinished Mulready proof in brown

Cole's suggestion for an embossed die for stamped paper

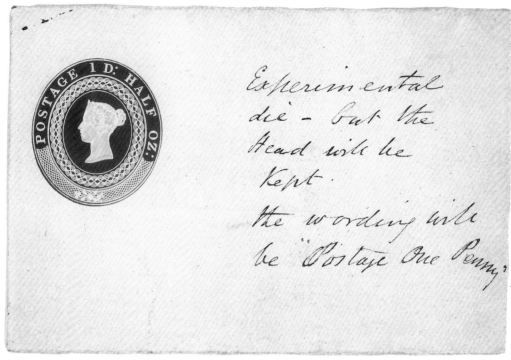

Wyon's first embossed design for stamped paper

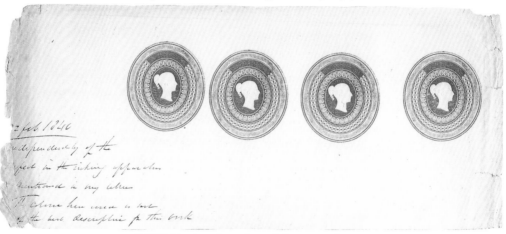

C F Whiting's embossed proofs for stamped paper

Medal of William Wyon engraved by his son, Leonard Charles Wyon, 1854

John Thompson's woodcut of the Mulready with the lines standing proud

He then referred to Thompson's original wood cut. If it were clichéd in a modified version of stereotype metal, this would last nearly as long as type.

Thompson was primarily a wood engraver, though he could, and did, work in hard metals such as brass and steel. It would be likely, therefore, that the first engraving he produced would be in wood. One such exists, exquisitely engraved with the skill for which Thompson was famous. Names of the artist and engraver are finely cut, as is the legend 'POSTAGE ONE PENNY' exactly in the style as finally printed. The next stage would have been to produce a mould and from this a brass plate, with some of the finer points engraved out.

The original brass plate is still extant with a hole for the value (see page 92). Close examination of the background shows the marks of chisel on wood, though these do not accord with the marks on the wood cut that exists. Exact facsimile woodcuts were often made at the time. From this brass die, together with the typecast panels, stereotypes were taken to make up into the printing forme. It took a long time to prepare the die, and Thompson had only finished all the rough work by 8 March, having been visited by Cole quite regularly to check up on progress.

The work was obviously hard but little evidence of the effort involved remained in the finished product. When Thompson appended an explanatory note to Queen Victoria on 3 April to accompany the proof he was rather defensive:

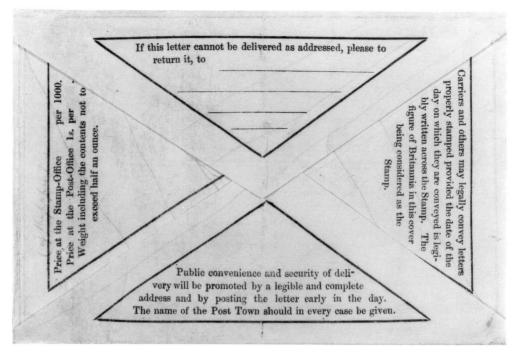

Proposed information panels for the envelope

The Engraving, though having the appearance of a slight etching, is produced by a very difficult and tedious process, being done in relief on brass. The lines from which the impression is produced stand up above the general surface. This mode of engraving is necessary for the purpose of working at the common printing machine.[21]

Correspondence took place in early March between Edwin Hill who was supervising production of all 'stamps' and Thompson on whether he should rely on the printer to produce perfect stereotype plates. Thompson, the skilful craftsman, was adamant that the engraver should either do, or superintend, the work of clearing and picking the casts himself.

His letter was dated 9 March:

The reproduction of plates by means of Stereotyping being an imperfect process every cast being liable not only to an accumulation of extraneous matter in the form of globules or air bubbles but also to a want of sharpness arising either from imperfection in the mould, or from the metal not having properly entered the lines it is essential that every plate should be carefully inspected before it is sent to press.

When the stereotype plate consisted of type only for book printing a picker in the office was employed. Since he was well acquainted with the forms of letters he had no difficulty in doing what was required. Any resulting damage to the letters would have been immediately obvious:

But in stereotyping from engravings the case is materially different and it is absolutely necessary that the clearing be done by or under the superintendance of the artist who engraved the original – indeed it would be exceedingly unjust not to submit it to his inspection for from the nature of the work, the intricacy of the lines &c it is much more liable than type to imperfections in casting – and when it is considered on what minute touches the character and expression of heads and the propriety of the other parts of a design depend, the idea of trusting this to any other person than the engraver, whose professional reputation is at stake cannot be entertained. In all works that I have engraved for the purpose of casting, the plates have invariably been sent to me to be cleared, and I believe such a course is to be the case generally. I have done a great deal for the Religious Tract Society and have frequently returned to them, as totally useless, plates that their sterotype [sic] printer has sent to them, as perfect. At the Bank of England where no expense was spared and where they had the most careful moulding and casting, and the best metal that could be procured – every plate was submitted to my inspection, but it was the more necessary as *perfect identity* was required which will also be an essential feature in the post office stamps. Identity might certainly be rendered doubtful by careless or bad stereotyping.

And I must state that had I for a moment suspected that any deviation from this mode of proceeding would have been likely to take place in executing the post office stamps regard for my professional reputation would have compelled me to decline the undertaking.[22]

When the stereotypes were made, Thompson cleared and picked them at home, removing any imperfections.

Layout and Frame

When the envelopes were actually issued they consisted simply of the Mulready design, the word POSTAGE on an engine-turned background and the particular stereo number. The lettersheets on the other hand had side panels with type matter giving prices and postal information.

Initially, there was a suggestion that the envelopes should also have information panels on the reverse. Branston in his advice to Thompson had mentioned the possibility of the envelope being polytyped in two pieces, with 'the four triangular labels to be separated afterwards.'[23] This is undated but was probably written during January 1840 and probably refers to layout proofs of the envelope with four triangular information panels, which when folded made up the reverse. At some point, the information panels on the envelope were dropped.

With regard to the lettersheet, the layout seems to have been derived from an entry to the Treasury Competition. This was a sheet printed in green with various blank coloured panels, printed in letter-press (see page 109). One of the panels bears the word 'POSTAGE'. Unfortunately, this suggestion is undated and bears no Treasury number. However, it is annotated in pencil 'Submitted by "A B"'. In the Treasury register the initials 'A B' appear twice – with No. 20365 on 17 September and No. 22734 on 9 October. The layout and spacing of the

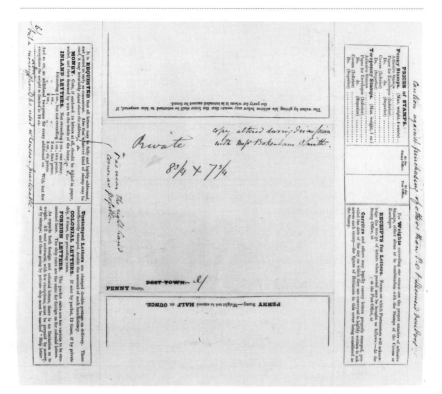

First layout proof for the lettersheet, February 1840

lines is the same as in subsequent Mulready proofs, and it was quite probably printed by Whiting. It seems likely that Cole and Whiting used this as the basis for the Mulready layout. In the Cole papers is a proof in red, clearly taken from the same block (see page 109). This has been marked in ink with panels including the words 'POSTAGE/POSTAGE ONE PENNY'. Again this is undated, but is presumably an early thought.

The first proofs that can be dated come from January 1840. These show a largely blank central area surrounded by information panels about postal regulations. Rowland Hill sent a copy to Maberly on 25 January and in the Cole papers is an annotated example marked 'copy altered during discussion with Messrs Bokenham & Smith' which must date from 11 February when they came to see Henry Cole at the Treasury about the legend to the covers.

There are many variations to the legend. The text alters considerably, as does the layout, before the final version appears. Various type fonts are also used, both serif and sans, and with different weights of bold. These were set by Charles Whiting. Some were proofed separately, others in the overall layout in combination with other parts.

Whiting submitted a choice of engine-turned backgrounds for the legend 'POSTAGE' on 27 February.

Layout proof for the lettersheet with a faint
impression of Thompson's engraving

Two different types of background were proofed in blue together
with solid panels as in the early versions (see page 110).

On 16 March Edwin Hill noted in his diary: 'Thompson's plate
and Whiting's frame to be put together in their present state, stereotyped,
and printed from for experiment.'[24] From this several proofs exist (see
page 127). The design is not yet complete. Inscriptions for Thompson
and Mulready at the foot of the design have not yet been engraved
showing normally as solid raised, and therefore printed, bars. There
are also distinctive printed marks on the left of the design covering
the Muslims crouched writing. A sheet of eight such essays in black is
dated 20 March. Another single example is in brown. Edwin Hill
mentions trying six plates in a forme on this date with Clowes printing
from them.

In the Phillips collection in the National Postal Museum is a proof
similar to this but without the uncut area at the foot of the design.
The engine-turned panels have been removed and pasted on to one
free area is a panel of engine-turning with the beginnings of a border.

Steam–driven printing machine at Clowes
(the hands of the second operator can be seen in the middle
of the machine removing the printed sheets)

From this the POSTAGE panel eventually derived. Two more variations exist from about the same time, one in blue, the other in black. Both have the same information panel wording, but one is without the design in the centre while the other has a faint impression of Thompson's engraving.

Stereotyping and Printing

Two printers were considered to produce the lettersheets and envelopes. Tenders had been invited from both Spottiswood and Clowes but the latter was preferred. William Clowes was one of the largest printers in London, based in Duke Street, off Stamford Street, Blackfriars. He had printed many of Charles Knight's publications and had come into contact with Rowland Hill in connection with the latter's rotary printing press. Hill had even been offered a partnership in the firm, but had turned this down to work on postal reform at the Treasury.

Clowes had some twenty steam presses driven by shafts and belts from two steam engines. There was also a foundry where the stereotype casts were made. The tender agreed on 18 March specified that Clowes would produce the stereotypes from Thompson's brass die and print the covers and envelopes at the rate of £25 per million. A special room had to be set aside for Post Office work and Edwin Hill was present to supervise production of the plates.

Production of casts commenced on 6 April and the registration of the die took place the next day. It was directed that the die and plates made from it had to be deposited at the end of each day in a box with two keys, one kept by Clowes and the other by Edwin Hill.

Both Cole and Rowland Hill took a keen interest, visiting the print works frequently to watch operations. On 9 April Rowland Hill noted:

Went again to Clowes's. E. H. is making great exertions – he is at Clowes's from 6 in the morning till 10 at night. They seem to think at the Stamp Office that the whole machinery is to be set to work without any trouble on their part.[25]

When the casts were made they were sent to Thompson for picking and then returned to Clowes for proofing and putting into formes. By Monday, 13 April matters were proceeding apace. Rowland Hill personally went to Thompson's to pick up some of the finished stereotypes:

Found that Clowes had, contrary to the arrangement made with him by E.H., taken away 24 plates last night. I took the remaining 12, & arranged with Thompson to send two assistants to complete the work at Clowes's. Found them "making ready" their machines. Went to the Stamp Office, & suggested to Pressley [the Secretary] that each plate should print a distinctive number as a means of narrowing the evidence if any fraud should be attempted by a comparison of the fraudulent impression with the genuine registered impression of the same number.[26]

The printing formes of the lettersheets and envelopes both consisted of twelve stereotypes. These were made up from various constituent parts. The side panels were set in type by Charles Whiting. Moulds were probably taken from these and stereotype casts produced. It is likely that these were placed round the brass die, as recommended by Branston, together with the POSTAGE panel rather badly produced by Whiting on an engine-turned background. This whole would then have been stereotyped again to produce the number required for each printing forme. The stereo number would have been individually inserted.

Proofs exist taken at various stages, from the original die, and from the stereotype casts, with and without numbers and on different types of paper. Many are on thin 'India' paper and some are known on green paper. Unfortunately, they are rarely annotated nor precisely dated but most would have been taken in the first two weeks in April. On 14 April printing began and Cole gleefully wrote to Mulready the following day: 'My dear Sir, here are specimens of the real thing now printing at the rate of seventy thousand per hour.'[27] Some six formes of the 1d. lettersheets were made with four of the 1d. envelopes. Only one each of the 2d. lettersheets and envelopes were made up.

Proof of the completed 1d. Mulready
(annotated 'Proof' in manuscript)

Trouble arose when it came to cutting them into single items. Although it was expressly stated on the lettersheets themselves that they would be available singly the Stamps and Taxes Office ordered that they should only be supplied in sheets. Rowland Hill was furious at what he regarded as yet another attempt by Wickham to sabotage his plan. Eventually, after much argument, it was agreed that Clowes should cut the lettersheets and envelopes as well.

The eventual bill for printing was £792 1s. 8d., of which £563 was for the printing alone, the remainder being for sundry expenses. This would indicate that a total of $22\frac{1}{2}$ million of the four types of lettersheets and envelopes was printed.

There seem to have been problems with the printing. Initially, Clowes did not execute the covers as well as had been expected, but he said that this would improve. There are indications that this did not happen for on 12 May Thompson was asked to inspect his brass die, which he pronounced to be perfect. On the same day a proof was taken from a cliché said to have been struck by the polytype process. It differs from other proofs in that it has no line round the design, nor any inscription.[28]

Quite what would have been the source of such a cliché is not clear. Polytyping was a method of producing casts from the original die that had been considered at the outset. Sometimes, it is stated, without any source being given, that this was the method by which the casts were produced. All contemporary references, however, always describe the process as stereotyping. In polytyping the method of reproduction is akin to die-sinking, a punch being created from the original die. The punch then strikes clichés to make up the printing plate. Stereotyping involves pouring molten metal on the mould taken from the original die.

Generally, polytyping was used only for the reproduction of small woodcuts. Duplicates could be produced more rapidly and more cheaply, and it was considered superior by some founders. However, the printed design would differ little, if at all.

Cutting of the envelopes remained a problem because of the time it took. Rowland Hill had to give permission for Clowes to continue cutting on the first Sunday after the issue date, and for a further two machines to be installed to speed up the work.

All the effort was to be in vain.

CHAPTER ELEVEN
Wyon's Embossed Stamp

William Wyon was born into a distinguished family of engravers and medallists in 1795. Apprenticed to his father at the age of fourteen, he soon attracted attention. While still quite young he won the Society of Arts' large gold medal in a competition of 1812/13. Already in 1816 he was appointed to a position in the Mint and he became Chief Engraver there in 1828. During the 1830s he produced new coin dies for William IV, and also for new Portuguese coinage. On 10 March 1838 Wyon became a Royal Academician, the first medallist to be so honoured. He also modelled and engraved the head of Queen Victoria for her coinage and various medals, to universal acclaim. One of the medals served as the basis from which the Queen's head on the adhesive labels was taken.

It was thus not surprising that Rowland Hill specified Wyon initially when artists were being considered for the various forms of 'stamps'. Work began on a die in December 1839, which was intended to be used on paper sent in by the public to be stamped. On 11 December Hill noted in his diary that he had 'directed Mr Wyon to commence a die of the Queen's head.'[1] Wyon's subsequent contacts were with both Hill and Cole.

In a letter of 23 December Wyon informed Cole that he was now proceeding with the Queen's head 'agreeable to the wish of Mr Hill & I am doing it in relief so that I can transfer it upon Steel of any size Mr Hill may require.'[2] He later added that as he had proposed to Hill, he was putting the tiara on the Queen's head.

In the same letter Wyon enclosed specimens of the 1d. and 2d. silver Maundy money as a result of a request by Cole. The following day Wyon wrote again explaining that there would be no difficulty in striking such coins in silver at the Mint, though it was possible there might be some delay.[3]

There is a design in the Victoria and Albert Museum which was drawn by Cole probably for Wyon's guidance (see page 127). The central feature is an embossed impression of a small coin but with the Queen's head facing to the right rather than to the left. Surrounding this is an impression in colour of engine-turning with two legends to be embossed white on a coloured ground. That at the top reads POSTAGE/HALF OZ 1D and at the bottom the instruction WHEN THE SHEET IS/FOLDED THIS STAMP MUST BE SEEN/ABOVE THE ADDRESS.

Wyon and Whiting Dies

Some of these ideas were incorporated into Wyon's first die. The head that Wyon engraved, facing left and without a pendent curl, was supplied to Charles Whiting for an engine-turned background to be added and proofs to be taken. It has been stated that this work was carried out by Arthur Deacon, who worked for Whiting. It was intended that the head, lettering and background be white embossing out of a coloured ground. There is a proof impression in colourless relief of the head alone with a manuscript note by Rowland Hill confirming Cole's wording: 'For letter paper. The head will be surrounded by a printed ground. Above the head will be the words Postage $\frac{1}{2}$ oz. 1d. Below: Write the address below'.[4]

When it came to proofing, problems arose with the presses, the result being imperfect strikes. On 4 January Wyon wrote to Cole about the imperfect manner of the striking but noted that they could be improved with an alteration of the presses. 'It is obvious from the impressions made by Mr Whiting that the fault of the impressions is not from the die as the impressions were very good.'[5] A week later he sought an interview with Hill to ascertain where the paper was to be stamped and which presses were to be used. He had not yet transferred the punch into a die.

The first die was ready by 25 January, proofs being known from that date. Hill sent examples 'as perfect as they could be obtained of the proposed stamps'[6] to Colonel Maberly on that date inviting suggestions. Whiting noted it as 'Mr Wyons head and legend' but 'our notion of the engine turned pattern to look well'. One of these proofs in brown is annotated 'Experimental die – but the head will be kept. The wording will be "Postage One Penny"' (see page 128).

A month passed and problems still remained in producing good impressions from Wyon's die. A letter of 22 February from Whiting to Hill explained what was happening:

I have to report to you the circumstances and results of our experiment with my Stamping Machine, so as to make it fitting to produce good impressions from Mr. Wyon's die, agreeably to your instructions of the 3rd inst. I have had a die made somewhat similar, because it was impossible to continue our experiment with Mr Wyon's, the Stamp Office requiring it for theirs; consequently interruption delayed proceedings. It seems to me that what the machine requires is very steady fixing and also weight on the surface.[7]

The proofs which accompanied the letter were a strip of four in brown of a design by Whiting (see page 128). The Queen's head, without tiara, faces to the right and there is a pendent curl to the chignon. This is surrounded by three ovals, with a blank tablet above the head. It was endorsed by Whiting 'independently of the defect in the inking apparatus mentioned in my letter, the colour here used is not of the best description for this work'. Other examples are known in black and other colours. Elsewhere, Whiting described this die as being suited for the Stamp Office machinery. It exists in two forms, one as here with a blank tablet in the oval above the Queen's head, the other with the word PAID inserted and the outer oval removed.

In the letter to Hill, Whiting continued:

The accompanying proofs establish the fact that the pressure is insufficient to bring up the head when cut in the die as the sheet exhibits and also for paper embossing; and then the occasional mackle is producing a double impression, which has been mentioned, arises from two causes, the one from lack of proper adjustment of the spring, the other from the method of holding the paper; these it appears are trifling difficulties easily to be remedied by the workmen.[8]

The most serious defect was the lack of power in inking the die properly. 'But even this, with an alteration of the inking apparatus, I suggest might be overcome. I therefore propose that the Engineer who made the machines should be consulted; and that our suggestions should be explained to him; and if he agrees to them that our machine be submitted to the test.'[9]

He then reported that Wyon was producing another die, not being satisfied with the effect of one that had just been finished.

Progress was slow. How the design changed can best be seen on two cards of proofs prepared by Whiting. Wyon's second die, dating from late February, had the wording changed to read POSTAGE ONE PENNY in sans lettering. Whiting described this as 'our doing except the head' but also that it was at Wyon's suggestion.

The next stage was to alter the lettering to a finer serif type and later to add a pendent curl to the chignon. Proofs exist of both states of the die. The latter version was supposed to be the die chosen according to Whiting but he noted that 'Mr Wyon called on the 17 March to say the die should be altered to be made smaller'.

To make the die smaller, the outer oval was removed and the legend placed on the inner oval. New lettering was required to fit the smaller oval and two versions of different sizes are recorded by Whiting in sans and serif typefaces. These are marked 'Lettering proposed by Mr Wyon / proof sent 27 March' and 'another experiment' (dated in

April). The second, undated, has reverted to having no pendent curl, presumably new impressions of the die of the Queen's head from Wyon.

Difficulties Leading to Abandonment

Unfortunately, there is very little documentary evidence of what Wyon and Whiting were doing at the time and deductions have to be made from the existing proofs. Unless dated these can be most misleading.

On 10 April Hill noted in his diary 'Went to see Wyon's progress. More blundering by Whiting has caused further delay.'[10] It is not clear exactly what this refers to but it presumably indicates that Whiting had either ruined a die or was incapable of obtaining good impressions from the presses. At this time many things seemed to Hill to be going wrong with obstruction from all quarters, but particularly the Stamps and Taxes office. His diary entries are often long and full of bitter complaint.

On 15 April the Stamps and Taxes office wrote to the Treasury informing them about progress in the production of the covers and envelopes at Clowes and of the adhesive labels at Perkins, Bacon & Petch. They also gave an estimate of when these could go on sale. At the end of their memorandum was the laconic note 'With respect to the Stamp which is in preparation by Mr Wyon for the purpose of Stamping the Paper which the Public may send in for that purpose we are unable at present to inform your Lordships when the same will be ready.'[11]

Work still continued, however, with further proofs all without the pendent curl to the chignon. On 6 May proofs were taken of the head and lettering alone ('Mr Wyon's idea of doing the lettering') and then with 'the engine turning done over the lettering' returned on 9 May. The two combined was the 'result of the above plan / die sent 29 May (late) proofs sent 2 June early'.

The idea of offering the public the facility of having their own paper stamped was not formally abandoned until October, and then only because of fears of forgery. On 13 October Hill noted 'that Palmer of Newgate St. had succeeded, after repeated trials, in making a very tolerable die which he has cast from some impressions in paper of the Queen's head by Wyon, the cast having been made by the new Electrotype process.'[12]

Hill doubted if this gave rise to fear of forgery of Wyon's embossed stamp but it did render insecure the ordinary bill and receipt stamps. However:

Mr Baring is of opinion that as the public evinces little or no anxiety to have the stamp in question, (which was to have been applied to any paper which might be sent

Mr Wyons head
and legend

our notion of
the engine turned
pattern to look well

our head &
engine turning

Sketch for the
Stamp Office
Machinery

Mr Wyons
Suggestion
from an Impression

one dying
except the head

Supposed to be
the die chosen

Mr Wyon called
on the 17 March
to say the die should
be altered to be
made smaller

Lettering
Proposed by
Mr Wyon

Proof Sheet
27 March

another
experiment

Die proofs showing the progress of Wyon's design
from January through to June 1840

to the Stamp Office for that purpose) it will be most prudent not to issue it lest the disposition which the public has evinced to try all sorts of experiments with the postage stamps should lead to frauds with regard to the bill and receipt stamps. I am sorry to give up Wyon's stamp for it is a beautiful thing.[13]

Wyon's stamp was not abandoned, but stamping-to-order facilities did not become available to the public until 8 October 1855. It had been intended that the stamping would take place at the Stamp Offices in London, Dublin and Edinburgh. In his report on the distribution of stamps of 27 March,[14] Hill specified that the quantity of paper to be received at one time should not be less than two reams (960 sheets) for 1d. stamps or one ream (480) sheets for 2d. stamps. An extra charge of 9d. per ream was to have been made to meet the cost of stamping.

When the Mulready stationery was so badly received by the public it became necessary to consider another design. As early as 6 June Hill was considering using the Wyon head as a replacement. By 14 October 1840 he could write 'It is settled to issue new Envelopes of two sizes made in the first instance of Dickinson's paper (of which we have a large stock) and stampt [sic] with Wyon's die.'[15]

Over a period of months work continued to perfect the dies and eliminate the printing problems and a modified version of the design was finally completed and registered on 20 January 1841. With variations it was then used on postal stationery right through to the end of Queen Victoria's reign.

Jacob Perkins, 1766–1849

The City Medal (enlarged) by William Wyon, 1795–1851

Original sketch for the Postage Stamp

Watercolour sketches for the Penny Black
and Twopenny Blue

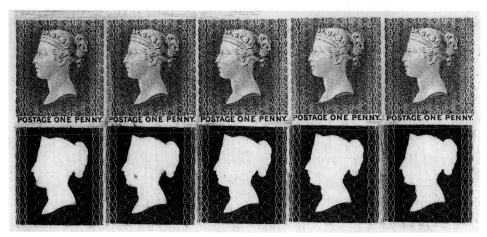

Proof impressions of the first and the experimental dies
for the Penny Black

Charles Heath, 1785–1848, by Henry Corbould

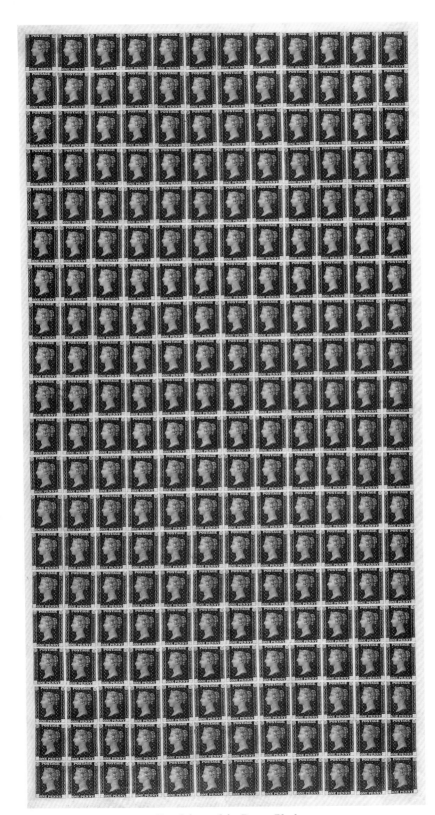

Proof sheet of the Penny Black

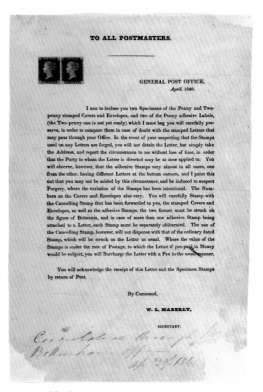

Letter from W Bokenham showing the first
Maltese Cross cancellations

Notice to postmasters announcing
the Penny Black

Penny Black used on the first day, 6 May 1840

CHAPTER TWELVE

The Penny Black

At the same time as Mulready was working on his design for covers and envelopes and Wyon was struggling with the embossed die for stamped paper, the task of producing the adhesive labels was entrusted to Perkins, Bacon & Petch of Fleet Street.

Jacob Perkins was born in 1766 in Massachusetts (see page 145). He invented a number of processes and machines for high quality printing, especially to do with the prevention of forgery of banknotes. On the advice of the British Minister to the United States he came to London in June 1819 to compete for the contract to print banknotes for the Bank of England. With him came some twenty-six cases of machinery. He also brought an agreement with Asa Spencer, the inventor of the geometrical lathe, for the latter to come to England to produce the white line machine-engraving which was used in Perkins' banknote designs and which was later to be used in the background of the Penny Black. Late in 1819 he entered into partnership with Gideon Fairman, an engraver from Philadelphia, and Charles Heath, then engraver to the King. Others in contact at this time included William Wyon and Henry Corbould. They failed, however, to gain the Bank of England contract.

Heath shortly went bankrupt and Joshua Butters Bacon, who had married Jacob Perkins' daughter, joined the firm in December 1821. By May 1829 the name had been changed to Perkins & Bacon, and the firm printed notes for the many British and Colonial banks of the time. In 1834, Henry Phillipson Petch, an engraver who had worked for the firm since 1823, was taken into partnership and the name was changed to Perkins, Bacon & Petch.

Hill was in contact with Perkins, Bacon & Petch in July and August 1839, enquiring about the possibilities of producing one of his 'stamps'. Little came of it, however. But in September Cole asked the firm to assist him with specimens for his Treasury Competition entry and it was Cole who again approached them on 2 December. He asked them to engrave steel dies less than one inch square. The following day the printers replied that they could produce such stamps at a rate of eight pence per thousand exclusive of paper.

There are virtually no references in Rowland Hill's or Henry Cole's diaries about the subsequent proceedings until the final versions of the labels were being printed. However, the correspondence and Engraving Books of Perkins, Bacon & Petch have survived and from these and proofs extant the story of the development of the design of the labels can be pieced together.

After Cole had made the initial contacts, an interview took place with Hill. The following day (14 December) Perkins, Bacon & Petch wrote to confirm what had been agreed:

That we would engage to prepare a die of the size pointed out by you [¾ inch square] – to be composed of the best Engraving of Her Majesty's Portrait which we can get executed by the best Artist, to be surrounded by white and black line Engine-turned work, (& of which Engine there is no copy in the British Dominions) and the appropriate wording – for the sum of Seventy-five Guineas, . . . and in case our plan is adopted the Seventy-five Guineas would be credited back in account.[1]

Hill replied that they should submit a sketch before beginning the work and that the Queen's head was to be drawn from Wyon's so-called City medal.

The City medal commemorated Queen Victoria's first visit to the City of London in November 1837 (see page 145). Although it was issued the following year it was based on a sketch originally drawn in 1834 when Princess Victoria was only fifteen. All postage stamps were to have a portrait based on this throughout Victoria's long reign. It was not the only basis, however, as other medals were supplied by a Mr Marriott to assist in the drawing.

Perkins, Bacon & Petch commissioned Henry Corbould to make a drawing of the Queen's head from Wyon's medal. Corbould had worked for the firm before from the time Perkins first arrived in Britain, and drawings of Victoria by Corbould for Perkins, Bacon & Petch exist from 1837. Born in 1787, he was a son of Richard Corbould, a landscape and miniature painter. He entered the school of the Royal Academy and later produced a large number of book illustrations and was then commissioned by the British Museum to make highly finished drawings of the recently acquired Elgin marbles. For his 'Queen's heads' for Perkins, Bacon & Petch he was paid £12.

In the Royal Collection is a small sketch annotated by Pearson Hill (Rowland Hill's son) as being the 'Original sketch for the Postage Stamp. (by Wyon)' (see page 146). This measures 19 x 19¾ mm, almost exactly ¾ inch square as originally required by Rowland Hill for the labels. It seems probable, therefore, that this was one of the first drawings, if not the first. Because Wyon was working on the embossed die for stamped paper, this drawing for an adhesive label is

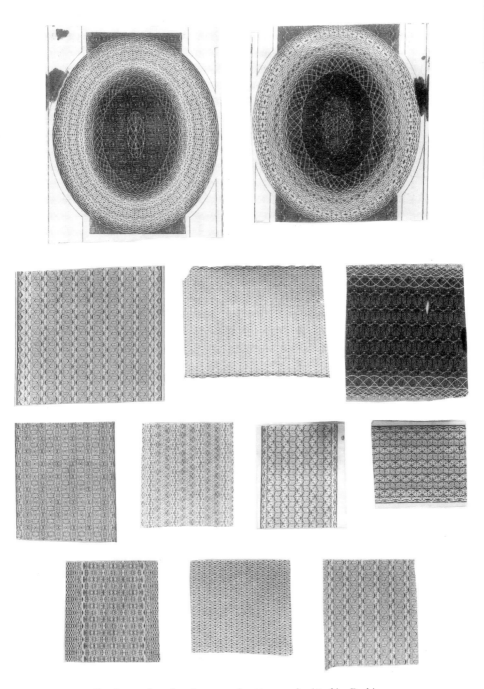

Stock samples of engine-turned patterns submitted by Perkins,
Bacon & Petch to be used for the background to the labels

unlikely to have been by him. Pearson Hill was writing at some considerable remove from the events in question and may well have been mistaken. Interestingly, when Henry Cole came to make his collection of drawings and proofs he also attributed trials to Wyon while, in fact, they clearly had been done by Perkins, Bacon & Petch.

This sketch may have been one, or a copy of one, by Henry Corbould. A similar sketch (though larger) is drawn on one of Corbould's drawings sent to Perkins, Bacon in 1837. The 'stamp' design has sometimes been described as a sketch for an embossed stamp, even as Wyon's entry to the Treasury Competition. Its size and form virtually preclude the former, and Wyon did not enter the Competition.

In December 1839, Perkins, Bacon & Petch submitted a number of stock samples of engine-turned patterns to be used for the background to the labels. Some twelve examples remain in the Cole collection. Most, though not all, come from a specimen sheet of different types of engine-turning originally submitted to the Bank of England in the 1820s. Also in the Cole collection are three examples of these backgrounds with a silhouette paper portrait of Queen Victoria pasted on top to simulate a stamp. One is clearly based on the earlier sketch, having the same wording (HALF OUNCE POST OFFICE ONE PENNY) surrounding the portrait in painted sans shaded capitals. It measures 21 x 20 mm, again approximately $\frac{3}{4}$ inch square.

It was possibly this last sketch that was submitted to Rowland Hill at the end of December 1839. At a meeting with Bacon on 31 December Hill agreed various detailed amendments:

> The 4 corners to be taken away but only to a slight extent.
> The length of the die to be one sixteenth of an inch more, equally divided between top and bottom, and one sixteenth of an Inch more to be taken at the bottom so as to insert in black letters without an underground, the words
> Half oz One Penny.
> Or if practicable increase the length One eighth and insert in white letters at the bottom
> $\frac{1}{2}$ oz One Penny.
> Certain letters to vary with each stamp to be placed at the top behind the head.
> Certain instructions as to the position of the stamp when used to be engraved round the margin of the plate.[2]

Hill concluded with calculations indicating a sheet of 240 stamps (12 × 20).

For the first die the background selected was that used in the drawing in the Cole collection. Bacon has described how this was transferred:

An impression . . . was transferred from the stock roller on to a flat piece of steel and the exact size of the background required for the stamp and a space for the head were

First trials with engine-turned backgrounds [No 4]
with that used for the first die

outlined on this die. An impression was then taken up on to another roller, the parts
of the pattern outside the indicated marks were removed, the space for the head was
cleared, and the background required for the stamp was then transferred to another
flat piece of steel, which became the actual die of the stamp. The die was then handed,
with the drawing made by Henry Corbould, to Charles Heath for the engraving of the
Queen's head.[3]

Charles Heath (see page 146) was formerly a partner of Jacob
Perkins. Born in 1785, he was the son of James Heath, engraver to the
Royal Family. His best work was in small plates for book illustration.
Larger plates were less successful. On more than one occasion (including
in April 1840) his engravings were dispersed by auction, apparently
because of money problems. He had several assistants and pupils and
the *Dictionary of National Biography* comments that 'Heath engraved
but little with his own hand in them.'[4]

It is clear that the work of engraving the Queen's head was
entrusted to Charles Heath but controversy surrounds who actually
carried out the work. His son, Frederick, was one of his assistants and
later statements ascribe the work to him. Certainly, the task was
given to Charles Heath's atelier but it seems likely that Frederick did
the engraving.

Subsequent progress in the engraving of the first die can only be
seen in extant proofs taken from the die at various stages. The first
was after the face had been faintly outlined and the diadem drawn in.
Then followed the engraving of the face and the filling in of the
surround, the proofs initially showing this by the addition of Indian
ink. This die was completed by the mid-January 1840. At the foot was
added the legend POSTAGE ONE PENNY in sans capitals probably about
the same time though this was not agreed by Hill until 30 January –
'Agreed with the C. of Ex. that the legend on the stamps should be
"Postage one penny" & "Postage twopence" & issued instructions to
the engravers accordingly.'[5]

Stages of the first rejected die

However, the background was too light to transfer well, as was the Queen's head, and so this first die was rejected. The die itself was still in the possession of Perkins, Bacon at the time they were taken over (1935), but it may have been destroyed at that time.

A new die was now required urgently. Part of the dark background which produced the central band in the specimen sheet alluded to before was selected:

In order to obtain this pattern on a flat steel surface for copper-plate printing, an impression was transferred from the engraved roller to another roller, and on this the borders of curved, interlaced lines, which appear white in the print, were cut with the engine-turning lathe. . . . A space for the head was cleared on this roller, and a portion of the design outside the part required for the stamp was also removed. The portion intended for the stamp was then transferred to a flat piece of steel, which in this case was used as an experimental die.[6]

This work is believed to have been done by George Rushall, an engraver with the firm. This experimental die still exists on the reverse of the piece of steel used to engrave the master die used for the penny black.

The Second Die

The experiment with the background for the second die was considered successful and so preparations were made for a completely new die. Surprisingly, this was not based on the roller impression made for the experimental die. As Bacon put it:

it was constructed in a circuitous manner. The die was obtained by transferring a piece of the unused background, left on the roller made for the experimental die, to a flat piece of steel. The space for the head, and the size of the background required were carefully outlined on this. An impression was then taken up on to another roller, the space for the head was cleared, and parts of the background round the portion required for the stamp were removed. The background was then transferred to another flat piece of steel, which became the actual die of the stamp.[7]

It was probably done in this manner to incorporate minor changes to the shape of the head, together with a rather larger background.

Background of
the second die

The experimental die
on the reverse of the 'Old Original'

When the background was completed five impressions in a row
were transferred from the roller to a steel plate, together with five
impressions from the first die. This was to compare the backgrounds
of the two dies and the spacing needed between impressions for the
final plate. Proofs printed in dark blue are known taken from this plate
(see page 146).

The second die was sent to Charles Heath on 16 January for the
head to be engraved. After this was done the space around the head
was filled in with lines to imitate the background. It was sent back to
Bacon on 20 February with the comment 'If that does not transfer
well nothing will.'[8]

It was a proof of this stage of the die that the Chancellor of the
Exchequer sent to Queen Victoria for her approval. On 20 February
he wrote to the Queen: 'The stamp is complete except as regards the
corners where it is proposed to introduce letters which will it is hoped
afford additional security against the possibility of forgery.'[9] On 2
March Rowland Hill wrote to Perkins, Bacon & Petch saying that the
Chancellor had shown him an autograph letter from the Queen 'ex-
pressive of "high appreciation" of the stamp.'[10]

At this time Rowland Hill was giving consideration to the layout
of stamps in the sheet. It had already been decided that these should
bear variable lettering and on a paper dated 22 February he laid out
the formula as it was to appear. In rows 12×20 the lettering would

Proof of second die, as approved

read a a to a l horizontally and a a to t a vertically in the sheet. The sketch is annotated 'The letters are to be arranged as above, but they are to be Roman Capitals.'

In the Cole collection there is a strange sheet layout in watercolours with corner squares and some different forms of the numeral '1' in the centre. It is annotated 'Early suggestion for Numbers of Stamps on the Sheet by H.C.' though its purpose is unclear.

During February trials had taken place with lettering in the corners and with the legend POSTAGE ONE PENNY. For these trials duplicate impressions of the background of die 2 with the vacant space for the head were used. First the legend was at the foot, as with essays of the first die. Then the word POSTAGE was separated from ONE PENNY and corner letters added. These are in the Cole collection, the letters used being A B / V R all in a sans face. Finer lettering in a serif face was then introduced with the four corners cut off to be replaced with pieces of paper bearing pencil letters B R / V R. This last specimen was mounted on card with the annotation on the reverse 'Approved R.H. 2.21.40'. These letters were then engraved in the centre of star-like ornaments.

At the end of February watercolour sketches were made for Rowland Hill, probably to show the effect of crosses in the upper corners and to indicate the colours proposed (see page 146). Two pairs now exist, originally part of one whole. On the pair now in the Royal Collection the left example in black is marked 1d. and the blue on the right 2d. The other pair is not annotated.

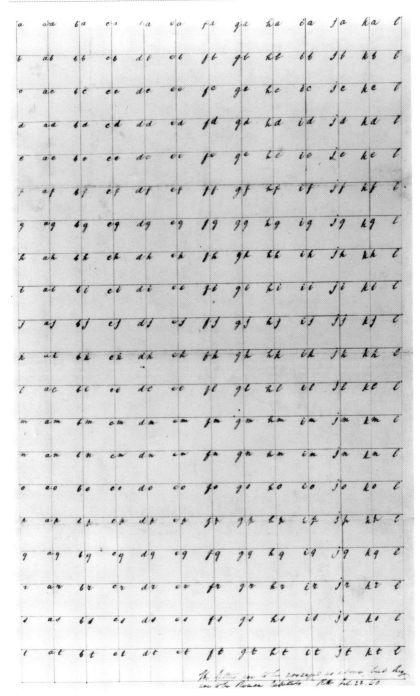

Hill's suggestion for the sheet layout

Trials for corner letters and legend

Stages of the final design and the
master 'Old Original' die

The beginning of March saw the engraving on the die of the agreed legend and of the crosses in the upper corners. The first plate from this die went into production on 11 March. This still had no corner letters at the bottom for they were to be punched in on the plate by hand.

Even at this time no formal contract had been drawn up with Perkins, Bacon & Petch. The Treasury had intimated in their Minute of 20 February that the work should be done by them but at the same time had put it under the superintendance of the Commissioners of Stamps & Taxes. Their description of what should be done was clear and precise:

For the adhesive stamps, a fine steel-plate engraving, by Heath, of Her Majesty's Head, reduced from Wyon's City Medal, with an engine-turned background by

Perkins, Bacon & Co., to be printed on sheets, each containing 240 impressions, these impressions being exact facsimiles of one another, except that they will be distinguished by certain combinations of the letters of the alphabet; the sheets of paper to have watermarks consisting of the word 'Postage' in the margin, and a small crown so placed as to occupy the lower part of each stamp.[11]

But it was only on 18 March that Wickham laid Perkins, Bacon's tender before the Board of Stamps & Taxes. Because of the care necessary in printing on copper plate he had confined his attention to Perkins' prices and not invited other tenders. He had, however, checked on the prices with Mr Rapley of the Stationery Office, who had agreed that it was a fair tender and might with propriety be accepted. The necessary steps were therefore to be taken. On the same day Wickham wrote to Rowland Hill informing him of the terms of the contract and stating officially that 'The 1d. value to be Black. The 2d. to be Blue.'[12] Perkins, Bacon had recommended two days earlier that the 1d. be in black and the colours needed to be distinguishable in both daylight and lamplight. Orders were given for the printing firm to prepare dies and plates for both the 1d. and 2d. values.

On 1 April 1840 the first plate for the 1d. was ready and a proof impression was taken from it (see page 147). There were still no corner letters but this sheet is the only complete example of any penny blacks still in existence.

The contract was finally signed on 13 April. The price paid was to be $7\frac{1}{2}$d. per thousand and the contract was to remain in force for one year from the date of the first delivery of stamps.

Printing

The method of printing by die and roller transfer was introduced into the security printing field by Jacob Perkins. The original design was engraved in reverse on a die of soft steel. This was then hardened in a furnace so that ordinary implements could not scratch it. A soft steel roller was put in a transfer press and rolled under great pressure backwards and forwards over the hardened die until the design was transferred to the roller. Sunk lines on the original die now became lines standing proud on the roller. In its turn the roller was hardened and from this any number of reproductions of the design were laid down on to a soft steel plate.

For the postage stamps this plate contained 240 impressions of the die minus the corner letters. These were then punched individually on to the plate.

Printing took place not at Perkins, Bacon & Petch's premises at 69 Fleet Street but at their works in Whitefriars Street. There were five (later six) flat-bed printing presses worked by a large diameter hand

Printing presses at Perkins, Bacon & Petch

wheel. Invented by Jacob Perkins, they were built by Messrs J & J Barrett of Finsbury and cost £70 each. Bacon has given a detailed description of the process:

The method of printing from the plate consists in mounting it on the bed of a hand printing press, which has a gas-jet fixed underneath the plate in order to warm it. The colour (or ink as it is called) is then rolled or dabbed over the whole of the plate. All the ink lying in the parts that stand up has then to be cleaned off with a rag, taking care however that the ink is left in the lines forming the design. The plate is finally cleaned and polished by the palm of the hand, after the application of a little whiting, a manipulation that required a good deal of practice and skill, and the sheet of paper to receive the impression, which has been previously damped, is laid smoothly on the plate. On the printer turning the wheel of the press, the paper is pressed into the sunken lines by the elasticity of the material – usually a sort of felt or cloth, called the blanket – on the cylinder that makes the pressure, and the design on the plate is thus transferred to the paper, the design, so to speak, standing up on the surface of the paper. The presses were so constructed that after the plate had passed under the cylinder it returned automatically to the operator, who then removed the sheet of paper covered with the design, and at once proceeded to ink the plate again for printing another sheet.[13]

These presses were each capable of printing some 800 sheets of stamps in 24 hours. Hill recorded on 10 May that 'the demand for labels is such that the contractors (Perkins Bacon), though they now have five presses, are obliged to work night and day; they are now producing 600,000 (stamps) daily.'[14]

Warrant to the printers for the first Penny Blacks,
public and Government

The first plate for the Penny Black was put to press on 11 April, with the second following on 22 April. In all there were 11 plates used from which over 68 million Penny Blacks were printed by the end of January 1841.

Printing of the twopenny blue stamps did not begin until 1 May 1840. Two plates were used between then and 29 August, and the total quantity printed was only 6,460,000.

Imprimatur or registration sheets from each plate were taken in the presence of officials of the Stamps & Taxes Board. These were kept at Somerset House but those from plates 4, 6, 7, 9, 10 and 11 of the penny and both plates of the twopenny disappeared while still in the custody of what became the Inland Revenue. Surviving sheets, minus the 20 to 30 stamps officially cut off each sheet between 1882 and 1914, are in the National Postal Museum. The plates were all destroyed by 1843.

Paper and Gum

Dickinson's silk-thread paper, adopted for use in the Mulready stationery, was clearly not suitable for printing miniature copper-plate engravings. So the idea of having a security watermark was transferred from the stationery to the labels. The paper was to be procured by the Commissioners of Excise.

Stacey Wise of Rush Mills just outside Northampton had been in contact with Perkins, Bacon & Petch in December 1839 and he responded to the invitation to tender published on 5 February 1840. Wise was not successful in the tender for the covers but at the beginning of March Rowland Hill indicated that he was in favour of his supplying the watermarked paper for the labels. A mould for the watermark had already been supplied by Edwin Hill.

In a letter dated 4 March[15] Rowland Hill specified that the size of each sheet was to be $22\frac{1}{4} \times 20$ inches, weighing $22\frac{1}{2}$lb per ream. Wise offered to supply this at 26s 3d per ream. When the paper was eventually supplied, however, it came in triple sheet size (rather than double) which caused delays in cutting at the printers. In the first contract (until August 1840) some 133 reams were supplied.

As early as 9 October 1839 John Rawsthorne of Manchester had written to Rowland Hill offering to furnish gum for the adhesive labels. In December he was asked to supply specimens of paper gummed with his preparation. It is not entirely clear as to what the ingredients were but when complaints arose that licking the gum was causing cancer Rawsthorne wrote indignantly that 'the material from which it is made is eaten daily in my own family in soups, milk etc.'[16]

Edwin Hill sent various samples printed by Perkins, Bacon & Petch to Rawsthorne in February 1840 asking that they be gummed. At the same time he insisted that all impressions, whether damaged or otherwise, should be returned to him. He thought that 'there is no doubt the wash must be applied in London but at first I think the solution of the gum had better be done in Manchester.'[17]

Reluctantly, the printers agreed to do the gumming and on 14 March wrote to Rawsthorne asking for particulars. Problems then arose as to cost and adhesive quality and the first supply did not arrive until the beginning of April.

When the printers came to gum the printed sheets in production there was further unforeseen trouble:

We have now been five days occupied in gumming the Stamps, and the difficulties we have met with are beyond description; some of them were natural to a new business in which we had never had any experience, and as far as the time required for drying goes, and the *cockling after pressing* we are better off than we expected to be; but after various experiments we find:-

1st.-That three persons can only gum and dry 600 sheets in 12 hours, whereas we shall probably require five times that quantity.

2nd.-That unless the gum is laid on rather thick, it will not adhere to the letter, when wet and put upon it, and consequently that it will not go near so far as you supposed.

3rd.-That after perfectly gumming the sheets it frequently happens that the gum separates, and leaves large spots upon the sheet, where the gum *has not taken at all.*

We do not believe this owing to any fault in the gum, but in the bleaching of the rag or sizing of the paper at the mill.

4th.-That the sheets do cockle and thus trouble us, while drying, and before we get them into the glazed boards for pressing.

If you can assist us by any suggestions we shall be glad to hear from you, for at present the cost to us of gumming is ruinous.

In the act of gumming we have tried three plans, one was the placing the sheets under a tympan – another was to place them in piles and gum the top, and remove them as done – and the last is placing them singly upon a block a fraction smaller than the sheet, and this is the best mode of the three.[18]

As a result, Rawsthorne supplied an improved version details of which were not given but which proved smoother in operation.

The 'VR' Penny Black

In the Treasury minute of 20 February provision was allowed for a separate stamp for official and Government business. This was to be distinguished from the public labels by colour. However, later, it was decided to use the same design as for the public stamps but to replace the corner crosses with the letters V R [Victoria Regina]. This was done by removing the upstanding metal on the roller. A memorandum from Rowland Hill to Bacon dated 26 March makes it clear that it was intended to have the same two Government stamps as for the public – i.e. 1d. black and 2d. blue – but only the former was produced. This plate was finished on 14 April and printing began from it on that day.

A total of 3,471 sheets were printed between 14 April and 3 June, but 148 were spoilt. Of the good examples, two sheets were kept for registration purposes, one was sent to Rowland Hill and 13 were delivered to Somerset House for specimens to be sent to postmasters with the printed circular of 7 May. Some 3,302 sheets were destroyed on 25 January 1843, leaving a balance of five sheets unaccounted for.

Quite when it was decided to abandon the idea is not certain, but these stamps were never distributed to the government departments they were intended for. A few specimens are known used, probably taken from the postmasters' circulars.

CHAPTER THIRTEEN

Success and Failure – The Public React

'Stamps issued to the public today (in London) for the first time. Great bustle at the Stamp Office.'[1] Thus did Rowland Hill note the Penny Black and the Mulready lettersheet and envelope going on sale. Initially, they were only on sale in London and only at certain locations. Cole indicated some of these when he wrote that on 6 May, the first day of validity, he called at the Stamp Office about the issue of the stamps 'and also at several shops in the Strand.'[2]

The Twopenny Blue was not available until 8 May, two days after the stamps were valid for postage.

Distribution and Sale

On 11 March, while work on the various printing plates was still continuing, Rowland Hill had submitted a report on the 'Distribution of Franking Stamps' to the Chancellor of the Exchequer.[3] This followed quite closely his proposals given in his report of 6 December on the Treasury Competition. It was later to be amended by a further report (of 27 March)[4] after he had consulted the Chairman of the Board of Stamps (Wickham) and the Secretary of the Post Office (Maberly).

In those days the Post Office did not sell items in the way we are accustomed to today. Thus, it did not automatically have the sole right to sell the new stamps and stationery. Since these were being produced under the auspices of the Board of Stamps and Taxes the latter decided that they should be sold by persons duly licensed by the *Stamp Office*, not, it is to be noted, the *Post Office*. This included all distributors and sub-distributors who already sold stamped paper for other duties in almost all the market towns throughout the country. But licences to vend stamps were 'to be granted freely to respectable applicants'[5] and an arrangement was to be made with the Postmaster General for all Deputy Postmasters and Receiving house keepers to be licensed.

This did not quite apply to everybody, however. The minutes of the Stamps and Taxes Board record on 7 April that Mary, Ann and Susan White had written requesting to be appointed Sub-Distributors at Coleford. It was ordered that 'they be informed that the appointment

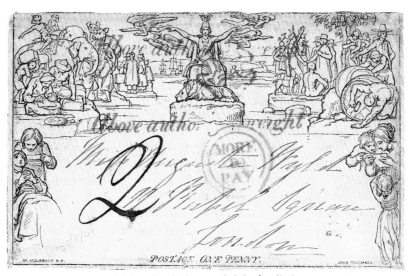

Mulready which exceeded the ½oz limit

Mulready caricature by John Leech

Ink trials for the new 1d. and 2d. labels

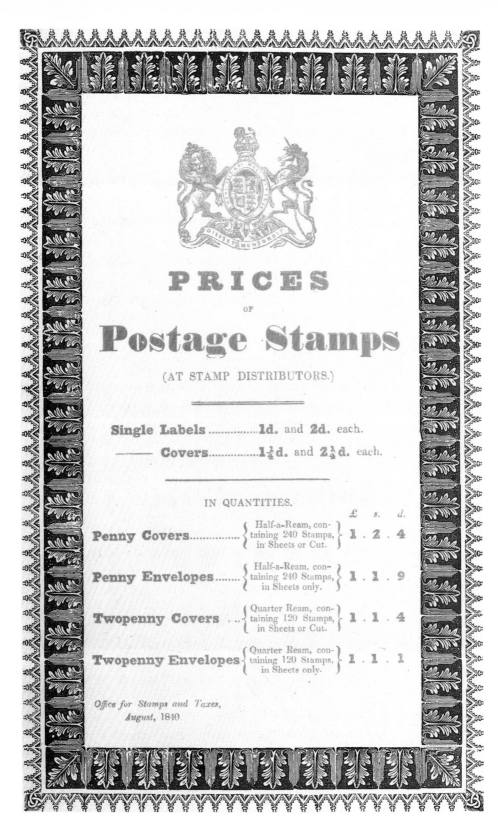

Stamps and Taxes Office poster advertising stamp and cover prices

Rowland Hill's diary for early May 1840

rests with the Lords of the Treasury, and . . . that it is contrary to the regulation of the office to confer such appointments on females.'[6]

With regard to where the stamps might be sold one Mark Barton wrote requesting information on selling postage stamps. He was informed that 'a licence will authorize him to deal in Stamps at a particular house or shop only, and that the law expressly prohibits under heavy penalties the carrying about of Stamps for Sale.'[7] Over the next few weeks the Board were inundated with requests for appointments as licensed vendors or sub-distributors of the stamps.

By now the Treasury was anxious to know when they would be in a position to supply distributors, and postmasters with the new stamps and when they would be ready to issue these to the public. After all, eight months had now elapsed since the passing of the Penny Postage Act. Referring to the Mulready stationery and the labels the Board of Stamps and Taxes minuted that they would be ready to issue these stamps in London on 27 April and to the Post Office and country distributors on 11 May. It was intended that in London the several stamps would be issued at the head office at Somerset House by Mr Cockell, the Distributor of receipt and other stamps, and in the City by Mr McQuoid, the Distributor of Sea Policy stamps.[8]

When the letter was sent a week later the position was somewhat clearer:

In our opinion we shall be ready to issue Stamps in London on the 20th of the present month but we strongly recommend to your Lordships that they should not be brought into use for Postage until the 1st of May next in order that a sufficient time may be given for the dealers to supply themselves with Stock.[9]

This would also prevent inconvenience if the first issue did not precede the date of use by several days. They thought that sufficient stocks could not be manufactured to supply the whole of the country before 1 June.

The Lords of the Treasury directed that the covers, envelopes and labels should be issued as soon as practicable and that they should come into use on 6 May. Issue of the stamps would in the first instance be confined to London but that it would 'be extended first to Dublin and Edinburgh, and afterwards to other parts of the Kingdom in such order as the Comm[issione]rs of Stamps & Taxes may determine and as rapidly as the necessary supply can be obtained.'[10]

On 5 May a notice dated 28 April was published in *The Times* announcing the forthcoming issue of the stamps. These could be used to prepay inland letters up to the weight limits prescribed and also foreign letters, though if the letter were only partly prepaid it would not be charged accordingly but rather would be sent to the Dead Letter Office and returned in all practicable cases to the writer. Notices to postmasters were sent out at the end of April bearing examples of the Penny Black (see page 148).

In practice, distribution of the stamps and covers was haphazard. There were particular problems with the London receivers. Hill was told that this was due to an administrative error on the part of the Treasury. On 7 May he recorded 'The London receivers have not been supplied with stamps. The delay is, I find, owing to an error in the Treasury. A minute directing that the issue may not be delayed till certain bonds are prepared was worked into a letter to the P.M.G. with the word *not* omitted.'[11]

This caused considerable dissatisfaction especially as licensed vendors in shops did have supplies and were selling them at a premium. However, it was not until 13 May that a letter from Maberly was received by the Stamps and Taxes Office asking for a supply of stamps so that the London receivers might be furnished with them. As a result a warrant was prepared for £1000 worth of 1d. labels and £600 of 2d. labels, with another batch to follow in a few days. 'Let a Warrant also be prepared for Conveying 500 reams of 1d. Covers cut and 200 reams of 2d. covers (if ready) but notify to Col. Maberly that it would be exceedingly inconvenient if the stamps were consigned in the numbers stated in his letter.'[12]

Poster advertising the correct prices for labels and covers

Problems still arose with cutting the covers and this was a cause of further delay.

When other parts of the country received supplies is not clear. Some of the earliest examples used (such as the Penny Black sent from Bath on 2 May) were probably taken from the postmasters' notices sent out before the issue date. By 6 May it is likely that only the Stamp and Taxes office, the Sea Policy office and the chief post office in London had supplies, and possibly the distributors in such large towns as Liverpool, places reachable by railway. Examples of Penny Blacks are known used from Liverpool on 6 May. But Mr Shuttleworth, the Distributor in Manchester, was told on 8 May that a certain quantity of stamps would be despatched to Manchester 'if possible' on Tuesday next (12 May).[13]

Scotland and Ireland were to be supplied from Edinburgh and Dublin respectively. Distributors and Sub-distributors were supplied direct by the Stamps and Taxes office; deputy postmasters by the Post Office. Licensed vendors could obtain supplies from either.

Prices were fixed at 1d. and 2d. for each of the labels with no discount or 'poundage'. Envelopes were only sold in complete sheets of twelve but the covers or lettersheets could also be sold cut singly at $1\frac{1}{4}$d and $2\frac{1}{4}$d each. Quantities were available at varying prices as advertised by the Stamps and Taxes office:[14]

2 Reams of 1d. covers containing 80 sheets or 960 Stamps	£4	7	0
Same quantity of Stamps for Envelopes	£4	5	0
1 Ream of 1d. Covers containing 40 sheets or 480 Stamps	£2	4	6
Same quantity of Stamps for Envelopes	£2	3	6
Half a Ream of 1d. Covers containing 20 Sheets or 240	£1	2	4
Same for Envelopes	£1	1	9
One Ream of 2d. Covers containing 40 Sheets or 480 Stamps	£4	3	6
Same for Envelopes	£4	2	6
½ Ream of 2d. Covers containing 20 Sheets or 240 Stamps	£2	2	8
Same for Envelopes	£2	2	2
¼ Ream of 2d. Covers containing 10 Sheets or 120 Stamps	£1	1	4
Same for Envelopes	£1	1	1

Because of the poor distribution initially some licensed vendors charged more for single items and the Stamps and Taxes office wrote to one of their Distributors who had complained 'that Licensed Vendors may charge what they please for the Labels'.[15] Many firms bought the lettersheets in quantity and printed advertisements on the reverse. These could then be supplied more cheaply to the public. Attractively printed notices were printed to indicate the official prices of the covers and envelopes on sale (see page 166).

The Maltese Cross Cancellation

To prevent re-use of the labels and covers some device was required to mark them. On 31 March William Bokenham, Superintending President of the Inland Office, wrote to Maberly with examples of a design (see page 148). 'I beg to submit to your notice specimens of the stamps proposed for destroying the One Penny and Two Penny Letter Stamps which, if approved of, the Contractors have undertaken to supply at a cost of 1/- each and at the rate of 1,000 per Week.'[16]

On the same sheet are three proof impressions of what has come to be called the Maltese Cross. The design is in fact rather more a combination of a Maltese Cross, a Cross Patée and a Tudor Rose (with four petals). There is no indication of the origin of this design nor of who produced it. Cost and the need for durability indicates the use of brass as the material. Two thousand handstamps were ordered and despatched in April 1840.

Perkins, Bacon & Petch had supplied a number of different types of red ink to the chemist Professor Richard Phillips on 18 March. A month later they sent Hill 'two small pots of red ink similar to that from which you tried specimens, the price of which would be five shillings and sixpence per pound'.[17] One week later, on 25 April, a Post Office notice was sent out to postmasters and sub-postmasters in England and Wales on the obliteration of stamps and the composition of the ink (the Scottish notice was sent two days later):

627

TO ALL POSTMASTERS

AND

SUB-POSTMASTERS.

GENERAL POST OFFICE,
25th April, 1840.

IT has been decided that Postage Stamps are to be brought into use forthwith, and as it will be necessary that every such Stamp should be cancelled at the Post Office or Sub-Post Office where the Letter bearing the same may be posted, I herewith forward, for your use, an *Obliterating Stamp*, with which you will efface the Postage Stamp upon every Letter despatched from your Office. *Red Composition* must be used for this purpose, and I annex directions for making it, with an Impression of the Stamp.

As the Stamps will come into operation by the *6th of May*, I must desire you will not fail to provide yourself with the necessary supply of Red Composition by that time.

Directions for Preparing the Red Stamping Composition.

1 lb. Printer's Red Ink.

1 Pint Linseed Oil.

Half-pint of the Droppings of Sweet Oil.

To be well mixed.

By Command,

W. L. MABERLY,
SECRETARY.

Notice concerning the obliteration of stamps
and the composition of the ink

It has been decided that Postage Stamps are to be brought into use forthwith, and as it will be necessary that every such Stamp should be cancelled at the Post Office or Sub-Post Office where the Letter bearing the same may be posted, I herewith forward, for your use, an Obliterating Stamp, with which you will efface the Postage Stamp upon every Letter despatched from your Office. Red Composition must be used for this purpose, and I annex directions for making it, with an Impression of the Stamp.

As the Stamps will come into operation by the 6th of May, I must desire you will not fail to provide yourself with the necessary supply of Red Composition by that time.

Directions for Preparing the Red Stamping Composition.
1lb. Printer's Red Ink.
1 Pint Linseed Oil.
Half-pint of the Droppings of Sweet Oil.
To be well mixed.

By Command,
W. L. Maberly,
Secretary.[18]

With the exception of the linseed oil, it is not clear exactly what the ingredients were. This was as true then as today and so a large number of varying shades of red, and even other colours, obtain, from brown through orange to blue.

The office datestamp was also to be applied to the envelope or cover but not to cancel the stamp.

When it came to the Mulready stationery, Hill suggested that the cancellation should always be struck on the figure of Britannia in order to prevent its re-use. 'If the Britannia were always struck it would be fair to assume that a label placed over the Britannia was put there to cover the obliterative Stamp, & to charge accordingly.'[19] Maberly had been thinking along the same lines and that is where the cancellation was invariably placed.

Removal of Cancellations

After the stamps had been issued a letter appeared in *The Morning Herald* referring to the possible re-use of the stamps. In its edition dated 13 May a correspondent identified only as 'P.W.T.' wrote:

I do not recollect having observed that any plan has been adopted to prevent a person from using the stamps a second time. I inclose the first I have seen (which was on a London letter I received this morning), and think it is like a marine, in the same way that an empty bottle is – viz., 'It has done its duty once, and is ready to do it again.'

[The suggestion of our correspondent is ingenious, but *non-possible*, so long as her Majesty's postmasters continue to dab red mud in their royal mistress's face – leaving her, like a newly-shorn sheep, bedaubed with the red brand-mark of its owner – or like a painted courtesan after a night's brawl, or a she savage prepared for the war dance. Those sanguinary bedaubings, our correspondent will perceive, extend beyond the sticking-plaster; and without them the plaster would not pass. – Ed. M.H.]

These comments were unfair in that Hill had always been conscious of the possibility of the re-use of labels. As early as 24 April he had written to Maberly 'to call his attention to the power of creosote to wash out the Post Office stamp, & enclosed a specimen of red ink by Perkins & Co., which is free from this objection.'[20]

When the stamps were introduced country postmasters in particular were lax at cancelling them properly and this gave rise to complaints. More seriously some people began to remove the cancellations. Hill became very concerned and spent the next six months working at a solution. On 21 May came the first intimation:

Several more cases of stamps wholly unobliterated, or very nearly so, have come within my knowledge, & all sorts of tricks are being played by the public who are exercising their ingenuity in devising contrivancies for removing the obliterating stamps by chemical agents & other means. One contrivance is to wash over the stamp before the letter is posted with isinglass or something else which acts as varnish & as the obliterating stamp falls on this varnish it is easily removed with soap and water.[21]

He went on to say that he was making every effort with the aid of Richard Phillips, the chemist, and others to prevent these frauds.

Hill asked Perkins, Bacon & Petch to produce new inks to print the two labels. They created a special printing plate of twelve impressions specially made from the 1d. die. The upper right corner of each stamp was made void to prevent any examples being used to prepay postage. These stamps were printed in a wide variety of colours – black, blues, lilac-rose and shades of green and red – and have become known as the Rainbow trials.

Hill's first 'Report on the Obliteration of Postage Stamps'[22] was dated 17 September and was prepared in haste as a result of a letter from the Postmaster General, though he pointed out that he had been conducting experiments for some time:

In conducting these inquiries I have assumed that the only practicable deviation from the present plan, was to alter the colour and composition of the inks now employed in printing the Postage Labels, and in obliterating them in transit through the Post Office.[23]

Officials of the Post Office had raised serious practical objections to other methods for cancelling the stamps such as tearing them or by pricking or abrading the surface. An ink cancellation was best but the composition of the ink would have to be changed. 'Of the many inks that have been tried that which on the whole appears to be best is good black letter-press printing ink diluted with an equal weight of cold drawn linseed oil.'[24] The ink had to be good, that used in the experiments costing 5s per lb. Its basis was carbon which, Hill was assured, was indestructible by any chemical agent, that is without also destroying the label as well.

The obvious objection to a black cancellation was the fact that the 1d. label was printed in black and the cancellation would thus not be readily apparent. A red label, however, would be much better. Perkins, Bacon & Petch manufactured several red inks to comply with the necessary conditions and then printed stamps with them from the trial plate. These trials were subjected to many experiments and one was chosen (16G) as being the best and most satisfactory. It was affected by creosote, turpentine and all oleaginous liquids quite as much as the proposed obliterating ink.

As far as the 2d. label was concerned, although it was not considered necessary, a new blue ink (No.3 plain) had been prepared with similar advantages and so it was proposed that the 2d. be printed in this. The cost would be slightly higher, about $\frac{1}{4}$d per 1,000.

Hill recommended that Perkins Bacon should print the labels in the new inks and that the Maltese Cross cancellation change from red to black. He was cautious, however: 'In the present state of chemical knowledge I believe [the arrangement] to be absolutely secure; but I cannot forget that the red obliterating ink adopted by the Post Office was once considered safe and that for a long time it successfully resisted all attempts to remove it.'[25]

On 18 November Hill reported that his apprehensions had been well grounded. His clerk, John Ledingham, had improved upon a process discovered by a Mr Watson which enabled the black cancelling ink to be removed from the labels then in use. 'The process consists simply of soaking the label for a short time in a strong solution of potash and then washing it with soap and water.'[26] It could be done at the rate of one a minute. Happily, this was not successful with the proposed red penny stamps but a new blue ink would be required for the twopenny. Perkins, Bacon & Petch were experimenting with one regarded as suitable.

Nevertheless, another black obliterating ink would be required, even better than that proposed in Hill's first Report. After experiment alkanet root (one ingredient of an ink suggested by Perkins Bacon) was added to black printing ink and this was found to be satisfactory.

At the end of this second Report Hill returned to the subject of the labels. He recommended that the Commissioners of Stamps and Taxes be instructed to print the penny labels in the red colour previously chosen and to suspend the printing of the twopenny labels until the new blue ink was approved. 'As it may be important hereafter to be able to distinguish the new from the old Twopenny labels I would recommend that the new ones be printed with a white line above and below the head . . . This alteration in the plate will readily be made.' [27]

In a postscript he strongly urged that all the obliterating ink should be prepared in London and thence supplied to the country offices.

Printing of the new penny red stamps began on 30 December 1840 and they were to be put on sale on 10 February 1841. The twopenny followed with printing beginning on 27 February (to be put on sale in March).

Despite the problems, however, this was a story of success. Not so with the Mulreadys.

Press Reaction

Rowland Hill had taken a proof of the Mulready design to the National Gallery on 10 April where it was 'much approved by the R.A.s who were met in council.'[28] Similarly, Wyon had liked it very much when it was first drawn. 'I am very anxious to hear if Mulready's design is adopted although I expected much from him it exceeded my expectations & I should really regret if so admirable a design should be lost to the Public but that cannot be – for I hear the Chancellor is a Man of taste.'[29]

A more ominous note was struck in April. Cole noted he had gone to his club 'wherein Whiting like a shabby fellow has thought fit to attack the Stamps.'[30]

The first comment in the newspapers came in *The Times* on 2 May. It was typical of much that was to come:

We have been favoured with a sight of one of the new stamp covers, and we must say that we never beheld anything more ludicrous than the figure or allegorical device by which it is marked with its official character – why not add embellished. Cruikshank [George Cruikshank (1792-1878) famous caricaturist and illustrator] could scarcely produce anything so laughable. It is apparently a spirited attempt to imitate the hieroglyphic which formed one of the ornaments to *Moore's Almanac*, Britannia is seated in the centre with the lion couchant (Whigish) at her feet; her arms are distended scattering little flying children to some elephants on the left, and on the right to a group of gentlemen, some of whom at all events are not enclosed in *envelopes*, writing on their knees, evidently on account of a paucity of tables. There are, besides, sundry figures, who, if they were to appear in the streets of London or on any of our highways, would be liable to the penalties of the Vagrant Act for indecent exposure. Under the table land by which these figures are supported some evidence of a laudable curiosity is depicted by three or four ladies who are represented reading a billet-doux or valentine, and some little boys evidently learning to spell, by the mental exertion which their anxious faces disclose. One serious omission we must notice. Why have those Mercuries in red jackets, who traverse London and its environs on lame ponies, been omitted! We must admit that, as they have recently been better mounted, perhaps that is one reason why they should not appear in this Government picture.

Much more along the same lines appeared in *The Times* and in all the other papers. Derision was the common response to the Mulready design. It was caricatured in words and imitative drawings. A lot of the comment made bitter use of Mulready's Irish origins and also of the missing leg on one of the angels – a mistake instantly spotted.

One piece in *The Morning Herald* of 25 May made deliberate use of this with a discourse described as 'The Puppet Show and the Post-Covers':

'Ladies and gentlemen, – and you, my very pretty little dears, – here you will see the whole allegorical and pictorial history of her Most Gracious Majesty's post-covers – and all for the low charge of *one penny*. For the accommodation of the short-sighted, the figures are magnified beyond the *natral* size, and the history of the same humanely adapted to the very lowest comprehensions. The post-covers, ladies and gentlemen – only one penny, and don't breathe upon the glasses!'

'Very faithful, quite extraordinary," mutters an old gentleman in a faded apple-green coat, yellow waistcoat, and drab breeches and gaiters – 'a beautiful work,' he exclaims, as with eye intent at the lens of a showman's box, and quite unconscious that he is rubbing elbows between a baker and chimney-sweep, he gazes on the magnificent Government work of art; and listens, with gaping ears, to the revealings of the master of the show, who, with extraordinary sagacity, thus interprets the hieroglyphics of the Treasury:-

'Look directly to the centre, and you will perceive the figure of Britannia with her shield upon her knee. She has just put up a covey of postmen with the wings of wild geese, naked in the *pictur*, but here, you will perceive, clothed for families. One of the postmen, you will observe, is making for the ear of a camel on the left, having, doubtless, a letter of importance to deliver to that sagacious animal.

'At the foot of Britannia is the British lion, looking as mild as *if* suckled upon ass's milk, and having not so much as a growl in the whole inside of him. His front paws is benevolently put out of sight, and his terrible tail hangs as limp as a thread-paper!

'The group on the immediate right is considered by Mr. Hume to be very beautiful. Observe that gentleman, without buttons to his coat, shaking hands with a wild Indian. That is the portrait of Mr Pease, the Quaker, as he appeared after his first motion in the House of Commons.

'The Red Indian as holds Mr. Pease, is the famous Chief Cut-and-come-again, of the Splitskull tribe. He and the other wild men are making a bargain with the whites for rum and powder, for which the savages are to give only their skins. Mr. Pease seems to say that all orders must be post-paid.

'You will observe a dog standing very respectful among the legs of the Indians. He was taken when a puppy from the wife of a general officer in the first American battles; was suckled by a squaw, and is therefore tenderly attached to the Splitskulls. A close observer may perceive that the dog has his own opinions of the Quakers.

'On the extreme right is a majestic man in a broad hat, talking to himself, and, as it appears, much delighted with the conversation. Name not known.

'In the centre, a woman with a baby at her breast, supplies a beautiful allegory, which I will not insult your capacities to attempt to describe. Only the back part of the baby is seen, but that is from life.

'A naked Indian that sits, and seemingly says nothing, is a most important figure. You will perceive that his arm affectionately encircles his knee; by which the artist infers that *'all is as right as his leg.'*

'A man rolling one cask, and one man hammering at another – making much noise and doing little work – are portraits from Parliament; to be supplied according to the politics of the beholders.

'A most umbrageous tree – said to be a portrait of the tree of knowledge – springs from the centre of the group, as meaning to shadow forth the blessings of the penny postage.

'Your polite attention is now requested to the group on the left. In the front is a gentleman on his knees, writing. Do you see him? That is a fancy portrait of Lord Palmerston, writing a *'communication'* to the innocent Hong merchants in the distance, – known by their long tails – and at the moment selling a chest of fine Pekoe to an English trader. The men-of-war, still further in the distance, are sailing for Canton.

'Now particularly observe the man with a heavy load upon his shoulder at the back of his lordship. That is a portrait of the Chancellor of the Exchequer, taken at the happy moment when making up his budget. You see that he is about to get the load upon the back of the elephant in front. Now, particularly mark the eye of the elephant as it is cast back upon the Chancellor; being as much as to say *'What the dickens is he going to put upon me now?''* The second elephant evidently shares in the curiosity of his companion.

'Observe that gentleman in earnest conversation with another gentleman, between the elephants, and before the camels. They are talking of the war in China, and other subjects of polite society.

'At the extreme back to the right is a Laplander in his sledge, drawn by a stag. He is on his journey to ship a cargo of ice, having received a large order from Messrs. Gunter, by penny post, for that commodity.

'You are now earnestly requested to consider what has been happily called the domestic parts of this wonderful composition. Observe the group at the right hand lower corner. A wife is reading a letter in confidence to a female friend – a letter from an absent husband, desiring the partner of his bosom to have prepared on his arrival by the late train, hot lamb chops and a dish of sparrow-grass. A little girl (their pledge of mutual love) is eagerly struggling for the letter.

'Now look to the opposite corner. There is the portrait of a venerable old lady of the name of Smith. She is bedridden, ladies and gentlemen, and is listening to a letter read by her *nevey*. Mark the figure of Mrs. Smith. She is looking all sorts of gratitude, and her two hands is clasped. The letter is from her grandson, John Smith, reported to have been hanged for burglary and murder; whereas that letter, just received by the penny post, assures the delighted parent that her grandchild is transported for life, for robbing on the highway, with the minor offence of slitting an attorney's nose.

'And that, ladies and gentlemen, and my very pretty little dears, concludes the whole of the hieroglyphical history of the covers of the penny post. Vivat Regina, no money returned.'

One of the letters to appear in the press caused Mulready to be particularly incensed. It was quoted in *The Morning Herald* of Friday, 22 May although it had been addressed originally to *The Glasgow Courier*.

From one James Mackenzie jun of 5 Grosvenor Gate, Park Lane, it read:

Sir,

I have the pleasure of Mr Mulready's acquaintance, and have, in common with others
of his friends, complimented him upon the talent he has displayed in the design of the
post covers; but I found it a subject which he is sorely vexed at, and of which he
protests being quite innocent of. It would indeed seem that he has had nothing to do
with the design, more than having brought it into a reduced scale; for the whole has
been forced upon him from the Treasury, with the assurance that the invention of the
drawing being that of a lady high in station, left him no alternative but to submit to
have himself published as its author.

I do think you owe this artist some reparation for your severe remarks, by stating
this fact to your readers.

The Editor added that 'Mr Mulready's friend may be assured that
we could not mean to wound the feelings of that gentleman by any
remarks we might make on the pictorial letter-cover, seeing that Mr
Mulready is a perfect stranger to us. If Mr Mulready, who we now
understand to be an academician and a person of distinction in his
profession, has been obliged to adopt the progeny of a lady of rank, the
sooner he renounces the functions thus forced upon him the better,
since he can gain no credit by the assumed paternity of one of the
silliest sketches we ever saw.'

Mulready immediately wrote a satirical letter anonymously to
The Morning Herald, though it was clear who the author was:

Sir,

I have found myself placed in a very peculiar situation by the insertion of the letter of
my friend Mr Mackenzie in your paper of to day relative to the Postage Envelopes of
which I am the . . . author. Since their appearance I have been subjected to so much
inconvenience that I acknowledge in self defence that out of a perhaps improper
anxiety to gratify the fancy of so illustrious a personage as the one whose invention it
was intimated to me by the treasury it was, I felt myself bound to fall in with his
wishes, although I did make some representations relative to several parts of the
details but which were not received. As the circumstances of my name being attached
to the covers has much injured my reputation as an Artist, it will much oblige me if
you will intimate to the public through your valuable paper & on my authority that
you have reason to know, the invention of the Envelope is due to the highest
personage in the realm.

> I am sir
> Your obedient Servant
> a forged signature [sic][31]

The Editor replied in a letter two days later presenting his compli-
ments. He would 'be much obliged to him if he will say whether or not
the enclosed letter is genuine.'[32]

Mulready had now calmed down, but remained hurt. He replied on
25 May:

The letter that appeared in the Morning Herald of Friday the 22 and which was signed James Mackenzie Jun 5 Grosvenor Gate Park Lane is evidently, to me, a mere witticism and intended to express in a droll and attractive manner, some person's contempt for the design of the postage cover. I should have been ashamed to endure it, but if you think it possible that anybody should take it for anything but a joke upon the outline as my composition, I cannot hesitate to disclose (?) that I am not acquainted with anybody named James Mackenzie, nor with anybody at Grosvenor Gate Park Lane, and that I have never uttered a word to any person whatever that could have given rise to the falsehood of his subject and composition not being entirely mine. On a parallelogram $3\frac{3}{8}$ by $5\frac{1}{4}$ a space was marked out which I was not to exceed, but which I was at liberty to fill. These were the only bounds set to me. I did not touch those bounds but I alone am answerable for what I have placed within them.

You can make what use you please of this statement.[33]

Nothing of Mulready's views appeared in the paper.

Caricatures

One remarkable result of the controversy was the printing of a large number of caricatures of Mulready's design. Many were extremely witty but some exposed the anti-Irish prejudice current at the time.

Two examples will suffice to give an idea of what was produced. One was designed by John Leech and published by Messrs Fores of 41 Piccadilly (see page 165). Each aspect of Mulready's work has been caricatured. Britannia has become a rather large lady. The angels are now penny postmen and as in the original one has only one leg. At Britannia's feet the lion now has a black patch over one eye and on the left are a group of Chinese one of whom is sitting on a bale of opium (a reference to the Opium War with China).

The other caricature shows some of the Irish jokes. Published by Thomas White, it is described as 'The New Post-Office Envelope – from a Design by Moll-Roony, R.A.M.' Here the lion has a spotted nightcap with the inscription beneath 'The British Lion Asleep. If you want to Wake him you must Hit him *very Hard*'. One of the camels has been transformed into a huge cat singing 'Moll row' and the naked Indians are being accosted by policemen.

The outcry against Mulready's design was universal and over-whelming. Even on 12 May it was clear to Hill that it was a mistake:

I fear we shall be obliged to substitute some other stamp for that designed by Mulready, which is abused & ridiculed on all sides. In departing so widely from the established "lion & unicorn" nonsense, I fear that we have run counter to settled opinions & prejudices somewhat rashly. I now think it would have been wiser to have followed established custom in all the details of the measure where practicable. The conduct of the public, however, shows that although our attempt to diffuse a taste for fine art may have been imprudent, such diffusion is very much wanted.[34]

Mulready caricature by Thomas White

Some forty years later Cole gave as his final opinion that the design was quite unsuitable for its purpose.

> The postage cover was for a dry commercial use, in which sentiment had no part. The merchant who wishes to prepay his letter rejects anything that disturbs his attention. I now think that anything, even a mere meaningless ornamental design, would have been out of place. The baldest simplicity only was necessary.[35]

Vast quantities of the Mulready envelope and lettersheets remained unsold. They were eventually destroyed, a special machine having been constructed as it proved impossible to burn them in secure conditions.

There were fewer comments about the adhesive labels. Perhaps the most amusing was the rhyme in the weekly sheet *The Town* entitled 'Lines on the Post Office Medallion':

> You must kiss our fair Queen, or her pictures, that's clear
> Or the gummy medallion will never adhere;
> You will not kiss her hand, you will readily find
> But actually kiss little Vickey's behind.[36]

Postal Traffic

For Rowland Hill, it was not the success of the covers or the labels
which mattered. It was the overall plan. He complained that many
aspects of it were not implemented and so it could not be judged fairly.
Perhaps the most objective viewpoint can be gained by looking at
postal and financial statistics over a period.[37]

	Chargeable letters (m)	Gross revenue (£)	Cost of management (£)	Net revenue (£)	Cost per 100 letters (£)
1839	75.9	2,390,763	756,999	1,633,764	1.0
1840	168.8	1,359,466	858,677	500,789	0.5
1845	271.4	1,887,576	1,125,594	761,982	0.4
1850	347.1	2,264,684	1,460,785	803,899	0.4
1853	410.8	2,574,407	1,400,679	1,173,728	0.3

As can be seen postal traffic increased dramatically and continued
to grow. The cost of carrying a letter gradually came down and
although Post Office revenue was initially cut considerably it grew
again with the increase of letters.

Rowland Hill was showered with honours and gifts. When he died
in 1879 he was buried in Westminster Abbey. The final accolade came
from the Liberal statesman William Gladstone:

his great plan ran like wild-fire through the civilised world, and never, perhaps, was a
local invention . . . and improvement applied in the lifetime of its author for the
advantage of such vast multitudes of his fellow-creatures.[38]

Notes to the Chapters

Chapter One

1 Carlton, C., *Charles I – The Personal Monarch*, 1984, p. 156.
2 Post Office Green Paper No. 15, *The Birth of the Postal Service*, pp. 13/18.
3 *Ibid.*
4 *Ibid.*
5 Fowler, K. A. *The Demand for and Provision of Postal Services during the Seventeenth Century*, 1984 (Post Office Archives, unpublished).
6 Stone, J. W. M. (ed.), *The Inland Posts 1392–1672: A Calendar of Historical Documents*, 1987, p. 109.
7 Gammons, T., *The Early Days of the Postal Service*, 1986, p. 6.
8 Ashley, M., *John Wildman: Plotter and Postmaster*, 1947, p. 169
9 *Ibid* p. 171.
10 Alcock R. C. & Holland F. C., *The Postmarks of Great Britain and Ireland*, 1940, p. 17.
11 Staff, F., *The Penny Post 1680–1918*, 1964, p. 43.
12 Gladstone, E. S., *Great Britain's First Postage Stamp*, 1924.
13 Bond, F. W. (ed.), *A General Survey of the Post Office 1677–1682 by Thomas Gardiner*, 1958, p. 42.
14 Post Office Act, 1711 (quoted slightly differently by Allen).
15 Robinson, H., *The British Post Office – A History*, 1948, p. 105.
16 Clear, C. R., *John Palmer (of Bath) Mail Coach Pioneer*, 1955, p. 19.
17 Robinson *op. cit.*, p. 137.
18 *Ibid* p. 139.
19 *Ibid* p. 211.
20 *Ibid* p. 213.
21 *Ibid* p. 157.
22 Post Office Archives, Post 107/75, 131, 132.
23 Post Office Archives, Post 59/34.
24 Twopenny Post-Office – Letter Carriers General Instructions, May 1, 1815 (Post 107/74, Post Office Archives).
25 Instructions to Letter Carriers (Post 107/231, Post Office Archives).
26 Stone, *op. cit.*, p. 133.

Chapter Two

1 PP 'A Return showing which of the Recommendations made by the Commissioners of Revenue Inquiry . . . have been carried into effect', dated 14 July 1835, p. 14.
2 *Ibid* p. 8.
3 *Ibid* p. 18.
4 *Ibid* p. 18.
5 *Ibid* p. 25.
6 Post Office Archives, Freeling papers Post 40, 221/1830 and Gammons, T., 'The First Whiting Essay?', *Stamp Collecting*, vol. 147, p. 813.
7 Knight, C., *Passages of a Working Life during Half a Century*, 3 vols., 1864/5, vol. 2, p. 122.
8 *Ibid* pp. 56/7.
9 *Ibid* p. 182.
10 *Ibid* p. 180.
11 *Ibid* p. 249.
12 *The Mirror of Parliament*, 1834, vol. II, p. 1837.
13 Knight, *op. cit.*, p. 250.
14 *Dictionary of National Biography*, vol. LIX, 1899, p. 105 (by A H Millar).

15 Printed address dated 31 March 1845, Post Office Archives 'Portfolio' Personalities.

16 Robinson, *op. cit.*, p. 248.

17 Robert Wallace papers, Watt Library, Greenock, No. 126.

18 PP 1837–8 XLV 'A Return in Abstract of the Recommendations contained in the Ten Reports of the Post Office Commissioners'.

19 Robinson, *op. cit.*, p. 256.

20 Post Office Archives, Post 107/434.

21 Post Office Archives, Post 30/35 (E1402/1838).

Chapter Three

1 Hill, R. and G. B., *The Life of Sir Rowland Hill and the History of Penny Postage*, 1880, vol. 1, p. 241.

2 Hill, R., *Post Office Reform*, 1st edition, 1837, p. 16.

3 *Ibid* p. 17.

4 *Ibid* p. 21.

5 *Ibid* p. 29.

6 *Ibid* p. 31.

7 *Ibid* pp. 33/4.

8 *Ibid* pp. 43/4.

9 *Ibid* p. 47.

10 PP 'The Ninth Report of the Commissioners appointed to inquire into the Management of the Post-Office Department', 1837. p. 32.

11 *Ibid* p. 32.

12 *Ibid* p. 33.

13 *Ibid* p. 8.

14 Parliamentary Debates, 3rd s. XXXVIII, p. 1464.

Chapter Four

1 PP 'First Report from the Select Committee on Postage', April 1838, p. ii.

2 Croker, J. W., *'Post Office Reform'*, *Quarterly Review* Vol LXIV, October 1839, p. 518.

3 Map, PP 'Third Report from the Select Committee on Postage', August 1838.

4 Third Report, *op. cit.*, p. vi.

5 *Ibid.*

6 *Ibid* p. viii.

7 *Ibid* p. 3.

8 *Ibid* p. 4.

9 First Report, *op. cit.*, p. 84.

10 *Ibid.*

11 *Ibid.*

12 Third Report, *op. cit.*, 'Abstract of Evidence', p. 18.

13 Public Record Office, T1/4127, pp. 145–8.

Chapter Five

1 *Dictionary of National Biography*, vol. XI, 1887, p. 269.

2 Bonython, E., *King Cole*, 1982, p. 10.

3 Cole, Sir H., *Fifty Years of Public Work*, vol. 1, 1884, p. 40.

4 *The Post Circular* No. 4, 5 April 1838, p. 17.

5 *A Report on a Scene at Windsor Castle*, 1839.

6 *Ibid.*

7 Cole, *op. cit.*, pp. 44/5.

8 *The Post Circular* No. 12, 30 April 1839, p. 58.

9 Cole, H. *op. cit.*, p. 52.

Chapter Six

1 Parliamentary Debates, vol. XLIX (third series), p. 626.

2 *Ibid* p. 627.

3 Cole, H., diary, Victoria & Albert Museum, 24 July 1839.

4 Parliamentary Debates, *op. cit.*, p. 1221.

5 *Ibid* p. 1237.

6 *Ibid* p. 1238.

7 Hill, R. & G. B., *op. cit.*, p. 370.

8 Bonython, E., *op. cit.*, p. 22.

9 Hill, R., diary, (Post Office Archives) Post 100/1, 17 September 1839.

10 Cole, H., diary, *op. cit.*, 30 October 1839.

11 Hill, R. & G. B., *op. cit.*, p. 370.

12 Public Record Office, T1/4127, pp. 193/204.

13 *Ibid.*

14 *Ibid.*

15 *Ibid.*
16 *Ibid.*
17 Post Office Archives, Post 107/586.
18 *Ibid.*
19 Hill, R., diary, *op. cit,* 6 December 1839.
20 *Ibid* 9 December 1839.
21 Mackay, J. A., *Scottish Postmarks from 1693 to the Present Time* (1978).
22 Mackay, J. A., *Irish Postmarks since 1840,* 1982, p. 9.
23 Whitney, Dr J. T., *Collect British Postmarks* (Fifth Edition), 1990.
24 Lillywhite, B. 'Uniform Fourpenny Postage', *Postal History Society Bulletin,* No. 124, March/April, 1963, pp. 23/6.
25 Post Office Archives, Post 107/377.
26 *Ibid.*
27 Incidental Bills, Post Office Archives, Post 6/30.
28 Hill, R., diary, *op. cit.,* 22 October 1839.
29 *Postal History Society Bulletin,* No. 211, September/October 1979, pp. 12/3.
30 Crawforth, M. 'Patent Postals: A Survey of Postal Scales patented in Britain 1840 to 1940', *Equilibrium,* 1981, pp. 398/400; see also *Equilibrium,* 1978, pp. 2, 10/11; Brass B, 'Candlesticks', *Equilibrium,* 1982, pp. 403/8; and Crawforth, D. 'Pop it in the Post', *Equilibrium,* 1989, pp. 1219/33.

Chapter Seven

1 Public Record Office, T1/4127, pp. 62/8.
2 *Ibid.*
3 Public Record Office, Treasury registers T2/166 and T2/169.
4 Treasury Nos. 18823, 19243.
5 Post Office Archives, Post 100/54, file 3.
6 Lowe, R., 'The Birth of the Adhesive Postage Stamp', *Penny Postage Centenary* (ed. S. Graveson), 1940, p. 72.
7 *Ibid.*
8 Public Record Office, T1/4127, pp. 149/78.
9 Post Office Archives, Post 30/429 (E1106/1883); Treasury Nos. 20063, 20316, 20412/18, 23377, 24592, 24620, 25102.
10 Royal Collection, album page 81.
11 *Ibid,* text p. 3.
12 *Ibid,* text p. 2.
13 *Ibid,* text p. 3.
14 *Ibid.*
15 *Ibid,* p. 5.
16 Cole, H., *Fifty Years, op. cit.,* vol. 2, p. 111.
17 *Ibid* p. 113.
18 *Ibid* p. 123.
19 *Ibid* pp. 123/4.
20 Royal Collection, album page 23.
21 Cole, H., diary, *op. cit.,* 5 September 1839.
22 *Ibid* 6 September 1839.
23 *Ibid* 11 September 1839.
24 *Ibid* 4 October 1839.
25 Cole, H., *Fifty Years, op. cit.,* vol. 2, p. 134.
26 Royal Collection, album page 24.
27 Cole, H., *Fifty Years, op. cit.,* vol. 2 p. 115.
28 Chalmers, L., *How the Adhesive Postage Stamp was Born,* 1939, p. 15.
29 *Ibid* p. 17.
30 Marshall, C.F. Dendy, 'The Winners of the Treasury Competition of 1839', *Stanley Gibbons Monthly Journal,* September 1925, p. 271.
31 Crawford, Earl of, 'Benjamin Cheverton', *The London Philatelist,* vol. XIX, 1910, p. 287.
32 *Ibid* p. 293.
33 *Ibid* p. 294.
34 *Ibid.*
35 Cole papers, Victoria & Albert Museum, vol. 1, p. 59.

Chapter Eight

1 Cole, H., diary *op. cit.,* 4 November 1839.
2 Hill, R., diary *op. cit.,* 27 November 1839.

3 Lowe, R. *The British Postage Stamp of the nineteenth century*, 1968, 1979 p. 48.

4 Public Record Office, T1/4127 pp. 258/309, and pp. 1/15.

Chapter Nine

1 Royal Archives, Queen Victoria's Journal 7 December 1839.

2 RA, MP 1/42.

3 RA, Queen Victoria's Journal 21 December 1839.

4 RA, MP 1/42.

5 RA, Queen Victoria's Journal 21 December 1839.

6. Hill, R. and G. B., *op. cit.* p. 387.

7 Hill, R., diary *op. cit.* 21 December 1839.

8 Public Record Office, T1/4127 pp. 246/57.

9. Hill, R., diary *op. cit.* 10 January 1840.

10 *Ibid* 11 January 1840.

11 Wright, H. E. and Creeke, A. B., *A History of The Adhesive Stamps of the British Isles*, 1899, pxx.

12 Hill, R., *Results of the New Postage Arrangements*, 1841, p. 15.

13 Hill, R., diary *op. cit.* 13 January 1840.

14 Bacon, E. D., 'The Houses of Parliament Envelopes of 1840', *The London Philatelist*, Vol. XLIII, 1934, pp. 26/9.

15 *Ibid.*

16 Hill, R., diary *op. cit.* 16 January 1840.

17 National Postal Museum.

18 Post Office Archives, E2146/1842 bottom.

19 Lowe, R., *The Encyclopaedia of British Empire Postage Stamps*, Volume I: 'Great Britain and the Empire in Europe', Second Edition, 1952.

20 Evans, J., *The Endless Web: John Dickinson & Co Ltd 1804–1954*, p. 72.

21 *Ibid.*

22 Hill, R. & G. B., *op. cit.* p. 390.

23 *Ibid* Vol II p. 91.

Chapter Ten

1 Royal Collection, album page 12.

2 Cole, H. diary *op. cit.* 28 November 1839.

3 *Ibid* 11 December 1839.

4 Cole, H., *Fifty Years op. cit.*, Vol. 1, p. 63.

5 Cole, H., diary *op. cit.* 15 December 1839.

6 RA VIC B2/59.

7 Royal Collection, album page 18d, NPM Phillips Collection, Vol. I/35.

8 Public Record Office, T1/4127 pp. 436/41.

9 Hill, R., diary *op. cit.* 22 February 1840.

10 Public Record Office, T1/4127 p. 667.

11 *Ibid* p. 445.

12 *Ibid* pp. 446/7.

13 Hill, R., diary *op. cit.* 25 February 1840.

14 *Ibid* 26 February 1840.

15 Public Record Office, T1/4127, pp. 407/12.

16 *Ibid* p. 557.

17 *Ibid* pp. 484/7.

18 *Ibid* p. 553.

19 Royal Collection, album pages 12b, d.

20 NPM Phillips Collection, Vol. II/2.

21 RA VIC B2/59.

22 Royal Collection, album page 12g.

23 *Ibid* album page 12b.

24 Hill, E., diary volume 1, *The British Philatelist*, Volumes X and XI, 1917/8 (later volumes are in the Public Record Office but the original volume 1 is missing), Vol. XI, p. 6.

25 Hill, R., diary *op. cit.* 9 April 1840.

26 *Ibid* 13 April 1840.

27 NPM Phillips Collection, Vol. II/13.

28 Royal Collection, album page 13.

Chapter Eleven

1 Hill, R., diary *op. cit.* 11 December 1839.

2 Cole papers, Victoria & Albert Museum, 55BB box 12.

3 *Ibid.*

4 Royal Collection, album page 308.

5 Cole papers, *op. cit.*.

6 Hill, R., diary *op. cit.* 25 January 1840.

7 NPM, Phillips Collection, Vol. I/39.

8 *Ibid.*

9 *Ibid.*

10 Hill, R., diary *op. cit.* 10 April 1840.

11 Public Record Office, IR 13/61 (1).

12 Hill, R., diary *op. cit.* 13 October 1840.

13 *Ibid.*

14 National Postal Museum, QV oversize album 1/21.

15 Hill, R., diary *op. cit.* 14 October 1840.

Chapter Twelve

1 Bacon, E.D., *The Line-Engraved Postage Stamps of Great Britain Printed by Perkins, Bacon & Co.*, 1920, Vol. II, pp. 21/2.

2 *Ibid* pp. 22/3.

3 *Ibid* Vol. I, p. 16.

4 *Dictionary of National Biography*, 1891, Vol. XXV p. 341.

5 Hill, R., diary *op. cit.* 30 January 1840.

6 Bacon, E.D., *op. cit.*, Vol. I p. 21.

7 *Ibid* p. 24.

8 *Ibid* Vol. II, p. 25.

9 RA VIC B2/53.

10 Bacon, E.D., *op. cit.* Vol. II, p. 30.

11 *Ibid* p. 8.

12 *Ibid* Vol. I, p. 27.

13 *Ibid* p. 12.

14 Hill, R., diary *op. cit.* 10 May 1840.

15 Post Office Archives, Post 100/54 (RH771).

16 Bacon, E.D., *op. cit.* Vol. II, p. 252.

17 *Ibid* p. 239.

18 *Ibid* 22 April 1840, p. 245.

Chapter Thirteen

1 Hill, R., diary *op. cit.* 1 May 1840.

2 Cole, H., diary *op. cit.* 6 May 1840.

3 National Postal Museum – album QV oversize, volume 1.

4 *Ibid.*

5. *Ibid.*

6 Public Record Office, Stamps & Taxes Minutes, IR 31/105, 7 April 1840.

7 *Ibid* 1 May 1840.

8 *Ibid* 9 April 1840.

9 Public Record Office, IR 13/61 (1).

10 Public Record Office, IR 13/59.

11 Hill, R., diary *op. cit.* 7 May 1840.

12 Public Record Office, IR 31/105, 13 May 1840.

13 *Ibid* 8 May 1840.

14 *Ibid* 23 April 1840.

15 *Ibid* 8 May 1840.

16 NPM Phillips Collection, Vol. VIII/25.

17 Bacon, E.D., *op. cit.* Vol. II, p. 39.

18 Post Office Archives, Post 107/627.

19 Hill, R., diary *op. cit.* 29 April 1840.

20 *Ibid* 24 April 1840.

21 *Ibid* 21 May 1840.

22 Public Record Office, T1/4127, pp. 19/43.

23 *Ibid* p. 21.

24 *Ibid* p. 24.

25 *Ibid* p. 32.

26 Second Report, Post Office Archives, Post 30/52–4 (Eng 2146/42).

27 *Ibid.*

28 Hill, R., diary *op. cit.* 10 April 1840.

29 Cole papers, *op. cit.* 11 January 1840.

30 Cole, H., diary *op. cit.* 22 April 1840.

31 W. Mulready letters, Victoria & Albert Museum, 86.NN.1 (283).

32 *Ibid* (336).

33 *Ibid* (230).

34 Hill, R., diary *op. cit.* 12 May 1840.

35 Cole, H., *Fifty Years, op. cit.*, Vol. 1, pp. 64/5.

36 De Righi, A. G. Rigo, *The Story of the Penny Black and its Contemporaries*, 1980, p. 40.

37 Daunton, M., *Royal Mail, The Post Office since 1840*, 1985, p. 23.

38 Farrugia, J., *The Life & Work of Sir Rowland Hill 1795–1879*, 1979, p. 2.

Henry 'King' Cole by James Tissot

Chronology

1829/30		
		Commissioners' Reports published inquiring into the Post Office.
1830		
1	February	Charles F. Whiting proposes 'go-frees' (prepaid wrappers by weight).
1832		
	December	Robert Wallace elected MP for Greenock.
1834		
	May	Charles Knight suggests 1d prepaid wrappers.
1835		
	May	Commission into the Management of the Post Office established (under Duncannon).
1836		
	June	Death of Sir Francis Freeling.
	September	Appointment of Lt.-Col. William Maberly as Secretary of the Post Office.

1837		
4	January	Rowland Hill sends his pamphlet 'Post Office Reform: Its Importance and Practicability' to the Chancellor of the Exchequer.
13	February	Giving evidence to the Commission, Hill proposes adhesive stamped labels as a means of prepaying postage.
	February	Publication of Hill's pamphlet.
7	July	Ninth Report of the Commission published recommending Hill's proposals and including examples of Dickinson's envelopes and lettersheets.
12	July	Post Office Acts revised and repealed.
23	November	Select Committee (under Wallace) appointed to inquire into Hill's proposals.
4	December	Chalmers writes to Wallace about stamped 'slips'.

	1838	
	February	Mercantile Committee on Postage formed.
8	February	James Chalmers produces stamped 'slips' in a letter to the Post Office.
14	March	First issue of *The Post Circular*.
4	April	First Report of the Select Committee.
1	August	Second Report of the Select Committee.

	1839	
	March	Final Report of the Select Committee.
6	May	Lichfield reports on the Select Committee's findings.
18	July	Postage Duties Bill introduced in the House of Commons.
17	August	Postage Act receives the Royal Assent.
23	August	Treasury Minute announcing a competition for the best plan for covers under the Uniform Postage Act.
6	September	Treasury Minute published in *The Times*.
7	September	Rowland Hill begins his diary *Post Office Journal*.
16	September	Rowland Hill appointed to the Treasury.
13	October	Henry Cole officially begins work as Hill's assistant.
15	October	Official close of Treasury Competition.

2	November	Hill submits his plan for implementing Uniform Postage.
4	November	Cole begins reading Treasury Competition entries.
12	November	Treasury Minute to introduce uniform postage.
2	December	Perkins, Bacon & Petch asked by Cole to engrave steel dies less than one inch square.
3	December	Final adjudication of prizes for Treasury Competition.
4	December	Chancellor authorises Hill to apply to Wyon, Harvey and another for designs.
5	December	Uniform Fourpenny Postage introduced.
6	December	Hill's Report on the Treasury Competition.
9	December	Corbould shows Cole his first drawing for the envelope.
11	December	Chancellor of the Exchequer authorises Hill to commence preparations for stamps. Wyon commissioned to engrave die of Queen's head for stamped paper. Corbould brings his finished drawing for the envelope.
12	December	Cole sees Mulready to obtain a design for the envelope.
13	December	Agreed that Perkins, Bacon & Petch prepare a die for the labels.

15 December	Mulready produces his first 'highly poetic' design.	
16 December	Perkins Bacon ordered to engrave die for postage label. Hill proposes 6 January for introduction of uniform penny postage.	
26 December	Treasury minute authorises four different types of stamps and sets 10 January as date for Uniform Penny Postage.	
(end) December	Sketch for label submitted to Rowland Hill.	
31 December	Hill and Bacon agree detailed amendments to label design.	

1840

6 January	John Thompson commissioned to engrave Mulready die.
10 January	Introduction of Uniform Penny Postage.
15 January	First label die completed and rejected.
16 January	Houses of Parliament prepaid stationery issued. Second label die sent to Charles Heath.
25 January	First Wyon die for stamped paper.
28 January	Treasury minute puts control of paper manufacture under the Excise department.
30 January	Legend on stamps agreed.

31 January	Edwin Hill appointed Superintendant of Stamps at Stamps & Taxes Office.
5 February	Invitation to tender for paper published.
11 February	Bokenham & Smith discuss legend on covers with Cole.
20 February	Completed head die for label shown to the Queen. Paper tenders to be submitted. Treasury minute allows for separate stamps for public and Government mail.
22 February	Dies for stamped paper by Whiting sent to Hill. Corner letters for labels arranged by Hill.
(end) February	Watercolour sketches of labels made for Hill.
2 March	Queen expresses 'high appreciation' of label die.
11 March	First plate for labels in production. Hill's first report on the Distribution of Franking Stamps.
18 March	Clowes' tender agreed. Perkins, Bacon & Petch tender agreed.
20 March	Mulready letter sheets proofed in a sheet of eight.
27 March	Hill's second report on Distribution of Franking Stamps.
31 March	Bokenham submits specimens of Maltese Cross.
1 April	Mulready die completed.

1	April	First proof sheet of the Penny stamp printed and approved by the Chancellor of the Exchequer.
3	April	Mulready proofs shown to the Queen.
6	April	Production of Mulready stereotype casts begins.
10	April	Mulready design much approved by R.A.S
11	April	First Penny Black plate put to press.
13	April	Perkins, Bacon & Petch contract signed.
14	April	Printing of Mulreadys begun.
15	April	Imprimatur sheets of Penny labels, public and official, taken.
22	April	Second Penny Black plate put to press.
1	May	Mulreadys and Penny label put on sale in London.

1	May	Printing of Twopence label begins.
2	May	First press comment on Mulready stationery.
6	May	Labels and Mulready stationery become valid for postage. Proofs of lettering and head of Wyon's die.
8	May	Twopenny label put on sale in London.
12	May	Thompson inspects Mulready brass die, and cliché struck by the polytype process.
17	September	Hill's first Report on the Obliteration of Postage Stamps.
18	November	Hill's second Report on the Obliteration of Postage Stamps.
30	December	Printing of Penny Red labels begins.

APPENDIX TWO

Treasury Competition Entries

This listing is a combination of three sources. All were written by several different clerks at the time but often in haste and without due care. As a result the registers are difficult to decipher and sometimes contradictory. Some of the entries are also wrong transcriptions by the clerks from poor signatures on the original letters. At this period no distinction was made between I and J in the registers. Here this has been rendered as J unless the letter had to be I. Alternatives from different sources are indicated by square brackets. Entries are normally noted as being Penny Post Plans or Suggestions or simply PP.

The first listing is of suggestions sent in during 1839 up to 21 August. These have a consecutive numbering system and are listed in T1/4127 pages 683 – 698.

1	5	February	Ed: Bowles Symes
2	11	March	Donald Bain
3	20	March	William Exton
4	12	April	Revd R B Bourne
5	19	April	Wm Mason
6	1	May	J Justin Thomson
7	11	May	Revd J Hebbach
8	18	May	C F Giesler
9		May	H
10	25	May	Wm Wray
11	25	May	Robt. Workman
12	30	May	William Clive
13	30	May	Fred: Smith
14	30	May	Sir Wm Heygate
15	30	May	S Springfield
16	31	May	James Swann
17	1	June	Messrs Fleming & Hope
18	1	June	A.B.
19	3	June	H Bovill
20	–		Reginald Jennings
21	4	June	D T
22	5	June	Ed. Gem
23	6	June	A Well wisher to Govt.
24	–		W. A.
25	7	June	G. V.
26	7	June	Eaton D Denton
27	7	June	John Mason
28	7	June	(R. Hill)
29	10	June	S. J.
30	10	June	John Snicket?
31	7	June	George Dickinson
32	11	June	Dr Cope
33	17	June	Thos. Bewlay
34	14	June	John Norris
35	18	June	Henry Buckley
36	20	June	R. W. Dickinson
37	29	June	John F Davies
38		June	John Fellowes
39	1	July	J A Taylor
40	–		AB from Cambridge
41	–		Anabatis
42	–		A Stationer
43	1	July	Dr Bowring
44	4	July	John Hamilton

45	4 July	John Key		69	19 July	William Hunter
46	6 July	J E Death		70	19 July	Charles Whiting
47	8 July	Wm Oldham		71	22 July	John Jackson
48	10 July	Ed: Bewley		72	22 July	C J Ivory
49	12 July	M.J.L.		73	22 July	John Neale
50	11 July	W. Hunt		74	23 July	John Evans (thro'
51	9 July	David Richards				W Attwood and
52	10 July	Abraham Francis				Sir R. Peel)
53	10 July	Wm. Goodhugh		75	25 July	J Page Bailey
54	11 July	T B Miller		76	24 July	N Clarke
55	10 &			77	24 July	J Wilson
	12 July	John Dickinson		78	25 July	M. Lambert
56	17 July	ditto		79	25 July	C. Duffield
57	9 July	W. Oldham		80	29 July	W. Eastlake
58	10 July	Revd T H Kingdom		81	29 July	Augustus
59	10 July	G A Procter				Stapleton
60	12 July	K. Drake				(thro' C Gore)
61	13 July	W K Osborne		82	August	George Reynolds
62	16 July	J Deans		83	3 August	George Dickinson
63	16 July	D B Hickey		84	3 August	Joseph Hanson
64	16 July	Isaac Davy		85	5 August	John Jackson
65	17 July	Ed: Hughes		86	31 July	W Kingsford
66	17 July	James Robertson		87	6 August	Jas Merrilees
67	18 July	A Hamilton		88	15 August	Jas Albery
68	19 July	A Country		89	21 August	T Shanks
		Gentleman		90	17 August	George Hadley

The main listing comes from the Treasury registers – T2/169 and T2/166 together with additions from Post Office Archives files – Post 30/52 file bottom.

Date received	Register number	Date sent	Name		Date received	Register number	Date sent	Name
19/8	17980	17 Aug	F G Waldron		4/9	19191	2 Sept	David Morrison
20/8	18067	19 Aug	John Hosmer					that his new
22/8	18197	21 Aug	R Bourne					discovery in
22/8	18229	10 June	C. Whiting					printing be made
23/8	18309	20 Aug	J Williams					applicable to
24/8	18446	22 Aug	R Bain					stamped envel-
27/8	18609	26 Aug	Seneca					opes for letters
			Hughes		5/9	19243	4 Sept	F Coffin with
27/8	18612		Edwd F Orson					Specimen of a
	18614		B Shaw					Steel engraved
	18615	22 Aug	T Wilkinson					label for the
29/8	18747	28 Aug	R Bourne					Penny Postage
30/8	18797	29 Aug	M. Neely		6/9	19313	5 Sept	G Elliott
	18823	30 Aug	F. Coffin			19314		B Drew
3/9	19072	2 Sept	Mr Bourne			19325	6 Sept	J Elpwis?
	19073		J C Dalwig			19326		S Netz

Date received	Register number	Date sent	Name		Date received	Register number	Date sent	Name
7/9	19357	5 Sept	R Yarston		9/9	19545		C Ritchie
	19390	6 Sept	J C Nelson			19546		Mr Singer
	19391		H R Rugg			19547	8 Sept	G St Julian
	19392		R C Willis			19548	6 Sept	T J Triebner
	19393		Rev. R H Shepherd			19549		Mr Woodhouse
						19550		J Walsh
	19394		J Edwards			19551	7 Sept	J Woodhouse
	19395	7 Sept	J S Walpole			19552		S Watts
	19396		J W Wright			19553		T Wellhave
	19397	6 Sept	Mr Beer			19554		J Weaver
	19398		S K Cook			19563	6 Sept	J Pyrie
	19399		C Ritchie			19564	9 Sept	C Burke
	19400		C West			19565		G Spencer
	19401	5 Sept	Anonymous		10/9	19633		Mr Fehan
	19402	4 Sept	Edinburgh Merchants			19634		P. Stoker
						19635		J. Jones
	19403	7 Sept	H Hill			19636		J. Barham
	19404		H Edwards			19637		Mr H Keltoe
	19418	7 Sept	H C Hamilton			19638		Clark J J
9/9	19490	7 Sept	J Olley			19639		E Negus
	19491		Mr F Bekerne?			19640		H R Matthew
	19492		Dr Moffatt			19641		J Findelam
	19493		H Riches			19642		C Stolman
	19494		Mr Mosley			19643		C Winterton
	19495	8 Sept	S Hardman			19644		Mr Tait
	19496	7 Sept	S W Bennett			19645		J F Tait
	19497	6 Sept	Anon (A Barrister)			19646	8 Sept	J Walsh
						19647	7 Sept	J C C Dawson
	19498		Anon			19648		E Otway
	19499		Anon (Competitor)			19649		J Skein
						19650		Mr Cannabee
	19500	7 Sept	Anon			19668	10 Sept	T H Willis
	19530	7 Sept	Anon			19669	9 Sept	B Baker
	19531	7 Sept	C Brewer			19670		Mr A Hodgson
	19532		C Booth			19671	10 Sept	C Bueke
	19533		Mr Bevan		11/9	19692	9 Sept	D R Rees
	19534		Mr Cooper			19693		Revd G Pigott
	19535		J Coppock			19694	8 Sept	G Lockey
	19536	8 Sept	Mr Connor			19695	10 Sept	Mr Tait
	19537	7 Sept	E C Everett			19696		T Davis
	19538		T Edwards			19697		G Hinde?
	19539	9 Sept	R Hovenden			19698	10 Sept	Mr Harris
	19540	8 Sept	H W Hooper			19699		C Jones
	19541	7 Sept	J Lumley			19700		S Mitchell
	19542	9 Sept	T Lloyd			19737		J Johnson
	19543	7 Sept	J McOwen			19738		J Jones
	19544		Mr Nias			19739		T Veale

Date received	Register number	Date sent	Name	Date received	Register number	Date sent	Name
11/9	19740		R Conway	12/9	19845	11 Sept	T Caspin
	19741		Revd H. Campbell		19846	11 Sept	H Barry
					19847	11 Sept	H de S Kingdom
	19742		J Weaver		19848	11 Sept	S Bannister
	19743	11 Sept	E Smallwood		19849	10 Sept	H Charry
	19744	9 Sept	C Williams		19850	11 Sept	G H Vaudeput
	19745		J Trevor		19869	7 Sept	C Vines
	19746	9 Sept	J McOwen		19870	7 Sept	R D'Oyley
	19747		A A Hutchinson	13/9	19890	11 Sept	Anonymous
	19748		J Tarrop		19891	11 Sept	Justin Brenan
	19749		T P Sutton		19892	11 Sept	T T Barnard
	19750	7 Sept	S Bigger		19893	12 Sept	George Brackett
	19752	9 Sept	H Flather		19894	12 Sept	G C Becker
	19753	8 Sept	J Nobell		19895	12 Sept	J Clarke
	19764	9 Sept	J Slade		19896	12 Sept	James Dutton
	19765	10 Sept	G Hornby	13/9	19897	12 Sept	Louis d'Elboix
	19766	8 Sept	Mr S Richardson		19898	12 Sept	John Green
	19767	11 Sept	G Spencer		19899	12 Sept	G W Hughes
	19772	9 Sept	Mr Glen		19900	12 Sept	Mr Hillyard
12/9	19794	11 Sept	J C Nelson		19938	12 Sept	Mr G Coleman
	19795	11 Sept	D Penny		19939	11 Sept	George Griffiths
	19796	11 Sept	J Crosley		19940	11 Sept	F S Hackman
	19797	9 Sept	P Murphy		19942	11 Sept	Mr Kingsford
	19798	10 Sept	J Lester		19943	11 Sept	Tho. Lewis
	19799	10 Sept	T Hunt		19944	10 Sept	F McNace
	19800	10 Sept	R Crawford		19945	12 Sept	Mr McCallum
	19826	10 Sept	S Creaghe		19946	12 Sept	Paul Measor
	19827	10 Sept	A Bain		19947	12 Sept	Mr S Morris
	19828	10 Sept	Mr Farrow		19948	12 Sept	John Noble
	19829	10 Sept	J Hickox		19949	11 Sept	Isaac Pitman
	19830	10 Sept	R Wallace		19950	12 Sept	Joseph Read
	19831	10 Sept	H F Cunning-ham		19951	11 Sept	J C Dalwig
					19952	11 Sept	C B Edwards
	19832	10 Sept	C Astley		19953	12 Sept	J Forder
	19833	7 Sept	J Buckingham		19954	12 Sept	R I Hills
	19834	11 Sept	Anonymous (JBS)		19955	12 Sept	Henry Harris
					19956	9 Sept	B Nolan
	19835	11 Sept	T Baker		19957	9 Sept	G Reynolds
	19836	11 Sept	J Moore		19958	11 Sept	Jas Stevens
	19837	11 Sept	R Graham		19959	12 Sept	Alfred Simpson
	19838	11 Sept	A Congenhien		19960	11 Sept	J S C T[h]om-gate
	19839	11 Sept	J J Cox				
	19840	11 Sept	Mr Ogden		19961	11 Sept	John Treggey & Son
	19841	11 Sept	C Calwell				
	19842	11 Sept	D & B W Jones		19962	12 Sept	George Van Sommer
	19843	11 Sept	G Jones				
	19844	11 Sept	J Dutton		19963	12 Sept	C M Wilkinson

Date received	Register number	Date sent	Name		Date received	Register number	Date sent	Name
14/9	19992	12 Sept	G C Becker		16/9	20178	10 Sept	JG
	19993	11 Sept	J Borthwick			20179	10 Sept	JG
	19994	13 Sept	T Cooke			20180	10 Sept	A Clergyman of Edinburgh
	19995	13 Sept	Mr Coombs			20181	10 Sept	RBH
	19996	13 Sept	J Creswick			20182	10 Sept	M Buckett
	19997	13 Sept	D Feltham			20183	10 Sept	I J Braine
	19998	13 Sept	J Jarman			20184	10 Sept	T Brighouse
	19999	12 Sept	S McKinnor			20185	10 Sept	R Buck
	20000	12 Sept	G Neave			20186	10 Sept	R Burgess
	20035	10 Sept	R Yarston			20187	10 Sept	Mr Bevan
	20036	9 Sept	D McCarthy			20188	10 Sept	Sir H L Bulever Chevalier Duvallier
	20037	11 Sept	J S Williams					
	20038	12 Sept	Mr Apsley			20189	10 Sept	G Bell Junr
	20039	12 Sept	Mr Robertson			20190	10 Sept	G H Brown
	20040	13 Sept	Mr Baker			20191	10 Sept	J J Brown
	20041	13 Sept	S Baylis			20192	10 Sept	T Brown
	20042	13 Sept	Mr W Withers			20193	14 Sept	Sir W Boyd
	20043	13 Sept	Miss Pyke			20194	14 Sept	B Budd
	20044	12 Sept	T Williams			20195	11 Sept	E Curry
	20045	12 Sept	C Williams			20196	9 Sept	R Crawford
	20046	12 Sept	Mr A Stoker			20197	8 Sept	J Cook
	20047	13 Sept	J Rawson			20198	13 Sept	J R Dymock
	20048	12 Sept	M Lambert			20199	12 Sept	C N Field
	20049	12 Sept	S Morrison			20200	14 Sept	Col. Fairman
	20050	12 Sept	D Porter			20201	14 Sept	H. Flower
	20060	14 Sept	J E Whinham			20202	7 Sept	Revd T Fenton
	20061	14 Sept	Anonymous Az			20203	29 Aug	R Fuge
	20062	13 Sept	H Cheesewright			20204	9 Sept	C Fowler
	20063	12 Sept	G Dickinson			20205	11 Sept	J Gardon
	20064	14 Sept	J Dickinson			20206	15 Sept	Dr Greville
	20065	14 Sept	G F Hudson			20207	10 Sept	Revd D Griffiths
	20066	13 Sept	J Mathews					
	20067	13 Sept	H Reece			20208	10 Sept	J Grant
	20068	13 Sept	I Rosewarne			20209	13 Sept	L Hindmarsh
16/9	20148	16 Sept	Mr Robb					
	20149	13 Sept	T Cullimore					
	20150	16 Sept	Revd J Caithness					
	20174	7 Sept	S Aykroyd					
	20175	10 Sept	S Aykroyd					
	20176	10 Sept	SDY					
	20177	10 Sept	Anonymous					

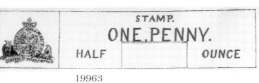

19963

20201

Date received	Register number	Date sent	Name	Date received	Register number	Date sent	Name
16/9	20210	13 Sept	Mr Harper	16/9	20255	14 Sept	W D Treganing
	20211	13 Sept	R Hendrick		20256	14 Sept	E Taylor
	20212	16 Sept	R Hills		20257	12 Sept	Mr Watson
	20213	12 Sept	J Hare		20258	13 Sept	A Warnock
	20214	12 Sept	B Harrison		20259	13 Sept	G P Wallen
	20215	13 Sept	C Hill		20260	14 Sept	T Woodward
	20216	11 Sept	G Hollings		20261	14 Sept	J Weaver
	20217	7 Sept	J S Huicks		(20316		Not George Dickinson)
	20218	15 Sept	G Jackson				
	20219	14 Sept	J Keane	17/9	20364		Anonymous
	20220	9 Sept	T S Lee		20365		Anonymous AB
	20221	6 Sept	T S Lee		20366		Anonymous MLS
	20222	13 Sept	J P Milford		20367		Anonymous A Stationer
	20223	12 Sept	C R Millar				
	20224	12 Sept	J Mark		20368		J Albery
	20225	12 Sept	Revd F O Morris		20369		Anonymous
					20370		Anonymous WN
	20226	14 Sept	Sir G S Mackenzie		20371		Anonymous DT
	20227	14 Sept	S Moore		20372		Anonymous GV
	20228	13 Sept	G Murphy		20373		Anonymous SJ
	20229	9 Sept	Mr Neely		20374		Anonymous WH
	20230	14 Sept	D Noott		20375		Anonymous A Well Wisher to G..o!
	20231	14 Sept	J Newman				
	20232	14 Sept	R A Norman				
	20233	16 Sept	H Ockerley		20376		Anonymous
	20234	14 Sept	J Olley		20377		Mr Bavill
	20235	16 Sept	E Otway		20378		Anonymous HB
	20236	26 Aug	Mr Pidding		20379		Anonymous CH
	20237	16 Sept	F D Puddy		20380		Anonymous
	20238	11 Sept	Revd J Roberts		20381		Anonymous
	20239	14 Sept	H Robinson		20382	16 Sept	Mr Banzell
	20240	15 Sept	Mr Rand		20383	16 Sept	Sam: Bannister
	20241	2 Sept	T Roberts		20384	16 Sept	T Bewley
	20242	3 Sept	J S Rilie		20385	16 Sept	Dr Bowring
	20243	12 Sept	B Read		20386	16 Sept	D Bain
	20244	10 Sept	C J Sassell		20387	16 Sept	D Bain
	20245	5 Sept	J Stangroom		20388	16 Sept	Revd R B Bourne
	20246	5 Sept	M Schiereck		20389	16 Sept	H Buckley
	20247	5 Sept	Mr Stewart		20390	16 Sept	Mr Bevan
	20248	15 Sept	J Simpson		20391	16 Sept	E Bewley
	20249	29 Aug	M Tennant		20392	16 Sept	Mr Butcher
	20250	3 Sept	Rvd J Tyso		20393	14 Sept	L Biggar
	20251	10 Sept	M Tennant		20394	14 Sept	M Braill
	20252	27 Aug	M Tennant		20395	14 Sept	J P Bailey
	20253	30 Aug	D Tod				
	20254	10 Sept	J Treganing				

Date received	Register number	Date sent	Name	Date received	Register number	Date sent	Name
17/9	20396	14 Sept	D Cope	17/9	20440	16 Sept	Mr Hunter
	20397	14 Sept	N Clarke		20441	16 Sept	J Hickox
	20398	14 Sept	L J Deans		20442	16 Sept	Mr Hamilton
	20399	14 Sept	J Davy		20443	16 Sept	E Hughes
	20400	14 Sept	E D Denton		20444	16 Sept	D B Hickie
	20401	14 Sept	C Duffield		20445	16 Sept	J Jackson
	20402	14 Sept	Chevalier Alt De Castello		20446	16 Sept	R Jennings
					20447	16 Sept	S Jones
	20403	14 Sept	J F Davies		20448	16 Sept	C J Ivory
	20404	14 Sept	R Drake		20449	16 Sept	J Jackson
	20405	14 Sept	T E Death		20450	16 Sept	Sir J Key
	20406	14 Sept	J F Davis		20451	16 Sept	Mr Kingsford
	20407	14 Sept	G Davidson		20452	16 Sept	Revd R Knox
	20408	14 Sept	J Dick[in]son		20453	16 Sept	T Lawes
	20409	14 Sept	J Dick[in]son		20454	16 Sept	R Litchford
	20410	14 Sept	J Dick[in]son		20455	16 Sept	N B Lack
	20411	14 Sept	R W Dick[in]son		20456	16 Sept	M Lambert
					20457	16 Sept	E Morton
	20412	14 Sept	G Dick[in]son		20458	16 Sept	T B Miller
	20413	14 Sept	G Dick[in]son		20459	16 Sept	J Merrielees
	20414	14 Sept	G Dick[in]son		20460	16 Sept	J Mason
	20415	14 Sept	G Dick[in]son		20461	16 Sept	J Mason
	20416	14 Sept	G Dick[in]son		20462	16 Sept	F R Lewes
	20417	14 Sept	G Dick[in]son		20463	16 Sept	J Norris
	20418	14 Sept	G Dick[in]son		20464	16 Sept	R C Northcote
	20419	14 Sept	Revd J H Kingdom		20465	16 Sept	J Neale
					20466	16 Sept	R Owen
	20420	14 Sept	T Evans		20467	16 Sept	Mr Oldham
	20421	14 Sept	Mr Exton		20468	16 Sept	Mr Oldham
	20422	14 Sept	Mr Eastlake		20469	16 Sept	Mr Olive
	20423	14 Sept	Mr E Evans		20470	16 Sept	Mr R Osborne
	20424	14 Sept	I Evans		20471	16 Sept	G A Procter
	20425	14 Sept	T Fetherston		20472	16 Sept	A Peacock
	20426	14 Sept	J Fraser		20473	16 Sept	D Richards
	20427	14 Sept	J Fellowes		20474	16 Sept	Mr Remington
	20428	14 Sept	A Frances		20475	16 Sept	B Read
	20429	14 Sept	Fleming & Hope		20476	16 Sept	G Reynolds
	20430	14 Sept	Mr Goodhugh					
	20431	14 Sept	E Gun					
	20432	14 Sept	C F Greisler					
	20433	16 Sept	J Hill					
	20434	16 Sept	Mr Hunt					
	20435	16 Sept	J Hamilton					
	20436	16 Sept	J Hanson					
	20437	16 Sept	R Hill					
	20438	16 Sept	Sir D. Heygate					
	20439	16 Sept	Revd T Hebback					

20474

Date received	Register number	Date sent	Name
17/9	20477	16 Sept	G Reynolds
	20478	16 Sept	G Reynolds
	20479	16 Sept	J Robertson
	20480	16 Sept	Mr Scanlan
	20481	16 Sept	T Shanks
	20482	16 Sept	E B Symes
	20483	16 Sept	E B Symes
	20484	16 Sept	J Shaw
	20485	16 Sept	J S Schroder
	20486	16 Sept	F Smith
	20487	16 Sept	J Scaiffe
	20488	16 Sept	Mr Stapleton
	20489	16 Sept	J Sarchel
	20490	16 Sept	J Swann
	20491	16 Sept	T Springfield
	20492	16 Sept	Mr C Turner
	20493	16 Sept	S Turner
	20494	16 Sept	J A Taylor
	20495	16 Sept	T T Thomson
	20496	16 Sept	R Workman
	20497	16 Sept	T Wingham
	20498	16 Sept	Mr Wray
	20499	16 Sept	R Workman
	20500	16 Sept	T Wilson
	20501	16 Sept	C Whiting
	20502	16 Sept	C Whiting
	20503	10 Sept	Mr Lovell
18/9	20608	17 Sept	Anonymous
	20609	14 Sept	C Alexander
	20610	18 Sept	G Bissager
	20611	12 Sept	R H Bow
	20612	16 Sept	R Corbett
	20613	16 Sept	E Connell
	20614	17 Sept	C Croft
	20615	13 Sept	T Champion Postage on periodicals
	20616	13 Sept	R Crawford
	20617	13 Sept	J Creshwish
	20618	17 Sept	B Drew
	20619	16 Sept	H D Egg
	20620	16 Sept	C R Field
18/9	20621	16 Sept	Mr Florence
	20622	16 Sept	J Foy
	20623	16 Sept	Mr Harris
	20624	16 Sept	Mr S Hartley
	20625	16 Sept	D C Higgs
	20626	15 Sept	T Howard
	20627	17 Sept	Revd J. Ingram
	20628	17 Sept	J Johnson
	20629	16 Sept	J Jarvis
	20630	18 Sept	T Jackson
	20631	17 Sept	C W Lascombe
	20632	17 Sept	J Lang
	20633	14 Sept	J Lawes
	20634	14 Sept	J Macdonald
	20635	16 Sept	D Moffatt
	20636	17 Sept	P Measor
	20637	14 Sept	T McLachlan
	20638	18 Sept	J Matthews
	20639	16 Sept	Sir G S Mackenzie
	20640	12 Sept	Mr S Stevenson
	20641	18 Sept	Mr I Stannard
	20642	17 Sept	Mr Tyers
	20643	16 Sept	T Tisdall
	20644	17 Sept	J H Williams
	20645	16 Sept	F Wyke
	20646	17 Sept	Capt. Webb
19/9	20724		Anonymous
	20725		Anonymous AZ
	20726		Anonymous
	20727		Anonymous HBJ
	20728		J Baft
	20729	18 Sept	G Bissager
	20730	13 Sept	J R Bell
	20731	18 Sept	H Barker
	20732	18 Sept	Mr H Carroll
	20733	18 Sept	L Cotton
	20734	17 Sept	Mr Cowing
	20735	17 Sept	J Dwyer
	20736	17 Sept	E Davis
	20737	17 Sept	T Duasberry
	20738	17 Sept	Revd W. Fletcher
	20739	16 Sept	Fleming & Cope
	20740	16 Sept	H Fleming
	20741	16 Sept	H Grange
	20742	16 Sept	E L Hall

20639

Date received	Register number	Date sent	Name
19/9	20743	16 Sept	R G Hall
	20744	18 Sept	C Hassan
	20745	18 Sept	R Hovenden
	20746	17 Sept	J Harmer
	20747	17 Sept	D Jarman
	20748	18 Sept	J Jackson
	20749	17 Sept	P M C Kerr
	20750	16 Sept	N B Lack
	20751	18 Sept	T Lawes
	20752	18 Sept	J Lumley
	20753	18 Sept	T Morgan
	20754	16 Sept	J Macdonald
	20755	18 Sept	F Matthews
	20756	16 Sept	M Mulreany
	20757	16 Sept	G Miller
	20758	16 Sept	E Manico
	20759	16 Sept	R Newman
	20760	16 Sept	G F Somerville
	20761	16 Sept	Revd G Taylor
	20762	16 Sept	Mr A Thompson
	20763	18 Sept	E L Williams
	20764	14 Sept	Revd W Wall
	20765	18 Sept	C Walkden
	20766	18 Sept	R White
	20767	17 Sept	R O Warwick
	20768	16 Sept	J S Young
20/9	20828	18 Sept	Anonymous
	20830	19 Sept	J Blackwell
	20831	18 Sept	J F Benwell
	20832	18 Sept	J Borthwick
	20833	18 Sept	F Blayney
	20834	18 Sept	E Brown
	20835	16 Sept	R Crawford
	20836	17 Sept	J Carruthers
	20837	19 Sept	J Clarke
	20838	19 Sept	Mr Dyce

Date received	Register number	Date sent	Name
20/9	20839	17 Sept	Mr Dickson
	20840	18 Sept	R J Fisher
	20841	19 Sept	F Freshfield
	20842	19 Sept	Mr C Frielth [Frieth]
	20843	19 Sept	T W Hart
	20844	18 Sept	Revd Hall
	20845	17 Sept	T Head
	20846	5 Sept	Mr Haughton
	20847	19 Sept	G Jackson
	20848	16 Sept	Revd R Knox
	20849	17 Sept	A W Maclean
	20850	17 Sept	R Monck
	20851	19 Sept	Capt MacCarthy
	20852	18 Sept	F C Nanley
	20853	19 Sept	R Prosser
	20854	18 Sept	B Read
	20855	19 Sept	R Rowe
	20856	20 Sept	J Ridley
	20857	20 Sept	Mr Sharp
	20858	16 Sept	J Senior
	20859	19 Sept	Mr J Stannard
	20860	17 Sept	G Taylor
	20861	19 Sept	C Vizer
	20862	18 Sept	Mr Woods
	20863	18 Sept	Mr Warren
	20864	16 Sept	Mr Wood

20853

20763

20912

Date received	Register number	Date sent	Name	Date received	Register number	Date sent	Name
20/9	20865	17 Sept	Mr Watts	21/9	20939	20 Sept	E Triot
	20866	19 Sept	Mr Yeldham		20940	20 Sept	Thomas Woodward
	20867	20 Sept	Mr Rogers		20941	19 Sept	John Williams
21/9	20911		Anonymous		20942	20 Sept	Charles Wake
	20912		Anonymous	23/9	21053	21 Sept	Anonymous
	20913	16 Sept	John Barnet		21054	21 Sept	Anonymous A
	20914	18 Sept	Mr Ball		21055	21 Sept	Anonymous Credo (John Henry Clive)
	20915	20 Sept	John Brent		21056	21 Sept	Mr Bacquinoir
	20916	19 Sept	Justin Brenan		21057	23 Sept	C W Bevan
	20917	19 Sept	William Collins		21058	23 Sept	Rev James Booth
	20918	19 Sept	T W Cox		21059	19 Sept	Stephen Brooks
	20919	19 Sept	William Curtis		21060	19 Sept	Mr Bevan
	20920	19 Sept	Benjamin Ellison		21061	18 Sept	Walter Brushe
	20921	19 Sept	Samuel Hitch		21062	19 Sept	Peter Bedwell
	20922	19 Sept	Samuel Haydon		21063	20 Sept	E Basseth [Bazeth]
	20923	19 Sept	Richard Hillier		21064	20 Sept	Mr Buchanan
	20924	16 Sept	John Henderson		21065	21 Sept	Mr Crouch
	20925	19 Sept	Lieut. Higginson		21066	20 Sept	D Campbell
	20926	19 Sept	John Sanderson Laws		21067	23 Sept	J Stirling Cooper
	20927	19 Sept	Dr Lardner		21068	20 Sept	R Creighton
	20928	20 Sept	William Morgan		21069	20 Sept	Peter Caldwell
	20929	20 Sept	David Morison		21070	20 Sept	Chas Chapple
	20930	17 Sept	James Macnamara		21071	19 Sept	John Cook[e]
	20931	20 Sept	Aaron Miller		21072	21 Sept	M De Baring
	20932	20 Sept	R Owen		21073	19 Sept	J A Dalzell
	20933	20 Sept	Eddell Penny		21074	20 Sept	Alex Dick
	20934	20 Sept	Mrs Elizabeth Strode		21075	23 Sept	J B Edwards
	20935	18 Sept	David Scarlett		21076	20 Sept	R Elnbrook?
	20936	20 Sept	George Smith		21077	19 Sept	H Flather
	20937	20 Sept	Robert Seaton		21078	21 Sept	Revd W Fordyce
	20938	20 Sept	Revd Joseph Tyso		21079	21 Sept	J Findlane
					21080	20 Sept	John Gibson

20924

21055

Date received	Register number	Date sent	Name		Date received	Register number	Date sent	Name
23/9	21081	22 Sept	Joseph Gibbs & Danl Poth		23/9	21110	21 Sept	Isaac Smith
	21082	20 Sept	Chas Garland			21111	20 Sept	H L Swale
	21083	21 Sept	Benjn Gall			21112	18 Sept	Alexr Smith
	21084	21 Sept	Jas Greenfield			21113	23 Sept	T J Triebner
	21085	21 Sept	J Harris			21114	19 Sept	G H Wardale
	21086	21 Sept	J Hayward			21115	21 Sept	Revd George Wilson
	21087	21 Sept	J F Handley			21116	21 Sept	Mr Wright
	21088	21 Sept	Chas Hargreave			21117	23 Sept	E J O Whitford
	21089	19 Sept	Thos Hart		24/9	21193	23 Sept	M Adams
	21090	23 Sept	Chas Jackson			21194	20 Sept	G Robertson
	21091	23 Sept	M Lazenby			21195	20 Sept	S Young
	21092	21 Sept	Wm Lyon			21196	24 Sept	J Cheesewright
	21093	19 Sept	Revd A Lyon			21197	24 Sept	Mr Nutsford
	21094	19 Sept	James MacDonald			21198	23 Sept	R Rowe
	21095	19 Sept	H Mullins			21199	19 Sept	J McLachlan
	21096	20 Sept	D McAdam			21200	23 Sept	T Evans
	21097	18 Sept	Francis Matthews			21211	21 Sept	T Baker
	21098	17 Sept	Peter McLaren			21212	21 Sept	J McOwen
	21099	18 Sept	Robert Meredith			21213	21 Sept	Mr Durno
	21100	19 Sept	J C Maccall			21214	23 Sept	Mr I Stannard
	21101	18 Sept	Mr J H Moreland			21215	22 Sept	Mr Hammond
	21102	21 Sept	James E McCabe			21216	22 Sept	Mr Dykes
	21103	20 Sept	H T O'Neill			21217	19 Sept	J Nixon
	21104	20 Sept	Mr Lyss Pearce			21218	21 Sept	Mr Slaughter
	21105	21 Sept	P Read			21219	21 Sept	R Williams
	21106	20 Sept	J B Russell			21220	23 Sept	C Jeffery
	21107	20 Sept	M M Robertson			21264	24 Sept	G Evans
	21108	21 Sept	Messrs Read			21265	24 Sept	J S Coyne
	21109	21 Sept	R Smith			21266	24 Sept	J Tillot
						21267	23 Sept	Mr Apsley
						21268	23 Sept	Mr H Phipps
						21269	22 Sept	T S Westlake
						21270	23 Sept	R Robertson

Sent from the Post Office

This listing is taken from Post Office Archives file Post 30/52 bottom, with Post Office numbers

24/9	Mr Coffin – 12,969	24/9	Mr Lane – 13,711
	Mr Bambridge – 13,019		Mr Myers – 13,759
	Mr Kearney – 14,591		Mr Lyon – 13,910
	Mr Read – 13,592		Mr Cockroft – 13,855
	Uxbridge Postmr: – 13,621		Mr Redwood – 13,929
	Revd W. Fletcher – 13,563		Mr Kittoe – 13,798
	Mr Dyson – 13,563		Mr Beasley – 13,945
	Mr Creery with Model – 13,734		Papyrus – 13,511

24/9 Mr Loscombe – 13,585
Mr Rettin – 13,576
Mr Bassett – 13,658
Mr Powell – 13,747
Mr Nutsford – 13,905
Mr Jackson – 13,502
Mr Bromage – 13,368
Mr Anderson – 13,332

24/9 Mr Dennison – 13,518
Anonymous from Dorchester –
13,775
Mr McGowan – 13,598
Revd J Olphert – 13,799
Mr Gall – 13,857
Mr Brown – 13,979
Mr Job – 13,976
Mr Clayton – 14,074

Date received	Register number	Date sent	Name
25/9	21292	24 Sept	Thomas Perry
	21293	21 Sept	Anonymous
	21294	23 Sept	Wm Knapp
	21295	21 Sept	John Lewis
	21296	23 Sept	Wm Hawthwaite
	21297	21 Sept	Mr Catchpool
	21298	23 Sept	E S Rogers
	21299	19 Sept	R Dougherty
	21300	23 Sept	Capt Hanchett
	21326	22 Sept	M Capelle
	21327	23 Sept	H Woodger
	21328	25 Sept	Mr Duncan
	21329	25 Sept	Mr Pitt
	21330	24 Sept	Mr Bearley
	21331	24 Sept	Mr C Wood
	21332	24 Sept	T Munro
	21333	23 Sept	H Quin
	21334	18 Sept	Mr M Duncan
	21335	23 Sept	H Corbett
	21336	23 Sept	Mr Stott
	21337	23 Sept	Mr Newmarsh
	21338	23 Sept	Mr Brown
	21339	23 Sept	C Daniel
	21340	21 Sept	Anonymous
	21341	21 Sept	T P O'Niell
	21342	24 Sept	Mr Allen
	21343	23 Sept	C Palmer
	21344	25 Sept	C Stovin
	21345	25 Sept	Anon ABDE
	21346	23 Sept	Mr Stigant
	21347	23 Sept	J McOwen
	21348	24 Sept	M Truscott
	21349	24 Sept	J Lumley
	21350	23 Sept	H Cockroft
	21351	24 Sept	H M Forbes
	21352	25 Sept	J Russell
	21353	24 Sept	Capt McCarthy

Date received	Register number	Date sent	Name
25/9	21354	20 Sept	Mr Wall
	21371	25 Sept	Anonymous
	21372	25 Sept	T S Vickers
26/9	21443	21 Sept	R Tschiffely
	21444	6 Sept	G Lananton [Geo Lenderton]
	21445	16 Sept	Chas Riesenbech
	21446	20 Sept	John Lowe
	21447	24 Aug	Mr Cook
	21448	23 Sept	T Sherbrook
	21449	22 Sept	H G Warren
	21450	21 Sept	T Hopper
	21463	26 Sept	L Alman
	21464	23 Sept	Jerome N Flood
	21465	25 Sept	J A Bacon
	21466	26 Sept	H Gardner
	21467	20 Sept	John Hamilton
	21468	23 Sept	Dr Henderson
	21469	24 Sept	John Hudson
	21470	25 Sept	Wm Lyon
	21471	25 Sept	H E Mosner
	21472	24 Sept	Sidney Powell
	21473	23 Sept	C Carroll Roe [Rae]
	21474	24 Sept	John Richardson
	21475	23 Sept	Mr Sparkes
	21476	21 Sept	Anonymous Zabulon Pier
	21477	21 Sept	Anonymous DC
	21478	26 Sept	J Baleman
	21479	12 Sept	H Chalmer
	21480	24 Sept	E W Davis
	21481	24 Sept	E Golding
	21482	25 Sept	S Harlan
	21483	24 Sept	J N Jakins
	21484	25 Sept	E Morton
	21485	24 Sept	P Nielson

Date received	Register number	Date sent	Name
26/9	21486	24 Sept	Mr Otter
	21487	24 Sept	G Pedler
	21488	25 Sept	D Penny
	21489	25 Sept	Mr Slaughter
	21490	24 Sept	E A Starling
	21491	24 Sept	J Warde
	21492	25 Sept	Mr Wilson
	21493	24 Sept	G Weighton
	21494	25 Sept	D Walker
	21495	25 Sept	Mr Alsop
	21496	25 Sept	Anonymous TB
	21497	25 Sept	Anonymous P
	21498	25 Sept	Anonymous
27/9	21577	23 Sept	George Boyce & William Jackson
	21578	25 Sept	Th. Brumby
	21579	25 Sept	Justin Brenan
	21580	25 Sept	Nicholas Clarke
	21581	25 Sept	A Cullimore
	21582	25 Sept	E G Hiscock
	21583	25 Sept	Edwd Lythgoe Hopper
	21584	24 Sept	Thomas Home
	21585	24 Sept	Wm Hinson
	21586	24 Sept	John Kell
	21587	26 Sept	Thos D Knight
	21588	26 Sept	Wm Lane
	21589	24 Sept	Dr Lynn
	21590	22 Sept	D McHugh
	21591	12 Sept	T M Myers
	21592	22 Sept	J M Nolan
	21593	21 Sept	Thos. Phillips
	21594	25 Sept	John Pearce
	21595	23 Sept	Miss Pyke
	21596	26 Sept	Mr J Pope
	21597	25 Sept	Revd A Rennison
	21598	26 Sept	Richard Rowe
	21599	26 Sept	M Roumette
	21600	25 Sept	J Saunders
	21601	26 Sept	Mr Slaughter
	21602	16 Sept	F St Leger
	21603	24 Sept	Chas Winchester
	21604	24 Sept	T Wroughton
	21605	25 Sept	R Wallace
	21606	25 Sept	Mr Butcher

Date received	Register number	Date sent	Name
27/9	21607	24 Sept	John Beatty
	21608	23 Sept	J A Emslie
	21609	25 Sept	J Davis
	21610	23 Sept	Revd D McCrea
	21611	24 Sept	A T J Martin
	21612	25 Sept	J R Nicoll
	21613	26 Sept	T F Westlake
28/9	21646	26 Sept	Anonymous TG
	21647	26 Sept	I R Brewer
	21648	24 Sept	James Burgess
	21649	24 Sept	Henry Burnett
	21650	26 Sept	James Brand
	21701	26 Sept	Henri Blomfield
	21702	25 Sept	Alexr Brodie
	21703	25 Sept	R Brown
	21704	27 Sept	Henry Cook
	21705	17 Sept	Wm Cowing
	21706	26 Sept	E Connell
	21707		H A Canson
	21708	27 Sept	Mr Davis Jnr
	21709	25 Sept	H Deacon
	21710	28 Sept	C N Field
	21711	24 Sept	M Gambars
	21712	25 Sept	John E Herrick
	21713	24 Sept	Chas Hughes
	21714	27 Sept	James Holder
	21715	27 Sept	Fredk Ham
	21716	9 Sept	Jas John Kelly
	21717	27 Sept	Wm Lyon
	21718	26 Sept	Robert Morgan
	21719	24 Sept	James McGowan
	21720	26 Sept	Edmd Pearce
	21721	26 Sept	Rowe, Kentish & Co
	21722	27 Sept	Thos Richard

21592

Date received	Register number	Date sent	Name	Date received	Register number	Date sent	Name
28/9	21723	26 Sept	S Still	1/10	21930	30 Sept	Mr F Strangways with letter from Mr Bicaurt
	21724	26 Sept	R E Walker		21931	30 Sept	Dr Rees
30/9	21801	23 Sept	Anonymous JAA		21932	30 Sept	P Carter
	21802	26 Sept	Anonymous Penthaes?		21933	30 Sept	B B Turner
	21803	–	Anonymous		21934	30 Sept	Revd Jos Dear
	21804	21 Sept	John Beckley		21935	30 Sept	Mr Hammond
	21805	30 Sept	James Bell		21936	28 Sept	Mr Hannon
	21806	27 Sept	J Butchart		21937	28 Sept	Francis Best
	21807	27 Sept	Geo Bissager		21938	28 Sept	Chas N Bolton
	21808	23 Sept	Mr Dudley		21939	29 Sept	Joseph Suffield
	21809	27 Sept	F H Elliott		21940	26 Sept	Mr J H Moreland
	21810	28 Sept	John Fellows		21941	26 Sept	Joshua Newbold
	21811	26 Sept	John Harper		21942	27 Sept	A E McAllister
	21812	28 Sept	James Keane		21943	27 Sept	James Beatty
	21813	26 Sept	Wm McQueen		21944	27 Sept	E Atkinson
	21814	27 Sept	Wm McCune		21945	24 Sept	John Gordon
	21815	30 Sept	Thos P Mann		21946	23 Sept	T H Pasley
	21816	28 Sept	David McCleery		21947	–	James Skeene
	21817	28 Sept	John Nicholls		21948	–	John Tate
	21818	28 Sept	Revd F O Niell		21949	27 Sept	Richd Madden
	21819	28 Sept	T Watts		21950	27 Sept	J H Blofield
	21820	27 Sept	D Wilson & Mr Charles		21951	26 Sept	G F Onsen
	21821	–	Wm Stone		21952	–	D Bedmead
	21822	27 Sept	A T J Masters		21953	–	C Linder
	21823	27 Sept	James Deans		21954	1 Oct	J D Thompson
	21824	27 Sept	Edwin Watson		21955	30 Sept	Thomas Biggs
	21825	27 Sept	John Fellows		21956	30 Sept	Revd O Reynolds
	21826	27 Sept	C W Bevan					
	21827	28 Sept	Mr G Poole					
	21828	23 Sept	John Jackson					
1/10	21892	27 Sept	T Austin					
	21893	–	Anonymous					
	21894	30 Sept	Thomas Hopkins					
	21895	–	J R Brewer					
	21896	–	Anonymous					
	21897	28 Sept	E de Bath (de Baste)					
	21898	19 Sept	Wm Butcher					
	21899	–	John Thos Donlevy					
	21922	28 Sept	John Hux					
	21923	30 Sept	Edwd Morton					
	21924	30 Sept	W Boyd & Sons					
	21925	26 Sept	Sir F W Knight					
	21926	27 Sept	James Stowe					

Rough Sketch of the detached Stamp –

If adopted it may be rendered much more elegant in design; with the compartments in colours thus securing it against imitation –

21925

Date received	Register number	Date sent	Name
1/10	21957	30 Sept	John Fellows
	21958	30 Sept	Thomas Lovell
	21959	30 Sept	John Heywood
	21960	30 Sept	Alexr Brown
	21961	30 Sept	J Patton
	21962	29 Sept	John Hawkins
	21963	–	Morison Smith
	21964	28 Sept	F O'Rourke
	21965	28 Sept	James Bibby
	21966	30 Sept	George Sherwood
2/10	21997	28 Sept	Stephen Webb
	21998	28 Sept	Gordon W Bolt & I G Dunster
	21999	24 Sept	Brackstone Baker
	22000	1 Oct	John Jackson
	22001	28 Sept	Chas Nielson
	22002	28 Sept	James McGorrin
	22003	27 Sept	Robert Owen
	22004	29 Sept	Mr Apsley
	22005	30 Sept	J H Elliott
	22006	26 Sept	J C Orchard
	22007	30 Sept	H Flather
	22008	30 Sept	B Gregory
	22009	–	Mr H Fleet
	22010	–	Henry Jackson
	22011	1 Oct	Anonymous JRE
	22012	1 Oct	Edwd Keet
	22013	1 Oct	Fredk Moore
	22037	28 Sept	John Ennis
	22038	29 Sept	Sir G S Mackenzie
	22039	25 Sept	Thos Serle
	22040	28 Sept	Angus Martin
F	22041	27 Sept	Anonymous Delta
	22042	1 Oct	John Mosscrop
	22043	1 Oct	Wm Lukyn
	22044	1 Oct	Hugh Henry Jones
	22045	1 Oct	James Petherick
	22046	1 Oct	B Rowsell
	22047	1 Oct	Revd S Fenton
	22048	1 Oct	John Smith Hill
	22049	1 Oct	T T Westlake
	22050	1 Oct	A Hilton
	22051	30 Sept	Jas W Lyon

Date received	Register number	Date sent	Name
2/10	22052	2 Oct	H Keanney
	22053	1 Oct	Anonymous SDG
	22054	24 Sept	Capt Sterne
	22055	26 Sept	D Stevenson
	22056	27 Sept	Edwd Smith
3/10	22097	2 Oct	J Bennett
	22098	2 Oct	J Bland
	22099	2 Sept	Monsr A Daubin
	22100	2 Oct	Baron de Berenger
	22101	30 Sept	J Grieve
	22102	–	E Norris
	22103	30 Sept	Mr Singer
	22104	1 Oct	J Wilkinson
	22105	1 Oct	C Blake
	22106	1 Oct	Mr A Creevy
	22107	30 Sept	Revd E Dillon
	22108	2 Oct	Mr Franklin
	22109	28 Sept	T F Hall
	22110	30 Sept	H T O'Neill
	22111	–	Mr W Redpath
	22112	2 Oct	Mr Stone
	22113	1 Oct	J H Wright
	22114	1 Oct	S Boothroyd
	22115	3 Oct	J W Herbert
	22116	–	H Ingram
	22117	30 Sept	P Caldwell
	22118	1 Oct	Mr W Withers
	22119	1 Oct	Revd A Lyne
	22120	30 Sept	Postmaster of Paxton
	22121	2 Oct	H P Clark
	22122	2 Oct	Elizth Clutterbuck
	22123	2 Oct	J Morris
	22156	2 Oct	J Jenour
	22160	2 Oct	R Bourne
	22161	2 Oct	Dr Mayne
	22162	3 Oct	T Swinburne
	22163	3 Oct	R Carlile

(none for 4/10)

Sent from the Post Office

This listing is taken from Post Office Archives file Post 30/52 bottom, with Post Office numbers

4/10	Mr Holt – 13,978	4/10	Mr Dickinson – 14309
	Mr G Pealer – 14,172		Mr Suffield – 14,304
	Admiral Griffiths – 14,181		M M – 14,312
	Mr Herrick – 14,200		Mr Hall (G.P. Surveyor
	Mr Thomas – 14,180		Scotd:) – 14,522
	Postmaster of Havant – 14,201		Mr Dillon – 14,484
	Mr Newtown – 14,266		Mr Tully – 14,385

Date received	Register number	Date sent	Name	Date received	Register number	Date sent	Name
5/10	22287	30 Sept	John Burke [Stephen]	7/10	22400	4 Oct	T Newton
	22288	3 Oct	J A W Cook		22441	1 Oct	P Christmann
	22289	3 Oct	Dr Cumin		22442	–	Sir J Hausler
	22290	30 Sept	Jas Chalmers		22443	–	C Peacock
	22291	2 Oct	Harry Dix		22444	3 Oct	T T Triebner
	22292	30 Sept	A B Daniel		22445	3 Oct	J Stephens
	22293	3 Oct	Chas Duffield		22446	4 Oct	T Swinburne
	22294	3 Oct	E C Everett		22447	4 Oct	J Stangroom
	22295	1 Oct	Saml Ferguson		22448	3 Oct	J B Walker
	22296	1 Oct	Mich. Grealy		22449	3 Oct	Mr Wheatley
	22297	1 Oct	B K Hill		22450	–	Mr M Robertson
	22298	2 Oct	Edwd Houghton		22516	3 Oct	Anonymous JAA
	22299	24 Sept	Wm Lovell		22517	–	Anonymous JP
	22300	1 Oct	Mr Laws		22518	6 Oct	Anonymous A working man
	22301	3 Oct	Mr Lyon		22519	4 Oct	H Brown
	22302	3 Oct	H Love		22520	4 Oct	J Bloss
	22303	2 Oct	Adam Melrose		22521	4 Oct	R Barker
	22304	2 Oct	Henry Duncan		22522	4 Oct	J Bievens
	22305	2 Oct	Mr Montague		22523	5 Oct	G Bissager
	22306	–	Revd F O Morris		22524	3 Oct	P Cowan
	22307	3 Oct	Chas New		22525	4 Oct	J Arnott
	22308	3 Oct	Mr Oliver		22526	4 Oct	J Cook(e)
	22309	2 Oct	R Rittie		22527	4 Oct	H Cockroft
	22310	2 Oct	J S Shackilford		22528	5 Oct	C Clyatt
	22311	4 Oct	Edwd Slaughter		22529	5 Oct	Mr S Crowther
	22312	3 Oct	Comr Townsend		22530	–	J Cart
	22313	2 Oct	Mr Woods		22531	1 Oct	Mr Decuet (Ducut)
	22314	30 Sept	T Whalley		22532	4 Oct	Revd C R Fanshawe
7/10	22392	4 Oct	J Brenan		22533	4 Oct	R Foote
	22393	30 Sept	J Butchart		22534	–	F Francellon
	22394	2 Oct	Mr Brenan		22535	4 Oct	Mr Grillier
	22395	2 Oct	F Cook		22536	5 Oct	J Greenfield
	22396	2 Oct	J F Davies		22537	3 Oct	S Gault
	22397	3 Oct	E Davies		22538	2 Oct	H Greer
	22398	4 Oct	M Lyons				
	22399	1 Oct	J N Mosley				

Date received	Register number	Date sent	Name
7/10	22539	20 Sept	J Gibson
	22540	30 Sept	C F Greisler
	22541	7 Oct	H Harris
	22542	7 Oct	S Hughes
	22543	4 Oct	J T Hughes
	22544	4 Oct	J Hiscox
	22545	1 Oct	J Harsburgh
	22546	– Oct	A Harden
	22547	4 Oct	Lt. Col. Jerrard
	22548	5 Oct	Mr F Johnstone
	22549	5 Oct	Mr Lyon
	22550	5 Oct	J Muir
	22551	5 Oct	R Madden
	22552	5 Oct	M Montgomery
	22553	5 Oct	C Montgomery
	22554	4 Oct	M McKenna
	22555	–	F Matthews
	22556	5 Oct	D P Neale
	22557	5 Oct	E Norris
	22558	5 Oct	J K O'Donnell
	22559	5 Oct	M Perrin
	22560	4 Oct	J Pine
	22561	4 Oct	G J Pitman
	22562	4 Oct	Mr Pearse
	22563	5 Oct	Mr H Roache
	22564	28 Sept	Mr Rankin
	22565	29 Sept	G E Stevens
	22566	28 Sept	Mr F Stevenson
	22567	5 Oct	J Stowe
	22568	3 Oct	G S Shand
	22569	2 Oct	J Stawell
	22570	3 Oct	C Tulley
	22571	4 Oct	H B Thomson
	22572	5 Oct	T J Triebner
	22573	7 Oct	E J Townsend
	22574	4 Oct	S Wilkinson
8/10	22575	1 Oct	R K Thompson
	22576	9 Sept	J H Piercy
	22577	7 Oct	J Payne & J Fuller
	22578	7 Oct	J Brown

Date received	Register number	Date sent	Name
8/10	22579	7 Oct	J Jerrard
	22580	6 Oct	J Ham
	22581	6 Oct	L Fenwick
	22582	6 Oct	J Lang
	22583	7 Oct	B Read
	22584	3 Oct	C Gilmore
	22585	5 Oct	C McCulloch
	22586	25 Sept	Mr Abbott
	22587	7 Oct	R Sercombe
	22588	5 Oct	Mr H Kempton
	22589	5 Oct	J Alton
	22590	7 Oct	E J Filmore
	22591	–	H Wheatley
	22592	5 Oct	Mr Morton
	22593	4 Oct	S Cummins
	22594	30 Sept	J McGahey
	22595	4 Oct	H Clarke
	22596	28 Sept	Mr Hill
	22597	6 Oct	R Miller
	22598	–	Anonymous (MKS)
	22599	7 Oct	T K Verdon
	22600	25 Sept	W H Brown
	22646	–	E J Catlow
	22647	7 Oct	R Dickinson
	22648	7 Oct	B Davies
	22649	–	L Morand
	22650	5 Oct	R Sayer
	22661	4 Oct	R Bullock
	22662	30 Sept	J Chalmers
	22663	7 Oct	J T Carter
	22664	7 Oct	Mr Chany
	22665	7 Oct	C Golightly
	22666	4 Oct	J Green

22564

22592

Date received	Register number	Date sent	Name	Date received	Register number	Date sent	Name
8/10	22667	–	J Lang	9/10	22778	8 Oct	S C Sagar
	22668	7 Oct	R Normanfoster		22779	8 Oct	D Tod
	22669	5 Oct	J Riley		22780	8 Oct	S C Webb
	22670	7 Oct	E Woods	10/10	22793	7 Oct	J S Sabberner
	22671	5 Oct	S Wilkinson		22794	7 Oct	Mr Brown
9/10	22692	30 Sept	A W Harnett		22795	7 Oct	E Martin
	22693	4 Oct	J McLachlin		22796	7 Oct	J Slaney
	22694	7 Oct	Revd S Green		22797	4 Oct	J Powell
	22695	7 Oct	Col. Fairman		22798	8 Oct	J C Sparke
	22696	8 Oct	J A Smart		22799	–	J Chalmers
	22697	8 Oct	E Woodcock		22800	7 Oct	J Jones
	22698	8 Oct	C Watling		22836	7 Oct	Anonymous
	22699	8 Oct	J Hewett				(PZ)
	22700	9 Oct	T Gee		22837	8 Oct	Richd Brailey
	22734	9 Oct	Anonymous		22838	26 Sept	J Borthwick
			(AB)		22839	7 Oct	R Buxton
	22735	7 Oct	Dr Arnott		22840	7 Oct	K A Carrie
	22736	8 Oct	Mr Aldridge		22841	8 Oct	Elizth Clay
	22737	8 Oct	G Birch Jr		22842	9 Oct	G Cook
	22738	4 Oct	J Butchart		22843	9 Oct	G Donner
	22739	7 Oct	H Besley		22844	3 Oct	J Erckmann
	22740	7 Oct	Mr Curtis for		22845	9 Oct	George Francis
			an appointment		22846	7 Oct	Alexr Grant
			connected with		22847	7 Oct	T Gapes
			the Penny Post.		22848	8 Oct	Henry Heath
	22741	8 Oct	G Evans		22849	30 Sept	H Hamilton
	22742	7 Oct	L E F		22850	7 Oct?	J Moinet
			Gomersall		22851	10 Oct	J Miller
	22743	7 Oct	E Hastings		22852	7 Oct	G H Orchard
	22744	7 Oct	J Halliday		22853	2 Oct	M Peyre
	22745	7 Oct	J H Garrett		22854	9 Oct	Mr Patton
	22746	7 Oct	J Jackson		22855	6 Oct	John Reid
	22747	7 Oct	G Murphy		22856	10 Oct	J P Schilizzi
	22748	8 Oct	T T Triebner		22857	4 Oct	Mr W Seaward
	22749	8 Oct	J Wilson		22858	9 Oct	J Startin
	22750	8 Oct	J Wing		22859	9 Oct	M Trouillet
	22767	7 Oct	Mr A Andrew		22860	9 Oct	Mr H W
	22768	7 Oct	T Butler				Tetheridge
	22769	5 Oct	J Campbell		22861	–	E A Townsend
	22770	8 Oct	Mr Davis Jr		22862	10 Oct	A W Webster
	22771	8 Oct	Mr Glass		22863	8 Oct	J Watson
	22772	8 Oct	R Hake Jr		22864	9 Oct	C F Whiting
	22773	7 Oct	H A Kuble		22865	9 Oct	T W Webster
	22774	4 Oct	J L Popkin		22866	5 Oct	T Zuber & Co
	22775	–	J Q Rumball		22867	–	D Greig
	22776	8 Oct	F Reeves		22868	9 Oct	Mr Eales
	22777	8 Oct	Mr J Stannard		22869	8 Oct	Chas Blake

Date received	Register number	Date sent	Name
10/10	22870	1 Oct	Richd Drew
	22871	9 Oct	George Phillips
	22872	9 Oct	H Flather
	22873	–	J M Woodyear
	22874	9 Oct	Joseph Green
	22875	8 Oct	Ambrose Blacklock
	22876	9 Oct	I Gill
	22877	9 Oct	Jas Dutton
	22878	7 Oct	Geo: Buckham
	22879	8 Oct	Mr H Carroll
	22880	8 Oct	John Fleming
	22881	8 Oct	Capt Graham
	22882	9 Oct	M Houlston
	22883	10 Oct	R T Nicholson
	22897	23 Aug	H Cole (30 Sept)
11/10	22919	–	Anonymous
	22920	–	Anonymous
	22921	8 Oct	J Blakly
	22922	8 Oct	J Bell
	22923	6 Oct	C Bendia
	22924	10 Oct	Mr Bartlett
	22925	–	J Crew
	22926	28 Aug	Fran: Coffin
	22927	8 Oct	Fredk Charone?
	22928	8 Oct	Thos. Davidson
	22929	8 Oct	C Ensor
	22930	10 Oct	H R Fanshawe
	22931	10 Oct	R Hake Jr
	22932	8 Oct	Orlando Jones
	22933	10 Oct	G B Kemp
	22934	7 Oct	J W Lyon
	22935	9 Oct	Mr J Luff
	22936	10 Oct	Jas Macaulay
	22937	10 Oct	H J Middleton
	22938	9 Oct	J Miller
	22939	10 Oct	J Ridley
	22940	2 Oct	Mr H Spiller
	22941	9 Oct	J Summers
	22942	9 Oct	Edwd Smith
	22943	9 Oct	C M Smith
	22944	10 Oct	Thos Sheppard
	22945	24 Sept	R Tripp
	22946	10 Oct	Mr Wilson
	22947	11 Oct	R T Nicholson (not 8)

Date received	Register number	Date sent	Name
11/10	22949	10 Oct	R S Lundie
	22950	10 Oct	John Lamb
	22980	–	D Clark
	22981	10 Oct	J J Collins
	22982	16 Sept	Ch. Dykes
	22983	9 Oct	Mr C Featherstone
	22984	10 Oct	G Francis
	22985	10 Oct	R R Hills
	22986	9 Oct	D B Hickie
	22987	8 Oct	J Jones
	22988	9 Oct	E Jackman
	22989	9 Oct	John Kelly
	22990	10 Oct	Mark Marks
	22991	7 Oct	Jas Macdonald
	22992	9 Oct	Agnes Nicol
	22993	9 Oct	J Roberts
	22994	10 Oct	Jas Saunders
	22995	10 Oct	J A Brown
	22996	6 Oct	M C Duffin
	22997	10 Oct	Jas Moore

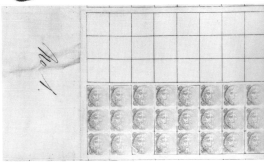

22983

23043

Date received	Register number	Date sent	Name		Date received	Register number	Date sent	Name
11/10	22998	8 Oct	Captn Cawley RN		12/10	23110	11 Oct	B H Edwards
	22999	9 Oct	M S Russell			23111	10 Oct	C J Field
	23000	10 Oct	J T Baillie			23112	10 Oct	Thomas Fisher
12/10	23042	6 Oct	A André			23113	9 Oct	Revd W Fraser
	23043	10 Oct	John Little			23114	9 Oct	J Fellowes
	23044	10 Oct	Mr Marshall			23115	9 Oct	Thos Gould
	23045	11 Oct	H R Matthew			23116	9 Oct	Alexr Grant
	23046	11 Oct	T Venner			23117	12 Oct	B Gregory
	23047	11 Oct	J Gray			23118	7 Oct	Amos Graham
	23048	11 Oct	J Dobson			23119	26 Sept	Edmund Hepple
	23049	8 Oct	T Popkins			23120	11 Oct	Robert Hake
	23050	12 Oct	Mr S Farquharson			23121	10 Oct	Revd W. Murray
	23051	22 Sept	H A Knott			23122	10 Oct	Robert Moir
	23052	10 Oct	B Burnell			23123	1 Oct	R Drew
	23053	9 Oct	Capt R Birch			23124	9 Oct	J McGorrier
	23054	10 Oct	B Read			23125	12 Oct	M E Mills
	23055	11 Oct	F Reeves			23126	7 Oct	A McCape
	23056	8 Oct	F W Scott			23127	8 Oct	Mr Nevill
	23057	1 Oct	J Salter			23128	11 Oct	J W Newberry
	23058	11 Oct	R S Sawerby			23129	10 Oct	Mr Pearson
	23059	8 Oct	Revd J F Gordon			23130	10 Oct	Raymond Perceval
	23060	–	L Thompson			23131	11 Oct	E A Porteus
	23061	10 Oct	G Payne			23132	10 Sept	R Retter
	23062	11 Oct	Mr Duncan			23133	11 Oct	Joseph Reid
	23063	11 Oct	Mr Backhouse with specimens of French Stamps			23134	10 Oct	J Redhead
						23135	12 Oct	J Rutherford
						23136	12 Oct	R Russell
	23095	10 Oct	H Atkinson			23137	–	C Ruby
	23096	11 Oct	Anonymous KC			23138	11 Oct	Joseph Suffield
	23097	11 Oct	Anonymous Credo			23139	–	C Sloman
	23098	–	Anonymous R			23140	12 Oct	Jeremiah Smith
	23099	9 Oct	Anonymous ZZ			23141	12 Oct	E W Twilou
	23100	–	Anonymous Fortuna			23142	(?)	A G Tyson
	23101	11 Oct	Josh Brown Jr			23143	10 Oct	Henry Todd
	23102	11 Oct	Jas Blake			23144	11 Oct	Joseph Tyro
	23103	10 Oct	do			23145	11 Oct	Mr Taylor
	23104	12 Oct	Jacob Bates			23146	11 Oct	John Toms
	23105	10 Oct	Dr Cumen			23147	–	Mr Tremlin
	23106	10 Oct	John Clark			23148	–	John Tillotson
	23107	–	Duncan Douglas			23149	–	Mr Tait
	23108	9 Oct	J C Dusourd			23150	9 Oct	Mr H Yate
	23109	8 Oct	J Delevarde			23151	11 Oct	Revd W B Woodman
						23152	11 Oct	George G Wall
						23153	11 Oct	H Windley
						23154	10 Oct	H W White

Date received	Register number	Date sent	Name
12/10	23155	10 Oct	W L Wharton
	23156	1 Oct	Joseph Zaeckel
	23157	11 Oct	R Sepper
	23158	10 Oct	J R Johnson
14/10	23240	–	M Harris
	23241	26 Sept	E Hepple
	23242	14 Oct	H McMahon
	23243	14 Oct	T Green
	23244	13 Oct	Anonymous Alpha
	23245	12 Oct	T Lanphier
	23246	12 Oct	S C Webb
	23247	12 Oct	T Watts
	23248	11 Oct	R Buck
	23249	11 Oct	J Cook(e)
	23250	11 Oct	J Sparrow
	23295	12 Oct	J Clark
	23296	11 Oct	J Johnstone
	23297	12 Oct	R Crowgey
	23298	11 Oct	J H Grafton
	23299	11 Oct	J Yates
	23300	–	T J Kent
	23331	12 Oct	Anonymous TR
	23332	14 Oct	do JR
	23333	11 Oct	do x y 1/1
	23334	–	do MG
	23335	9 Oct	do JPS
	23336	9 Oct	do SWB
	23337	–	C Allen
	23338	10 Oct	A Allardice
	23339	11 Oct	G W Aylen
	23340	11 Oct	J A Alger
	23341	12 Oct	S E Ash
	23342	10 Oct	M Boilleau
	23343	10 Oct	Saml Bennett
	23344	9 Oct	T Bennett
	23345	11 Oct	N Bennington jr

23338

Date received	Register number	Date sent	Name
14/10	23346	12 Oct	Chas Balfour
	23347	12 Oct	James Booth
	23348	12 Oct	J Bray
	23349	12 Oct	T Boys
	23350	12 Oct	J Brenan
	23351	–	Mr Bowler
	23352	14 Oct	S J Brown
	23353	8 Oct	A C Balfour
	23354	10 Oct	Mr Brenan
	23355	8 Oct	A Berrolla
	23356	14 Oct	Robert Bullen
	23357	11 Oct	R Banks
	23358	14 Oct	Mr Biggar
	23359	14 Oct	Mr C Black
	23360	–	J A Bown
	23361	14 Oct	J J Beardmore
	23362	–	M Bacquinoir
	23363	10 Oct	J Cummins
	23364	10 Oct	D Collins
	23365	10 Oct	J M Cooke
	23366	12 Oct	J Chiswick
	23367	12 Oct	H Colgate
	23368	12 Oct	P Coleman
	23369	8 Oct	T Cadett
	23370	9 Oct	Anonymous WC
	23371	14 Oct	Mr J Davies
	23372	12 Oct	Dr Dawson
	23373	11 Oct	H Dereks
	23374	12 Oct	B Dell
	23375	11 Oct	James Deans
	23376	12 Oct	G Dudgeon
	23377	5 Oct	G Dickinson
	23378	12 Oct	H Deacon
	23379	12 Oct	C Duffield
	23380	–	R P Davey
	23381	–	G F Duncumb
	23382	–	E Evershed
	23383	10 Oct	T Evans
	23384	12 Oct	J Essery Jr
	23385	12 Oct	James England
	23386	12 Oct	A Edmonds
	23387	14 Oct	G H Francis
	23388	5 Oct	J Fleming
	23389	12 Oct	Revd W Fletcher
	23390	10 Oct	Dr Fraser
	23391	12 Oct	Mr Farrow
	23392	8 Oct	R M Freeman

Date received	Register number	Date sent	Name	Date received	Register number	Date sent	Name
14/10	23393	12 Oct	J Greenfield	14/10	23438	12 Oct	M H Perigal
	23394	12 Oct	C Gaubert		23439	12 Oct	Eddell Penny
	23395	12 Oct	S Gray		23440	12 Oct	Eddell Penny
	23396	9 Oct	G Gardner		23441	11 Oct	Dr C Patterson
	23397	12 Oct	F W Gerish		23442	–	L Plaisant
	23398	7 Oct	John Gourlay		23443	12 Oct	J Prince
	23399	12 Oct	J Gilbert		23444	12 Oct	Payne & Bousquet
	23400	12 Oct	Mr Hargraves		23445	–	R Power
	23401	12 Oct	Mr H Hooper		23446	8 Oct	Mr Rogers
	23402	11 Oct	M J Hammond		23447	–	J Rowland
	23403	12 Oct	F J Hardy		23448	–	Mr T Radford
	23404	12 Oct	Mr Hammond		23449	11 Oct	Mr Raynes
	23405	11 Oct	J Hutchenson Jr		23450	13 Oct	Read P
	23406	11 Oct	D A Hughes		23451	10 Oct	Hughes Russell
	23407	14 Oct	A Higginson		23452	3 Oct	G Robinson
	23408	12 Oct	G Hutton		23453	–	Mr S Roberts
	23409	11 Oct	Taylor & Jones		23454	10 Oct	George Robertson
	23410	14 Oct	J Jones		23455	12 Oct	H Rankin
	23411	12 Oct	F Jones		23456	12 Oct	J H Relie
	23412	13 Oct	J Kirkhouse		23457	–	J Rutherford
	23413	12 Oct	P M C Kerr		23458	12 Oct	R P Rubie
	23414	11 Oct	H Logan		23459	12 Oct	T C Symons
	23415	–	R Lefevre		23460	11 Oct	J Skirving
	23416	12 Oct	F Larbalester		23461	14 Oct	H Schroder
	23417	9 Oct	M Lafabreque		23462	10 Oct	J W Symes
	23418	13 Oct	Mr Lyon		23463	10 Oct	J T Storey
	23419	10 Oct	Mr Marrogh		23464	14 Oct	T Swinburne
	23420	12 Oct	Henry Michael		23465	13 Oct	[J P C Surrey] Thomas Dyer
	23421	14 Oct	E Miles		23466	11 Oct	J Sutton
	23422	14 Oct	H Mopple		23467	12 Oct	A Specht
	23423	12 Oct	D Mahon		23468	14 Oct	Mr Smart
	23424	14 Oct	Mr Miller		23469	–	Mr A Sherwin
	23425	12 Oct	Simon McLennan		23470	10 Oct	J Sullivan
	23426	10 Oct	M Maiaire		23471	11 Oct	T Sanders
	23427	11 Oct	J Mounsher		23472	12 Oct	Andrew Shortrede
	23428	12 Oct	J Matthews Jr		23473	12 Oct	L W Tear
	23429	11 Oct	Robt Moir		23474	11 Oct	P M Taylor
	23430	14 Oct	Mr Neely		23475	11 Oct	Edwd Thornbill
	23431	14 Oct	Mr Oldham Jr		23476	13 Oct	John Tucker
	23432	9 Oct	J C Orchard		23477	12 Oct	S Travers
	23433	–	R Prendergast		23478	7 Oct	H Vasseur
	23434	14 Oct	Messrs Poupard & Co		23479	10 Oct	G R Tilling
	23435	13 Oct	J M Peniston		23480	12 Oct	J Wood
	23436	12 Oct	J W Penton				
	23437	13 Oct	Mr Parker				

Date received	Register number	Date sent	Name	Date received	Register number	Date sent	Name
14/10	23481	12 Oct	J Warcup	14/10	23490	12 Oct	J Thompson
	23482	10 Oct	R Wordsworth		23496	14 Oct	Fredk Crook
	23483	12 Oct	J M Wheeler		23497	14 Oct	Mr G
	23484	12 Oct	J Wood				Hemsworth
	23485	12 Oct	J Wilson		23498	14 Oct	Thos Flendell
	23486	14 Oct	Chas Watling		23499	9 Oct	George Gardner
	23487	–	J Wrothall		23500	–	Anonymous X Y Z
	23488	–	G Hardcastle	15/10	23548	15 Oct	Anonymous E B
	23489	12 Oct	M Cronellet		23549	10 Oct	C Vezee

Sent from the Post Office

This listing is taken from Post Office Archives file Post 30/52 bottom,
with Post Office numbers

15/10   Mr Gordon – 15,082
    Mr Jones – 15,108
    Mr Michell – 14,871
    Mr Hill – 14,927
    Mr Farrar – 14,924
    Mr Morris – 14,923
    Mr Winberry – 14,856
    Mr Combes – 15,118
    Mr Butler – 14,925
    M Le Capelain – 15,332
    (with model of Stamp)
    Amicus – 15,210
    Mr Hosmer – 15,216
    Mr Hillman – 15,287
    Mr Cockings – 15,253
    Mr Grimes – 15,292
    Mr Fort – 15,255
    John Mahony
    (Mail Guard) – 15,333
    Delta – 14,680
    A.A.A. – 14,706
    The Stranger – 14,983

15/10   from Dundee – 14,928
    (forwd by Duke of Richmond)
    Mr Jos Coates – 15,252
    Mr Manwell – 14,867
    Sig. Angeloni – 14,926
    Watford Pmr. – 14,865
    Sir John Robinson – 15,166
    transmitted by Sir E Lees
    Mr Martin – 14,585
    Mr John Spratt – 15,313
    Mr Wilkinson – 15,300
    Mr Nicol – 14,587
    Mr Heath – 14,586
    Mr Tupper – 15,369
    Mr Hooper – 15,339
    Boxford Pmr. – 15,345
    Mr H Durré – 15,371
    forwd by Mr Stephen – 14,997
    Mr Deaddes – 15,131
    Mr W. Apsley – 15,254
    M Belcour – 15,214]

Date received	Register number	Date sent	Name	Date received	Register number	Date sent	Name
15/10	23581	–	Anon	16/10	23608	–	do A Citizen
16/10	23601	–	Anon Simplex				of Hereford
			Munditus		23609	14 Oct	J J Alney
	23602	–	do TW		23610	11 Oct	B Ansell [R]
	23603	–	do X Y Z		23611	12 Oct	T Argand
	23604	–	do ED		23612	–	A Ainger
	23605	–	do		23613	–	S Portlock
	23606	–	do I P		23614	–	J Brett
	23607	–	do X Y		23615	–	R Brooks

Date received	Register number	Date sent	Name	Date received	Register number	Date sent	Name
16/10	23616	–	T Burbridge	16/10	23655	–	J W Edmonds
	23617	10 Oct	R Bambridge		23656	12 Oct	Mr J Evans
	23618	–	J O Burne		23657	14 Oct	B Frankland
	23619	11 Oct	J Booth		23658	14 Oct	R W Fox
	23620	12 Oct	Revd L J Boyce		23659	14 Oct	J Fraser
	23621	12 Oct	R Creighton		23660	14 Oct	J Forbes
	23622	12 Oct	P R Barron		23661	14 Oct	Mr Foote
	23623	12 Oct	C Black		23662	15 Oct	J Finch
	23624	14 Oct	J Brown		23663	14 Oct	Mr C Featherstone
	23625	14 Oct	J Bogardus				
	23626	14 Oct	T Bleads		23664	14 Oct	J Farnworth
	23627	14 Oct	G Barker		23665	14 Oct	Richard Faraday
	23628	15 Oct	G F Bennett		23666	14 Oct	Capt Graham
	23629	11 Oct	T E O Cavanagh		23667	14 Oct	Mr Gusenthwaite Jr
	23630	12 Oct	J Chalmers				
	23631	13 Oct	J Cooke		23668	15 Oct	T Garlick
	23632	14 Oct	E Chance		23669	13 Oct	Mr Hersee
	23633	14 Oct	T Caithness		23670	14 Oct	C Hopper
	23634	14 Oct	H Collen		23671	14 Oct	Thos Henwood
	23635	14 Oct	T G Craig		23672	14 Oct	Mr Huttmann
	23636	14 Oct	Thos Clutterbuck		23673	14 Oct	C Hessace?
					23674	14 Oct	G Hogarth
	23637	14 Oct	M Carly		23675	14 Oct	J W Haythorne
	23638	14 Oct	J Clark		23676	14 Oct	Messrs Halfhede & Cowper
	23639	15 Oct	Mr Calvert				
	23640	15 Oct	Mr T Coleman				
	23641	15 Oct	J Carter		23677	14 Oct	J Hamilton
	23642	11 Oct	J Crowther		23678	–	T Harwood
	23643	–	E Churton		23679	14 Oct	Heraud J A
	23644	–	B Cheverton		23680	–	J Innes
	23645	3 Oct	T F Dickinson		23681	15 Oct	C Johnson
	23646	12 Oct	J A Davies		23682	15 Oct	F Jackson
	23647	12 Oct	J Denny		23683	14 Oct	Thos Joyce
	23648	12 Oct	E Duverger		23684	14 Oct	E Jones
	23649	14 Oct	J Davison		23685	14 Oct	Mr James
	23650	14 Oct	Geo Downer		23686	–	R Johnston
	23651	–	G M Duncan		23687	–	Thos Kinder
	23652	15 Oct	J Dickinson		23688	12 Oct	Mr Knight
	23653	–	C P Eden		23689	14 Oct	Wm Kingdom
	23654	13 Oct	B Ellison		23690	14 Oct	H Knight
					23691	14 Oct	M Kennelly
					23692	14 Oct	Mr A Knott
					23693	12 Oct	E Keene
					23694	14 Oct	Mr J Lucas Jr
					23695	14 Oct	Mr Lambert
					23696	14 Oct	T Lowery
					23697	12 Oct	Thos Lacey

23676

Date received	Register number	Date sent	Name
16/10	23698	15 Oct	R S Lundie
	23699	14 Oct	J Lumley
	23700	12 Oct	J Meacham
	23701	14 Oct	B Munn
	23702	–	S Moore
	23703	14 Oct	David Morison
	23704	14 Oct	Mr Mann
	23705	–	Capt Montague
	23706	–	S Milne
	23707	14 Oct	Alexr Macdougal
	23708	12 Oct	Mr Morris
	23709	–	J W Middlewood
	23710	14 Oct	Edward O Neill
	23711	13 Oct	Mr J Newbold
	23712	14 Oct	R Nursey
	23713	14 Oct	G Ogilvie
	23714	13 Oct	T Powell
	23715	–	J Prince
	23716	12 Oct	J Patterson
	23717	14 Oct	D Potts
	23718	14 Oct	J Pollard
	23719	12 Oct	T S Prideaux
	23720	14 Oct	J W Pewtress
	23721	14 Oct	Mr W Price
	23722	12 Oct	P Patterson
	23723	14 Oct	F A Papps
	23724	14 Oct	J Pyne
	23725	14 Oct	W S Richard & Son
	23726	14 Oct	J V Richardson
	23727	14 Oct	J Rampley
	23728	14 Oct	J H Reddle
	23729	–	T Rilgby
	23730	13 Oct	Dr O Reilly
	23731	–	A W Reynard
	23732	3 Oct	F Renby

Date received	Register number	Date sent	Name
16/10	23733	14 Oct	Geo Russell
	23734	–	J Rutherford
	23735	14 Oct	J & F Ross
	23736	10 Oct	C Stainsbury (Sainsbury)
	23737	15 Oct	J W Southgate Jnr
	23738	15 Oct	T Shotsky
	23739	11 Oct	R W Swinburne
	23740	14 Oct	J Stowe
	23741	15 Oct	Mr Spring
	23742	12 Oct	C Storey
	23743	12 Oct	E Smith
	23744	15 Oct	Myers Sparrow & Co.
	23745	15 Oct	Marley & Saunders
	23746	–	A D Shiledor (A.G.Boilleau?)
	23747	15 Oct	Mr Thompson
	23748	–	E Turnbull
	23749	14 Oct	D Thomas
	23750	14 Oct	H Todd Jnr
	23751	14 Oct	James Tyler
	23752	14 Oct	P Young
	23753	14 Oct	T K Verdon
	23754	12 Oct	J Veitch
	23755	15 Oct	M Tennant
	23756	14 Oct	W M Williams
	23757	14 Oct	Mr Wylds [Mr Brown of Hertford]

23738

23743

23750

Date received	Register number	Date sent	Name
16/10	23758	–	J Whitehead
	23759	14 Oct	Mr Warren
	23760	14 Oct	Mr Washbourne
	23761	14 Oct	Joshua P Westhead
	23762	–	Mr Waldron
	23763	14 Oct	J Wright
	23764	14 Oct	T Welsh
	23765	9 Oct	George Wilson
	23766	12 Oct	Mr Woods
	23785	15 Oct	Anonymous JJ
	23786	14 Oct	Mr Apsley
	23787	–	J Cuber
	23788	–	Anonymous JMB
	23789	–	J Burch
	23790	15 Oct	C Bicke
	23791	13 Oct	Capt Davies
	23792	15 Oct	J Duncan
	23793	9 Oct	J Evans
	23794	14 Oct	J Elliott
	23795	–	J Edwards
	23796	12 Oct	D Forrest
	23797	–	R E Gavey
	23798	9 Oct	E Gadefrai
	23799	14 Oct	B Hope
	23800	–	H A Knott
	23801	14 Oct	H P Keighley
	23802	–	J Lane
	23803	–	J D Malcolm
	23804	10 Oct	H McCullagh
	23805	15 Oct	J Paterson
	23806	16 Oct	J Powell
	23807	–	T Popjoy
	23808	–	T Robson
	23809	–	J Rahles
	23810	15 Oct	J Stanton
	23811	14 Oct	R W Sievier
	23812	14 Oct	T Stockman
	23813	15 Oct	Schonberg & Bishop
	23814	16 Oct	R Taylor
	23815	–	Mr Tait
	23816	15 Oct	M Wickins
	23817	12 Oct	Mr Wood Jr
	23818	14 Oct	S S Webb
	23819	14 Oct	T Walker

Date received	Register number	Date sent	Name
17/10	23889	–	Anonymous
	23890	14 Oct	Henry Cockroft
	23891	14 Oct	Thos Henry Fletcher
	23892	12 Oct	Thos Fraser
	23893	12 Oct	Wm Gunn
	23894	14 Oct	Geo H Jay
	23895	13 Oct	Rob Geo Kelly
	23896	13 Oct	T B Mason
	23897	14 Oct	Surgeon Thomas
	23898	12 Oct	Thomas Walsh
	23899	15 Oct	D Webster
	23900	12 Oct	J H MacLorley
	23920	14 Oct	Joseph Clarke
	23921	15 Oct	Wm Hersee
	23922	15 Oct	Robert Kennan
	23923	15 Oct	Laxlord & Holland
	23924	14 Oct	Henry Mayfield
	23925	15 Oct	Robert Marle
	23926	12 Oct	James Reed
	23927	14 Oct	J Stephens
	23928	–	Edward Turner
	23929	15 Oct	Thos Woodborough
	23930	14 Oct	R Wordsworth
	23931	17 Oct	L Angelom Fransinati
	23932	–	F L Freud?
	23933	–	C R Brown
	23934	15 Oct	J W Parker
	23935	–	J Schmeltz
	23936	–	C Vezee
	23944	15 Oct	Mr Wheatley
	23945	16 Oct	J Wood
	23946	15 Oct	A Stenton

23757

Date received	Register number	Date sent	Name	Date received	Register number	Date sent	Name
17/10	23947	15 Oct	Mr J Mansell	21/10	24173	16 Oct	J O Bierne
	23948	16 Oct	J C Rose		24174	–	A Finnie Jr
	23949	16 Oct	Robert Seaton		24175	19 Oct	Thomas Robson
	23950	15 Oct	Dr Sayer		24176	17 Oct	Mr J Parr
18/10	23993	12 Oct	Anonymous		24177	18 Oct	H T ONeill
	23994	17 Oct	do		24184	18 Oct	Samuel Gordon
	23995	17 Oct	do HGB		24185	18 Oct	E Hepple
	23996	14 Oct	J O Beirne		24186	17 Oct	George Gardner
	23997	17 Oct	Mr Calvert		24187	18 Oct	R W Sievier
	23998	–	A G Hamilton		24188	19 Oct	James Crooks
	23999	5 Oct	Robert Kennan		24189	19 Oct	Thos Dyer
	24000	14 Oct	J M Lynn		24190	19 Oct	Saml Wells (Webb)
	24028	14 Oct	Anonymous		24191	19 Oct	H Cockroft
	24029	17 Oct	J W Armstrong		24195	21 Oct	E B Walmseley
	24030	16 Oct	R Creighton		24196	–	Wm Lyon
	24031	15 Oct	J Elliott		24197	16 Oct	W H Logan
	24032	14 Oct	G Gardner		24198	19 Oct	E B Walmesley
	24033	16 Oct	J Morris		24199	19 Oct	R Bush
	24034	15 Oct	S M P Reid		24200	17 Oct	Robert Plunkett
	24035	17 Oct	A Stanton				
	24036	–	Mr Watson		24204	18 Oct	P Le Chapelain
	24041	–	JJ		24205	18 Oct	H Collinson
	24049	–	FWF Woodman	22/10	24282	21 Oct	S C Webb
19/10	24091	–	Anonymous		24283	21 Oct	J G Craig
	24092	18 Oct	H Challinor		24284	17 Oct	E Smith
	24093	9 Oct	G Gardner		24285	17 Oct	C Freeth
	24094	16 Oct	Revd J P Leahy		24286	19 Oct	E A Davis
	24095	18 Oct	T May Jnr		24287	22 Oct	R Bullen
	24096	17 Oct	Mr Wills		24288	11 Oct	R K Douglas
	24125	16 Oct	Thos Donlevy		24289	28 Sept	C H Smith
	24126	16 Oct	Mr H Spiller		24290	21 Oct	W M Williams

Sent from the Post Office
This listing is taken from Post Office Archives file Post 30/52 bottom,
with Post Office numbers
22/10 Mr Rd Bennen – 13,777
Mr C A Holl (?Hill) – 15,407
Mr Byng Hall – 15,507
Mr W S Eagerty – 15,492
Mr W Tate – 15,476
Mr Gordon – 15,566
Mr Webster – 15,632
Mr Durré – 15,608
W. Neilson – 15,609
Mr Greenwood – 15,709
Mr Hampton – 15,706

25001

Date received	Register number	Date sent	Name	Date received	Register number	Date sent	Name
23/10	24344	22 Oct	Mr Connor	29/10	24795	26 Oct	R B Bennett
	24345	22 Oct	S Wright		24796	28 Oct	J S Cocking
	24346	19 Oct	H Flather		24797	28 Oct	Mr Gray
	24347	18 Oct	Mr J Mitchelson		24798	21 Oct	Mr Hammond
					24799	28 Oct	Mr Stannard
	24348	–	T J Bedford		24800	28 Oct	J Tillotson
	24349	21 Oct	J Cooke		24808	28 Oct	J Hiscox
	24350	22 Oct	Geo Gunning	30/10	24865	28 Oct	Mr Collins
24/10	24394	23 Oct	Annoyance [sic] J.J.		24866	28 Oct	J Rutherford
					24867	24 Oct	J T Thomson
	24395	22 Oct	Mr James		24868	29 Oct	S Webb
	24396	10 Oct	N Westray		(24871	27 Oct	G Colman to
	24400	23 Oct	T.T.Triebner				be appd to sell
	24441	21 Oct	Wm Cooper				Penny Post
	24455	–	P Richards				Stamps)
	24456	12 Oct	A Banfield	31/10	24945	28 Oct	A Didelot
	24457	21 Oct	J Williams		24946	28 Oct	GPO
	24458	22 Oct	C R Brown		24947	31 Oct	W Lyon
	24459	22 Oct	L Hewett		24979	28 Oct	Sir G Mackenzie
	24460	22 Oct	Mr Lyon		24980	29 Oct	J Cook
	24461	23 Oct	J Phillips		24981	30 Oct	H Cockcroft
25/10	24493	20 Oct	A Berrolla		24982	30 Oct	C Duffield for
	24494	21 Oct	J W Middlewood				an appt under
	24495	22 Oct	J Murray				the Penny Post
	24496	–	C George				Act
	24540	23 Oct	E Lacy		24983	29 Oct	Secy Post
	24556	24 Oct	Mr Seate				Office with
26/10	24592	25 Oct	G Dickinson				Penny Post
	24593	23 Oct	J Dickinson				Plans
	24594	23 Oct	J Groves Jr	1/11	24998	19 Oct	J Davis
	24595	25 Oct	J Houlston		24999	29 Oct	J A Forbes
	24596	23 Oct	E Hastings		25000	25 Oct	J Mathers
	24598	25 Oct	Mr J Stannard		25001	–	J Brett
	24599	22 Oct	John Davis		25040	31 Oct	Mr Adam
	24620	24 Oct	G Dickinson		25041	31 Oct	J Biddle
28/10	24697	25 Oct	R Creighton		25042	31 Oct	J Cox
	24698	25 Oct	C Mackenzie		25043	30 Oct	J Coleman
	24733	26 Oct	R Blenkinsop		25044	28 Oct	A Graham
	24734	26 Oct	H Cockcroft		25045	30 Oct	A Murray
	24735	24 Oct	T Clutterbuck		25046	31 Oct	T S Westlake
	24736	26 Oct	J Greenfield		25047	29 Oct	H Russell
	24737	25 Oct	H Lincoln		25074	1 Nov	J Rangeley
	24738	25 Oct	H T O Neill	2/11	25101	31 Oct	Mr Oldham Jr
	24739	26 Oct	J Reid		25102	30 Oct	G Dickinson
	24740	12 Oct	J H Relie		25103	31 Oct	J Greenfield
	24741	24 Oct	M Tennant		25104	–	H Davis
	24757	–	Anonymous		25114	–	J O Beirne

Date received	Register number	Date sent	Name
2/11	25115	31 Oct	T T Triebner
	25117	1 Nov	M De Baring
4/11	25196	–	George Ness
	25205	2 Nov	Mr Clarke
	25219	1 Nov	C Hughes
	25220	2 Nov	A Blacklock
	25245	1 Nov	Mr Harper
	25246	2 Nov	Mr Cockroft
5/11	25297	4 Nov	T Swinburne
	25298	4 Nov	R Crawford
	25299	3 Nov	H Harris
	25300	3 Nov	G Greenfield
	25339	2 Nov	Mr Butcher
	25340	2 Nov	H Bloomfield
	25341	2 Nov	R W Hume
	25342	3 Nov	T T Westlake
	25343	4 Nov	R Gill
	25344	4 Nov	Anonymous
	25370	5 Nov	L A Frusinati
6/11	25448	2 Nov	J Stirrat
	25449	4 Nov	F Clayton
	25450	4 Nov	H Atkinson
	25466	5 Nov	F Ham
	25483	6 Nov	A L Zambelli

Date received	Register number	Date sent	Name
	25500	–	JJ
7/11	[25536		Anon]
	25550	6 Nov	T Swinburne
	25552	6 Nov	Frederick Pilch
	25553	5 Nov	Mr Curtis
	25554	–	Mr Newton
	25555	–	H T O'Neill
	25564	6 Nov	J Triggey & Son
8/11	25648	6 Nov	T Fisher
	25649	–	Revd J P Alcock
	25650	–	Anonymous
	25657	8 Nov	M Carty
	25661	26 Oct	Inv De Hersfeldt
9/11	25782	8 Nov	Postmaster General with returns of the effect of reduction of rate of postage from 4d to 2d (?) between places within 8 miles

Date received	Register number	Date sent	Name
9/11	25783	–	Postmaster General Penny Post Plans

Rev H Barry – 16,065
Mr Ainswicke – 16,168
Braintree Postmr. – 16091
Mr Greenwood – 15,709
Mr Cox – 16151
Mr Mackay – 16,069

Mr Wilkinson – 16,424
Mr Lockwood – 16,408
Mr Kent – 16,508
Mr Scott – 16,507 (James)
Mr Hopkins – 16,506
Mr John Smith – 16529

PO Archives file
Post 30/52 bottom

Date received	Register number	Date sent	Name
9/11	25787	7 Nov	T T Triebner
	25788	6 Nov	F W F Woodman
	25789	5 Nov	R Worthington
	25790	8 Nov	J J Cox
	25791	–	S Forrester
11/11	25847	8 Nov	Mr Harper
	25894	8 Nov	J Halliday
	25895	9 Nov	J Meacham
	25896	7 Nov	D P Neale

Date received	Register number	Date sent	Name
11/11	25897	8 Nov	Kemp Sanby
	25898	8 Nov	T M Truscott
	25899	9 Nov	Thos Dixon
	25900	9 Nov	C S Conves
12/11	25947	7 Nov	T Argand
	25948	–	J C Wilcox Junr
	25949	9 Nov	R Owen
	25950	11 Nov	T Dousbery
	25988	11 Nov	H S Searle
	25989	11 Nov	C Norwood

Date received	Register number	Date sent	Name
12/11	25990	11 Nov	J Powell
	25991	10 Nov	R Hillier
	25992	11 Nov	J Goodfellow
	25993	–	J Biddle
	25994	9 Nov	J Biggs
	25995	12 Nov	A W Webster
	25996	12 Nov	Mr H Phipps
	25997	11 Nov	G P Hinton
	25998	12 Nov	J Jones (R)
	25999	11 Nov	F L Simes (Sims)
	26000	11 Nov	E Turnbull
13/11	26047	-	Anonymous
	26048	12 Nov	Mr Green
	26049	9 Nov	H Flather
	26050	12 Nov	J Houlston
	26091	11 Nov	T Smithson
	26094	13 Nov	J Wing
	26095	11 Nov	Postmr Ashby de la Zouche
	26125	8 Nov	J F Naylor
	26126	13 Nov	J Rungeley
14/11	26197	13 Nov	G Page
	26198	10 Nov	J Smyth
	26199	–	N H Eager
	26200	–	T T Triebner
	26225	–	D Cohen
	26226	–	G G Lowes
	26227	–	J M Woodyear
15/11	26250	–	Anonymous
	26299	14 Nov	J Pullen
	26300	–	J McDonald
	26315	15 Nov	R Bourne
16/11	26365	15 Nov	J F Naylor
	26366	15 Nov	G Parsons
	26367	15 Nov	R Miller
	26368	15 Nov	J W Walford
	26369	14 Nov	B B Turner
	26370	14 Nov	J Moon
	26371	14 Nov	E Keene
	26372	–	Anonymous
	26373	–	J Jackson
18/11	26477	17 Nov	Mr Lyon for return of his plan
	26481	17 Nov	J Moore
	26482	16 Nov	Mr W Tait
18/11	26483	–	Margt Williams
	26484	–	Anonymous
	26485	–	do
	26486	14 Nov	D Scarlett
	26487	15 Nov	H S O'Neill
	26488	15 Nov	Mr Slaughter
	26489	15 Nov	T Fisher
	26490	–	E Benham
	26491	16 Nov	T T Triebner
	26492	16 Nov	J Baker
	26493	16 Nov	C L Lee
	26494	16 Nov	B Smith
	26495	16 Nov	J Beardmore
	26496	16 Nov	H Cockroft
	26497	15 Nov	R Hillier
	26498	16 Nov	J Brigg
	26499	16 Nov	C Norwood
	26500	16 Nov	R E Marshall
	26513	18 Nov	John Prince res his process of making paper with threads with ref to penny post
	26528	–	E Browne
19/11	26596	16 Nov	JAA
	26597	18 Nov	J Briggs
	26598	18 Nov	J Tronbridge
	26599	18 Nov	H Cockroft
	26600	18 Nov	T Egan
	26638	18 Nov	F Moore
20/11	26649	18 Nov	M Lambert
	26650	18 Nov	J B Monmouth
21/11	26750X	19 Nov	Mr Rowland Hill Report on the Security in the delivery of letters as affected by prepayment of postage.
22/11	26802	18 Nov	R Bullen
	26835	–	T Cassin
	26836	21 Nov	H Harris
	26837	19 Nov	T H Moreland
	26838	21 Nov	Anon J J
	26839	20 Nov	P Bigger

Date received	Register number	Date sent	Name	Date received	Register number	Date sent	Name
22/11	26882	–	S Brett	30/11	27500	26 Nov	Harrn Flather
	26885	14 Nov	Revd F O Morris		27505	30 Nov	P Bruff
	26888	8 Nov	Sir G Mackenzie	2/12	27590	29 Nov	H Macaire
23/11	26947	1 Nov	R Percival		27601	2 Dec	Myers Sparrow & Co
	26949	20 Nov	J Stephens				
	26952	22 Nov	Mr Towndrow		27602	–	Pewtress Low & Co estimate for furnishing general labels
	26953	23 Nov	S C Webb				
	26956	20 Nov	R Simpson				
	26968	15 Nov	John Harris				
	26969	18 Nov	T S Lea	3/12	27689	2 Dec	Anon. rel to awarding Premiums for the best Penny Post plans
	26970	–	R Stevenson				
	26971	19 Nov	R Fuge				
	26972	17 Nov	S Aykroyd				
	26973	19 Nov	A W Webster				
	26974	14 Nov	J Bowden		27699	2 Dec	C Colvell
	26999	22 Nov	J T White		27700	2 Dec	Wm McCallum
25/11	27049	22 Nov	JJ	4/12	27750	29 Nov	J Rutherford
	27053	23 Nov	H Jackson		27751	2 Dec	J Wood
	27085	23 Nov	J Bishop		27752	3 Dec	E J Wheeler
	27086	23 Nov	J C Dalwig		27760	3 Dec	J Rawsthorne
	27087	23 Nov	Richard James		27929	4 Dec	Amelia Hilton
	27088	24 Nov	Mr Lyon		27791	3 Dec	Revd. J Simons
	27089	22 Nov	Wm Wheatley		27792	28 Nov	J H Pasley
26/11	27145	25 Nov	G Murphy	5/12	27842	3 Dec	T T Triebner
	27146	25 Nov	Mr G Poole		27900	5 Dec	Richard Jones
	27147	–	J Matthews	6/12	27929	6 Dec	J Prince paper made by him
	27148	23 Nov	T Mackintosh				
	27149	–	Anonymous		27939	5 Dec	Mr Hatch
	27150	21 Nov	D Bell		27940	4 Dec	P Neilson
	27164	23 Nov	D McClary		27941	3 Dec	Anonymous JAA
27/11	27217	25 Nov	C N Field		27952	5 Dec	C West
	27248	26 Nov	Postmr Genl	7/12	27997	3 Dec	Mr Alexander
	27256	27 Nov	L A Frusinati		27998	4 Dec	R B Baird
28/11	27297	27 Nov	T Barron		27999	4 Dec	Mr Stone
	27298	27 Nov	C Norwood		28000	5 Dec	J Fellows
	27299	26 Nov	H Bovill		28026	5 Dec	S C Webb
29/11	27365	26 Nov	JAA	9/12	28081	6 Dec	S M Reid
	27366	28 Nov	T Bagnold		28082	5 Dec	P Patterson
	27367	27 Nov	H Cockroft		28100	6 Dec	Mr R Hill Report on the Franking Stamp
	27368	27 Nov	J Hiscox				
	27369	27 Nov	B Harrison				
	27370	8 Nov	T Leonardos		28103	7 Dec	C Singleton
30/11	27448	29 Nov	G Daniel(l)	10/12	28175	-	G Boyce
	27449	–	C L Hughes	11/12	28296	10 Dec	Mr M Williams
	27450	29 Nov	J Ward(e)		28297	10 Dec	Revd W R Shirley
	27498	27 Nov	Hughes Russell				
	27499	28 Nov	J C Dalwig		28298	–	T Triebner

Date received	Register number	Date sent	Name
11/12	28299	10 Dec	J Gardener
12/12	28338	9 Dec	Revd W P Moore
	28400	11 Dec	J Fleming
13/12	28445	10 Dec	Anon J A A
13/12	28449	12 Dec	Mr T Haley for return of his Penny Post Plan
	28451		R Crawford re premium
	28485	13 Dec	L Angeloni
14/12	28497	13 Dec	E Stropling
	28504	13 Dec	T Woodward
	28527	–	R Fowke
	28528	12 Dec	J Stephens
16/12	28621	13 Dec	John Atkinson
	28622	13 Dec	Col. Holcombe
	28636	13 Dec	J Pedler
	28658	–	T T Triebner
17/12	28721	16 Dec	H Harris
	28737	16 Dec	Anonymous
	28738	12 Dec	A Banfield
	28739	16 Dec	G Harvey
	28740	12 Dec	M B Macalister
	28741	12 Dec	G Peacock
	28742	16 Dec	J Skuse
	28743	16 Dec	J F Towers
18/12	28857	16 Dec	J Menan res: the premium for Penny Post Plans
	28872	16 Dec	Mr Adam
	28873	16 Dec	Lieut Col Holcombe
	28874	14 Dec	C Dykes
19/12	28955	17 Dec	A T J Martin for the publication of the various plans
	28983	17 Dec	M Tennant
20/12	29050	17 Dec	R Tripp
	29063	17 Dec	J A A
21/12	29143	19 Dec	L Angeloni
	29144	20 Dec	T Beardman
	29145	18 Dec	R Crawford
	29146	18 Dec	R Crowther
21/12	29147	18 Dec	Mr F G Waldron
	29160	19 Dec	J H Evelyn
23/12	29239	23 Dec	F Moore
	29240	21 Dec	T T Triebner
	29248	21 Dec	H R Fanshawe
	29249	21 Dec	Edmund Hayes
	29250	21 Dec	Mr McQueen
	29256	21 Dec	George Allen
24/12	29349	21 Dec	R Crowther
	29350	21 Dec	J L Popkin
	29350 X	23 Dec	Mr Saml Forrester, an Excise officer Penny Post (plan – Royal Collection; essays NPM)
26/12	29440	15 Dec	Mr Alexander
	29441	24 Dec	Dr Cope
	29442	24 Dec	H Highton
	29443	24 Dec	B Read
	29444	25 Dec	P Read
	29449	24 Dec	S C Webb
	29450	23 Dec	Anonymous JAA
	29455	23 Dec	R Crawford
27/12	29591	26 Dec	Minute respecting the Penny Post to take effect from 10 Jany 1840 and awarding the Premiums
	29624	26 Dec	M Uzielli

EDINBURGH 1st QUAR: ONE PENNY 2ᴰ JULY 1840 QUARTO No 526 ½ OZ

29350X

Date received	Register number	Date sent	Name	Date received	Register number	Date sent	Name
28/12	29679	–	C W Bevan to be remunerated for his Penny Post	30/12	29758	29 Dec	Boykett Breeds
					29762	30 Dec	F G Waldson
					29782	28 Dec	Richd Crawford to be rewarded for his Penny Post
	29681	27 Dec	T C Craig				
	29682	28 Dec	J Ede (?W Jones)		29783	27 Dec	Baron de Berenger do
	29684	27 Dec	J Hux return of his plan & model		29786	28 Dec	G M Horton
	29687	26 Dec	T J R Kent to be remunerated		29787	28 Dec	James Lee
					29791	28 Dec	J Porter
	29689	27 Dec	J Ridley		29792	30 Dec	J Prince offering paper
	29690	27 Dec	S Webb to be remunerated for her Penny Post		29795	27 Dec	J Scouller
				31/12	29844	–	T Fleming
	29714	26 Dec	T E Death resl		29845	26 Dec	J Grierson
	29718	27 Dec	John Atkinson fur: respecting the Penny Post		29849	28 Dec	Mr Loder
					29851	29 Dec	Mr Pennell
					29865	31 Dec	Anonymous

APPENDIX THREE

List of Post Towns in
Great Britain & Ireland

Taken from Post Office Directory for 1840 pp8/11, retaining the spellings as given there (even where clearly wrong)

A List of Post Towns and Principal Places in the United Kingdom.

ENGLAND AND WALES

Abbots Bromley	Attleborough	Berkeley, Glo'ster	Botesdale
Abbotsbury	Axbridge	Berwick	Bourn
Aberaeron	Axminster	Betley	Boxford
Aberford	Aylesbury	Beverley	Bozeat
Abergavenny	Aylesford	Bewdley	Brackley
Abergeley	Aylsham	Bexhill	Bracknell
Aberystwith	Bagshot	Bicester	Bradford, Yorks.
Abingdon	Bakewell	Biddenden	Bradford, Wilts.
Acle	Bala	Bideford	Bradwell
Alcester	Baldock	Biggleswade	Braintree
Aldborough, Sufflk	Bampton, Devon	Bildestone	Brampton
Aldboro' Yorksh	Banbury	Billericay	Brandon
Alford	Bangor	Bilstone	Brecknock
Alfreton	Barkway	Binfield	Brentwood
Alnwick	Barmouth	Bingham	Bridgend
Alresford	Barnard's Castle	Bingley	Bridgenorth
Alstone	Barnsley	Birmingham	Bridgewater
Alton	Barnstaple	Bishop's Auckland	Bridlington
Altrincham	Barrow on Humber	Bishop's Castle	Bridport
Ambleside	Barton	Bishop's Stortford	Brigg
Amersham	Basingstoke	Bishop's Waltham	Brighton
Amesbury	Bath	Blackburn	Bristol
Amlwch	Battle	Blackpool	Brixham
Ampthill	Bawtry	Blakeney	Broadstairs
Andover	Beaumaris	Blandford	Broadway
Andoversford	Beccles	Bletchingley	Bromwich, West
Appleby	Beaconsfield	Blithburg	Bromyard
Arrington	Beaminster	Blyth	Broomsgrove
Arundel	Bedale	Bodmin	Broseley
Ashbourn	Bedford	Bognor	Brough
Ashburton	Bedwin, Great	Bolingbroke	Broughton
Ashby de la Zouch	Belford	Bolton	Bruton
Ashford	Belper	Bootle	Buckden
Ashton	Bensington	Boroughbridge	Buckingham
Askrig	Benson	Bossiney	Budleigh Salterton
Atherstone	Berkhemstead	Boston	Builth

Bungay
Buntingford
Burford
Burnham, Essex
Burnham, Norfolk
Burnley
Burslem
Burton in Kendal
Burton on Trent
Bury St. Edmund's
Bury, Lancash.
Buxton
Caistor, Norfolk
Caistor, Lincolnsh.
Callington
Calne
Camborne
Cambridge
Camelford
Campden
Cannock
Canterbury
Cardiff
Cardigan
Carleon
Carlisle
Carmarthen
Carnarvon
Castle Bromwich
Castle Carey
Castle Eden
Castle Rising
Catteric
Cave, North & S.
Caxton
Chalford
Chapel in Frith
Chard
Charing
Chatham
Chatteris
Cheadle
Chelmsford
Cheltenham
Chepstow
Chertsey
Chesham
Cheshunt
Chester
Chesterfield
Chester le street
Chichester
Chippenham
Chipping Norton
Chirk

Chorley
Christchurch
Chudleigh
Chumleigh
Church Stretton
Cirencester
Clare
Clay
Cleveland Inn
Clifton
Clitheroe
Cobham
Cobridge
Cockermouth
Coddenham
Colchester
Coggeshall
Coleshill
Collumpton
Collyton
Colne
Colnbrook
Coltersworth
Coltishall
Congleton
Conway
Corfe Castle
Corwen
Cosham
Coventry
Cowbridge
Cowes
Cranbourn
Cranbrook
Crawley
Crediton
Crewkerne
Crickhowel
Cricklade
Cromer
Cross
Cross Hills
Crowland
Cuckfield
Danbury
Darlaston
Darlington
Dartford
Dartmouth
Darwen
Daventry
Dawlish
Deal
Deddington
Dedham

Denbigh
Derby
Dereham
Devizes
Devonport
Dewsbury
Diss
Dolgelly
Doncaster
Dorchester
Dorking
Douglas, Isl. of Man
Dover
Downham
Driffield
Droitwich
Dudley
Dulverton
Dunchurch
Dunkirk
Dunmow
Dunstable
Dunster
Durham
Dursley
Eastbourne
East Grinstead
Easingwold
Eastham
Eccleshall
Egham
Egremont
Ellesmere
Ely
Emsworth
Enstone
Epping
Epsom
Epworth
Esher
Eton
Etruria
Evesham
Ewell
Exeter
Exmouth
Eye
Fairford
Fakenham
Falmouth
Fareham
Farnborough
Farnham
Farringdon
Fazeley

Felstead
Felton
Fenny Stratford
Ferrybridge
Feversham
Finchingfield
Fishguard
Flint
Folkingham
Folkstone
Fordinbridge
Fowey
Framlingham
Frodsham
Frogmill
Frome
Gaddesden
Gainsborough
Gargrave
Garstang
Gateshead
Gatton
Gerrard's Cross
Glastonbury
Gloucester
Godalming
Godstone
Goole
Gosport
Goudhurst
Grampound
Grantham
Gravesend
Grays
Greenhithe
Gretabridge
Grimsby
Guernsey
Guildford
Guisborough
Gwyndee
Hadleigh
Hagley
Hailsham
Hales Owen
Halesworth
Halifax
Halstead
Haltwhistle
Hanley
Harlech
Harleston
Harling
Harlow
Harpenden

Harrowgate	Hull	Ledbury	Malton
Hartfordbridge	Hungerford	Leeds	Malvern
Hartlepool	Hunmanby	Leek	Manchester
Harwich	Huntingdon	Leicester	Manningtree
Haslemere	Hurstgreen	Leigh	March
Hastings	Hurst Pierpoint	Leighton Buzzard	Mansfield
Hatfield	Hythe	Lenham	Margate
Hatherleigh	Ilchester	Leominster	Market Bosworth
Hawarden	Ilfracombe	Lewes	Market Deeping
Hawes	Ilminster	Leyburn	Market Drayton
Hawkhurst	Ingatestone	Lidney	Market Jew, or
Hawkshead	Iron Bridge	Lincoln	Marazion
Havant	Ipswich	Linton	Market Harborough
Haverhill	Isle of Man	Liphook	Market Raisin
Haverfordwest	Isle of Wight	Liskeard	Market Street
Hay	Ilsley	Litchfield	Market Weighton
Haywood, Great	Ivinghoe	Littlehampton	Marlborough
Hedingham	Ivy Bridge	Liverpool	Marlow
Hedon	Jersey (Isle)	Llandaff	Marsk
Helmsley	Keighley	Llandilo	Masham
Helstone	Kineton	Llandovery	Matlock
Hemelhempstead	Kelvedon	Llanelly	Maryport
Henfield	Kendal	Llanfylling	Melcomb Regis
Henley on Thames	Kenilworth	Llangaddock	Melksham
Henley in Arden	Keswick	Llangollen	Melton Mowbray
Hereford	Kettering	Llanidloes	Mere
Hertford	Kidderminster	Llanerchymed	Merthyr Tydvil
Hexham	Kidwelly	Llanrwst	Mevagissy
Heytesbury	Kildwick	Llantrissant	Middleham
Higham Ferrers	Kimbolton	Loddon	Middleton, Teesdale
Highworth	Kingsbridge	LONDON	Middlewich
Hinckley	King's Langley	Longmelford	Midhurst
Hindon	Kington	Longport	Milborn Port
Hitchin	Kirby Lonsdale	Long Sutton	Mildenhall
Hobbs Point	Kirby Stephen	Longtown	Milford Haven
Hockerill	Kirkham	Looe E. & W.	Milnthorpe
Hoddesdon	Knaresborough	Lostwithiel	Milton
Holbeach	Knighton	Loughborough	Milverton
Holkham	Knowle	Louth	Minchinhampton
Holmschapel	Knutsford	Lowestoff	Minehead
Holt	Lamberhurst	Ludlow	Missenden
Holdsworthy	Lambourn	Luggershall	Modbury
Holyhead	Lampeter	Luton	Mold
Holywell	Lancaster	Lutterworth	Monmouth
Honiton	Lane Delph	Lydd	Montgomery
Horncastle	Lane End	Lyme	Morpeth
Hornchurch	Langport	Lymington	Morton in Marsh
Horndean	Laugharne	Lyndhurst	Nailsworth
Horndon	Launceston	Lynn	Namptwich
Hornsea	Lavenham	Macclesfield	Narbeth
Horsham	Lavington	Machynlleth	Nayland
Houghton le Spring	Lawton	Maidenhead	Neath
Howden	Leamington	Maidstone	Needham Market
Hubberstone	Leatherhead	Maldon	Neston
Huddersfield	Lechlade	Malmsbury	Nettlebed

Newark	Pattrington	Rhuabon	Sedgefield
Newbury	Pembroke	Richmond, Yorks.	Selby
Newcastle on Tyne	Penkridge	Rickmansworth	Settle
Newcastle in Emlyn	Penrith	Ringwood	Seven Oaks
Newcastle under Line	Penryn	Ripley	Shaftesbury
Newenden	Pensford	Ripley, Yorkshire	Sheerness
Newent	Penzance	Ripon	Sheffield
Newhaven	Pennybont	Robertsbridge	Shelton
Newmarket	Pershore	Rochdale	Sheppy, Isle
Newnham	Peterborough	Rochester	Shepton Mallet
Newport, Glo'ster	Petersfield	Rochford	Sherborne
Newport, Mon.	Petworth	Rockingham	Shields, N. & S.
Newport, I. Wight	Pewsey	Romney, New	Shiffnal
Newport Pagnell	Pickering	Romsey	Shipstone
Newport Pembrk.	Pinner	Ross	Shoreham
Newport, Salop	Plymouth	Rothbury	Shrewsbury
Newton Abbot	Plympton	Rotherham	Sidmouth
Newton Bushel	Pocklington	Rottingdean	Silsoe
Newton, Lancas.	Pontefract	Rougham	Singleton
Newtown	Poole	Royston	Sittingbourne
Northallerton	Porchester	Rugby	Skipton
Northampton	Portland, Isle	Rugeley	Sleaford
Northfleet	Portsea	Runcorn	Sledmere
Northiam	Portsmouth	Rushyford	Slough
Northleach	Poulton	Ruthin	Snaith
Northop	Prescot	Ryde, Isle of Wight	Sodbury
North Petherton	Presteign	Rye	Solihull
North Walsham	Preston	Saffron Walden	Somersham
Northwich	Preston Brook	St. Alban's	Somerton
Norwich	Prittlewell	St. Asaph	Southam
Nottingham	Puckeridge	St. Austle	Southampton
Nuneaton	Purbeck, Isle	St. Clair's	Southend, Essex
Oakham	Purfleet	St. Columb	Southminster
Oakhampton	Pwllheli	St. Germain's	South Molton
Odiham	Queenborough	St. Helen's, Lanc.	South Petherton
Old Down	Radnor	St. Ives, Cornwall	Southport
Oldham	Ragland	St. Ives, Hunts.	Southwell
Ollerton	Ramsay, I. of M.	St. Leonard's	Southwold
Olney	Ramsbury	St. Mawes	Spalding
Ongar	Ramsey, Hunts.	St. Michael's	Speenhamland
Orford	Ramsgate	St. Neots	Spilsby
Ormskirk	Ravenglass	Salisbury	Spittal
Orset	Rawcliffe	Saltash	Stafford
Orton	Rawtenstall	Sandbach	Staindrop
Oswestry	Rayleigh	Sandgate	Staines
Otley	Reading	Sandwich	Stamford
Ottery St. Mary's	Redburn	Sawbridgeworth	Stanhope
Oundle	Redcar	Saxmundham	Stanstead
Overton, Hants	Redditch	Scarborough	Stevenage
Overton, Flintshire	Redruth	Scilly Islands	Steyning
Oxford	Reepham	Scole	Stilton
Padiham	Reeth	Seaford	Stockbridge
Padstow	Reigate	Seaton, Devonshire	Stockport
Painswick	Retford	Seaton, Norfolk	Stockton on Tees
Parkgate	Rhayader	Sedbergh	Stoke, Norfolk

Stoke, Staffords.
Stoke, Suffolk
Stokesley
Stone
Stoneham
Stonehouse
Stokenchurch
Stoney Cross
Stony Middleton
Stony Stratford
Storrington
Stourbridge
Stourport
Stow on the Wold
Stow Market
Stratford on Avon
Stratton, Cornwall
Stratton, Norfolk
Strood, Kent
Stroud, Glos'ter
Sudbury
Sunderland
Sunning
Sunning hill
Sutton Coldfield
Swaffham
Swanage
Swansea
Swindon
Tadcaster
Tamworth
Tarporley
Taunton
Tavistock
Teignmoth, E. & W.
Temple Sowerby
Tenbury
Tenby
Tenterden
Tetbury
Tetsworth
Tewkesbury
Thame
Thaxted
Thetford

Thirsk
Thornbury
Thorne
Thrapstone
Ticehurst
Tideswell
Tilbury Fort
Tipton
Titchfield
Tiverton
Todmorden
Topsham
Torbay
Torquay
Torrington
Totness
Towcester
Town Malling
Trecastle
Tregony
Trentham
Tring
Trowbridge
Truro
Tunbridge
Tunbridge Wells
Tunstall
Tuxford
Tynemouth
Uckfield
Ulverstone
Upminster
Uppingham
Upton on Severn
Usk
Uttoxeter
Uxbridge
Wadebridge
Wadhurst
Wakefield
Wallingford
Walsall
Walsingham
Walton on Thames
Wangford

Wansford
Wantage
Ware
Wareham
Warminster
Warrington
Warwick
Watford
Watlington
Watton
Wearmouth, Bishop's
Wednesbury
Weedon
Welchpool
Welford
Wellinborough
Wellington, Salop
Wellington, Soms.
Wells, Norfolk
Wells, Somerset
Welwyn
Wem
Wendover
Wenlock
Weobly
West Bromwich
Westbury
Wetherby
Weybridge
Weymouth
Wheatley
Whitby
Whitchurch, Hants
Whitchurch, Salop
Whitehaven
Whitstable
Whittingham
Wickford
Wickham Market
Wickwar
Wigan
Wigton
Wiley
Willenhall
Wilton

Wimborne
Wincanton
Winchcombe
Winchilsea
Winchester
Windsor
Wing
Wingham
Winsford
Winslow
Wirksworth
Wisbeach
Witham
Witney
Wiveliscombe
Woburn
Wokingham or
  Oakingham
Wolseley
Wolverhampton
Woodbridge
Woodstock
Woodyates
Wooler
Woolpit
Woore
Wootton Bassett
Wooton under Edge
Worcester
Workington
Worksop
Worthing
Wragby
Wrexham
Wrotham
Wycombe, High
Wymondham
Yarm
Yarmouth, I. of W.
Yarmouth, Norfolk
Yeovil
York
Yoxford

SCOTLAND

Aberdeen
Aberdour, Fife
Aberfeldy
Aberlady
Aberlour
Aboyne

Airdrie
Alford
Alloa
Alyth
Annan
Anstruther

Appin
Arbroath
Ardrossan
Arisaig
Arran
Arroquhar

Aross
Auchnacraig
Auchterarder
Auchtermuchty
Ayr
Ayton

Balfron
Ballantrae
Ballichulish
Ballindalloch
Banchory
Banff
Bannockburn
Barrhead
Bathgate
Beauly
Beith
Bellshill
Bervie
Biggar
Blackshiels
Blair Adam
Blair Athol
Blairgowrie
Boat of Forbes
Bonar Bridge
Bonaw
Borrowmuirhead
Borrowstownness
Bothwell
Bowholm
Bowmore
Braemar
Brechin
Bridge of Earne
Broadford
Brodick
Buckie
Bucklyvie
Bunessan
Burntisland
Burwick
Cairndow
Cairnish
Cairnryan
Callender
Cambuslang
Camelon
Campbeltown
Carnwath
Carronshore
Castle Douglas
Cathcart
Catrine
Chance Inn
Chirnside
Clachan
Clackmannan
Coldingham
Coldstream
Colinsburgh

Colinton
Coll
Comrie
Corstorphin
Craig Ellachie
Crail
Cramond
Creetown
Crieff
Crinan
Cromarty
Crook
Cullen
Culross
Cumbernauld
Cumnock
Cupar, Angus
Cupar, Fife
Currie
Dalkeith
Dalmally
Dalmellington
Dalry, Ayrshire
Denny
Dingwall
Dirleton
Dornoch
Douglas
Doune
Drymen
Dumbarton
Dumfries
Dunbar
Dunbeath
Dunblane
Dundee
Dunfermline
Dunkeld
Dunning
Dunoon
Dunse
Dunvegan
Dysart
Eaglesham
Earlston
Easdale
Ecclefechan
Eddlestone
Edinburgh
Elgin
Ellon
Ely
Errol
Evanton
Eyemouth

Falkirk
Falkland
Fettercairn
Fochabers
Ford
Fordon
Forfar
Forres
Fort Augustus
Fort George
Fortrose
Fort William
Fraserburgh
Fruchie
Fushie Bridge
Fyvie
Galashiels
Galston
Gartmore
Gatehouse
Gifford
Girvan
Glammis
Glasgow
Glenlivat
Glenluce
Golspie
Gourock
Graham's Town
Grangemouth
Grantown
Greenlaw
Greenock
Gullan
Haddington
Hamilton
Hawick
Helensburg
Helmsdale
Hermiston
Holytown
Huna
Huntley
Inchture
Invergordon
Inverkeithing
Inverness
Irvine
Jedburgh
Johnstown
Jura
Innerkip
Innerleithen
Inverary
Keith

Keithall
Kelso
Kenmore
Kennoway
Kettle
Kilbride, E. & W.
Killin
Kilmarnock
Kilmaurs
Kilpatrick
Kilwinning
Kilsyth
Kincardine
Kincardine O'Neil
Kinghorn
Kingussie
Kinross
Kintore
Kintra
Kippen
Kirkcaldy
Kirkcudbright
Kirkintullock
Kirkliston
Kirknewton
Kirkwall
Kirriemuir
Laggan
Lamlash
Lanark
Langholm
Larbert
Largo
Largs
Lasswade
Lauder
Laurencekirk
Lauriston
Leadhills
Leith
Leitholm
Lennox Town
Lerwick
Leslie
Lesmahago
Leuchars
Leven
Libberton
Linlithgow
Linton
Lochalsh
Lochcarron
Lochearnhead
Lochgilphead
Lochmaben

Lochwinnock	Newhaven	Portree	Strathmiglo
Lockerby	Newmills, Ayrshire	Portsoy	Strichen
Longtown	Newmills, Fife	Prestonkirk	Stromness
Luss	Newport	Prestonpans	Strontian
Lybster	Newton Stewart	Rachan Mill	Swinton
Markynch	Noblehouse	Rannoch	Tain
Maryhill	North Berwick	Ratho	Tarbat
Mauchline	North Queen Ferry	Renfrew	Tarland
Maybole	Oban	Rhynie	Tayinloam
Meigle	Old Meldrum	Roslin	Thornhill
Melrose	Old Rain	Rothes	Thurso
Mid-Calder	Paisley	Rothesay	Tobermory
Milnathort	Parkhead	Rutherglen	Tomintoul
Milngavie	Parkhill	St. Andrew's	Tongue
Mintlaw	Patrick	St. Boswell Green	Torryburn
Moffat	Pathhead	St. Ninians	Tranent
Moniave	Peebles	Saltcoats	Troon
Monimusk	Pennycuick	Sanquhar	Tullich
Montrose	Perth	Selkirk	Turriff
Mortlach	Peterhead	Slateford	Tyndrum
Morvern	Pitlochry	South Queen's Ferry	Tyrie
Muirdrum	Pitsligo	Stewarton	Uddington
Muirkirk	Pittenweem	Stirling	Ullapool
Monlochy	Pollockshaws	Stonehaven	West Salton
Musselburgh	Polmont	Stornoway	Whitburn
Nairn	Portaskaig	Stow	Whithorn
Neilston	Port Glasgow	Stranraer	Wick
Newburg, Fife	Port William	Strathaven	Widowell
New Castleton	Portobello	Strathblane	Wigton
New Galloway	Port Patrick	Strathdon	Wilsontown

IRELAND

To expedite the despatch from Dublin, Bags are now made up in London for Cork, Belfast, Donaghadee, Drogheda, Galway, Limerick, Londonderry, Newry, Sligo, Waterford and Wexford.

Abbeleix	Ashford	Ballibay	Ballyhaunis
Abbeyfeale	Askeaton	Ballina	Ballymahon
Adair	Athboy	Ballinakill	Ballymenagh
Ahascragh	Athenry	Ballinasloe	Ballymoe
Antrim	Athleague	Ballincolig	Ballymoney
Andraban	Athlone	Ballingarry	Ballymore
Ardara	Athy	Ballinrobe	Ballymote
Ardee	Aughnacloy	Ballycastle	Ballynacargy
Ardglass	Aughrim	Ballyclare	Ballynahinch
Arklow	Bagnalstown	Ballyconnel	Ballynamore
Armagh	Bailyborough	Ballygawley	Ballyragget
Arthurstown	Ballybuttan	Ballyglass	Ballyshannon
Arva	Balbriggan	Ballyjames Duff	Ballytore
Ashbourn	Ballaghaderin	Ballylongford	Ballyvary

Baltinglass
Banagher
Banbridge
Bandon
Bangor
Bantry
Beerhaven
Beer Island
Belfast
Bellagby
Belmullet
Belturbet
Blackwater Town
Blessington
Boyle
Bray
Broadway
Brookboro'
Broughshane
Bruff
Buncrana
Bunratty
Burrin
Burrosakane
Burrosoleigh
Burros-in-ossory
Bushmills
Buttevant
Cabinteely
Caherciveen
Cahirconlish
Cahir
Caledon
Callan
Camolin
Cappoquin
Carlingford
Carlow
Carn
Carnew
Carrickfergus
Carrickmacross
Carrick-on-Shannon
Carrick-on-Suir
Cashcarrigan
Cashel
Castlebar
Castle Bellingham
Castleblakeny
Castleblaney
Castlecomer
Castleconnel
Castle Dawson
Castlederg
Castledermot

Castlefin
Castle Island
Castlemartyr
Castle Pollard
Castlerea
Castletown
Castletown Delvin
Castletown Roche
Castlewellan
Cavan
Celbridge
Charleville
Church Hill
Clane
Clara
Clare
Clifden
Cloghan
Clogheen
Clogher
Clognakilty
Clonard
Clonaslie
Clonegal
Clonee
Clones
Clonmell
Clough
Cloughjordan
Cloyne
Colehill
Coleraine
Collon
Collooney
Cong
Cookstown
Cootehill
Cork
Cove of Cork
Craughwell
Croome
Crosdoney
Crosmolina
Crumlin
Cumber
Curofin
Cushendall
Dangan
Deelcastle
Delganny
Derry, London
Dervock
Dingle
Donaghadee
Donegal

Donerail
Down Patrick
Drogheda
Dromahair
Dromore
Dromore, West
Drumcree
Drumsna
Dublin
Dundalk
Dunamanagh
Dunfanaghy
Dungannon
Dungarvon
Dungiven
Dunlavin
Dunleer
Dunmanway
Dunmore
Dunmore, East
Dunshaughlin
Durrow
Edenderry
Edgeworth's Town
Elphin
Emo
Emyvale
Enfield
Ennis
Enniscorthy
Enniskillen
Ennistimon
Eyrecourt
Ferbane
Fermoy
Ferns
Fethard, Wexford
Fethard, Tipperary
Fintona
Five Mile Town
Florence Court
Flurrybridge
Fork Hill
Foxford
Frankford
French Park
Freshford
Galway
Garvagh
Geashell
Gilford
Glasslough
Glenarm
Glenavy
Golden

Gore's Bridge
Gorey
Gort
Gowran
Graig
Granard
Grayabby
Hacketstown
Headford
Hillsborough
Hollymount
Hollywood
Howth
Inistiogue
Innishannon
Irvinstown
Johnstown
Keaduc
Keady
Kells
Kenmare
Kenturk
Kilbeggan
Kilcock
Kilconnel
Kilcullen
Kildare
Kildorrery
Kildysart
Kilkeel
Kilkenny
Killala
Killaloe
Killarney
Killinchy
Killough
Killucan
Killybegs
Killyleigh
Killynaule
Killysandre
Kilmacthomas
Kilmallock
Kilrea
Kilrush
Kilworth
King's Court
Kinnegad
Kinnety
Kinsale
Kircubbin
Kish
Knock
Knocktopher
Lanesborough

Larne
Leighlinbridge
Leixlip
Letterkenny
Limerick
Lisburn
Lismore
Lisnaskea
Listowel
Littleton
Longford
Loughbrickland
Loughgall
Loughrea
Loughswilly
Lowtherstown
Lucan
Lurgan
Lurgangreen
Macroom
Maghera
Magherafelt
Malahide
Mallow
Manorhamilton
Market-hill
Maryborough
Maynooth
Middleton
Millstreet
Miltown
Miltown Malbay
Mitchelstown
Moate
Mohill
Moira
Monaghan
Monastereven
Moneygall
Moneymore
Monivae

Mountmelick
Mount Nugent
Mountrath
Mount Talbot
Moville
Moy
Moynalty
Muff
Mullingar
Myshall
Naas
Narin
Navan
Nenagh
New Birmingham
New Bliss
Newbridge
Newcastle
Newmarket
Newmarket on
    Fergus
Newport, Mayo
Newport Tipperary
Newry
Newtown Ards
Newtown Barry
Newtown Forbes
Newtown Hamilton
Newtown Limavady
Newtown Mount
    Kennedy
Newtown Stewart
Nobber
Old Castle
Omagh
Oranmore
Oulart
Outerard
Pallasgreen
Pallaskenry
Parsonstown

Passage
Passage, West
Philipstown
Pill Town
Portadown
Portaferry
Portarlington
Portglenone
Portlaw
Portumna
Ramelton
Randalstown
Raphoe
Rathangan
Rathcoole
Rathcormack
Rathdowney
Rathdrum
Rathfriland
Rathkeale
Rathlacken
Rathowen
Richhill
Roscommon
Roscrea
Ross
Rosscarberry
Rostrevor
Rusky
Rutland
Saintfield
Scaiff
Scrabby
Shanagolden
Shinrone
Sixmile Bridge
Skibbereen
Sligo
Stewartstown
Strabane
Stradbally

Stradone
Strangford
Stranorlor
Strokestown
Summerhill
Swanlibar
Swinford
Swords
Taghmon
Tallanstown
Tallow
Tanderagee
Tarbert
Templemore
Tempo
Thomastown
Thurles
Tinahely
Tipperary
Toome
Tralee
Tramore
Trim
Tuam
Tubbermore
Tulla
Tullamore
Tullow
Tulsk
Tynan
Tyrrel's Pass
Valentia
Virginia
Warrenspoint
Waterford
Westport
Wexford
Wicklow
Youghall

Illustration Acknowledgements

Index

* denotes an illustration